LATIN AMERICAN HISTORICAL DICTIONARIES SERIES

Edited by A. Curtis Wilgus

1. *Guatemala*, by Richard E. Moore, rev. ed. 1973.

2. *Panama*, by Basil C. & Anne K. Hedrick. 1979.

3. *Venezuela*, by Donna Keyse & G. A. Rudolph. 1971.

4. *Bolivia*, by Dwight B. Heath. 1972.

5. *El Salvador*, by Philip F. Flemion. 1972.

6. *Nicaragua*, by Harvey K. Meyer. 1972.

7. *Chile*, by Salvatore Bizzaro. 1972.

8. *Paraguay*, by Charles J. Kolinski. 1973.

9. *Puerto Rico and the U.S. Virgin Islands*, by Kenneth R. Farr. 1973.

10. *Ecuador*, by Albert W. Bork and Georg Maier. 1973.

11. *Uruguay*, by Jean L. Willis. 1974.

12. *British Caribbean*, by William Lux. 1975.

13. *Honduras*, by Harvey K. Meyer. 1976.

14. *Colombia*, by Robert H. Davis. 1977.

15. *Haiti*, by Roland I. Perusse. 1977.

16. *Costa Rica*, by Theodore S. Creedman. 1977.

17. *Argentina*, by Ione Wright and Lisa M. Nekhom. 1978.

18. *French and Netherlands Antilles*, by Albert Gastmann. 1978.

19. *Brazil*, by Robert M. Levine. 1979.

20. *Peru*, by Marvin Alisky. 1979.

Historical Dictionary
of
BRAZIL

by

ROBERT M. LEVINE

Latin American Historical Dictionaries, No. 19

CT.

The Scarecrow Press, Inc.

Metuchen, N.J. & London

1979

Library of Congress Cataloging in Publication Data

Levine, Robert M
    Historical dictionary of Brazil.

    (Latin American historical dictionaries ; no. 19)
    Bibliography: p.
    1. Brazil--Dictionaries and encyclopedias. I. Ti-
tle.
    F2504.L46   981'.003   78-10178
    ISBN 0-8108-1178-2

To

Kenneth M. and Jean Levine
and
Janice and Arnold Hirshon

TABLE OF CONTENTS

EDITOR'S FOREWORD

Brazil is a nation whose time has almost arrived, and it is now regarded as the leading Latin American country, with Mexico disputing the fact. The last American government to abolish Negro slavery, it has developed a "Cosmic Race" with a profound social conscience and a national economic compulsion which makes other nations jealous. This volume by Dr. Levine has caught the spirit of its people and leaders and its significant impatience in striving for rapid national development. All this and more can be seen in the scope and treatment of facts in this historical panorama.

Robert M. Levine is a native of New York State and he is now Professor of History in the State University of New York at Stony Brook. On his way to this position he has passed along an interesting academic and professional route. He received his B. A. degree from Colgate in 1962, and his M. A. (1964) and Ph. D. (1967) from Princeton, in which latter institution he briefly served as Instructor. In preparation for his career he studied in Argentina, Spain and Brazil where he lectured at University Centers in São Paulo, Belo Horizonte, Rio de Janeiro and Recife.

During most of these years his interest in teaching and research has centered on various aspects of Brazilian history and development. In his college activities he has served as a member of many administrative and advisory committees. Always interested in cooperating professionally with other scholars in the Latin American field, Dr. Levine has chaired national and international seminars, roundtables, and consortiums and has been a useful member of related committees and organizations.

During the last decade Dr. Levine has researched and written scores of conference papers, periodical articles, encyclopedia sections, scholarly monographs and three books, all (with a few exceptions) relating to Brazil. His contributions have been published in the United States, in Latin America and in Europe. These scholarly activities have attracted wide attention and he has been invited to serve as consultant by a number of organizations. Fortunately, in much of his research Dr. Levine has been aided by grants from the Ford Foundation, The Doherty Foundation, the New York State Research Foundation, Fulbright, the Social Science Research Council, United States Office of Education, and the American Philosophical Society.

Material included in this volume has been selected by Dr. Levine with the object of producing a well-balanced, comprehensive sketch of Brazilian history. Included is a lengthy bibliography confined to works in English, for to add Portuguese and other language references would have made the volume much too long, if not unrealistic. Some readers or reviewers may find omissions of facts of special interest to them, but Dr. Levine has presented a work which will be both welcome and useful, and it will make a valuable addition to the Latin American Historical Dictionaries Series.

A. Curtis Wilgus
Emeritus Director
School of Inter American Studies
University of Florida

INTRODUCTION

Brazil is the world's fifth largest nation after the Soviet Union, China, Canada and the United States. It has a population of nearly 120 million, and the majority of Brazilians are less than twenty-five years of age. More South Americans speak Portuguese than all other languages combined (Spanish, Quechua, French, English, Dutch); Brazil claims more nominal Roman Catholics than any country on earth.

Brazilian society illustrates paradox. It encompasses vast regional diversity, yet its national culture is impressively homogeneous. It is famed for its multi-racial plurality, yet its elite has always been, and continues to be, Caucasian. Historically tolerant and given to what Brazilian historians have termed "compromise and conciliation," Brazil has also seen insurrection, periods of repression, and harrowing treatment of the socially vulnerable.

Anachronism highlights its rich history. The only European colony in the hemisphere to embrace monarchy after Independence, Brazil remained a slave society until 1888, well to the end of the nineteenth century. Its Emperor, the titular head of the Church, was also a Freemason. Relatively free from military interference in civilian affairs until the proclamation of the Republic in 1889, in the 1960's Brazil became a model, to some, of authoritarian military-dominated national development. With one exception, Brazil avoided major wars with its neighbors, yet it was the only Latin American country to enter the First World War and to send troops in the Second. During that war, Brazil fought in the name of democracy on the Allied side, yet its own constitution reflected corporatist and fascist influences from the "Mediterranean" fascism of Salazar, Franco, Maurras, and Mussolini; many of its armed forces officers initially favored the Axis cause.

Brazil seeks to achieve world-power status in the

coming decades. It is fashionable in Brazil to speak, in
fact, of the twenty-first as the "Brazilian" century. Brazilians point to their new role as broker and mediator among
the Third World; their formidable reserves of natural resources; their newly-discovered off-shore petroleum deposits;
the human potential of their burgeoning population. Admirers
point to the post-1964 "economic miracle," while critics hold
that the "miracle" has benefited the affluent at the expense
of the poor.

Outsiders approaching Brazil for the first time find
the country and its society larger-than-life. Others see in
its evolving socio-political environment the trappings of Or-
wellian social control. Almost everyone is dazzled by Brazil's richness, its diversity, its physical grandeur, the
warmth of its people.

It is my intention to deal with Brazil in a broad manner. Entries in this dictionary--and readers should remem-
ber that it is not an encyclopedia--treat not only people and
events but Brazilian civilization in several dimensions: popular and folk culture as well as the fine arts; slang as well
as established terminology; women as well as men; popular
as well as erudite culture; sports as well as politics; the
obscure (to a limited degree) as well as the renowned.

The Dictionary was compiled by surveying the major
literature on Brazil, in Portuguese as well as English, with
an emphasis upon recent writing. As a result, some of the
interpretations may be surprising, but they represent current scholarly thinking. Sadly, some of the best books on
Brazil are rapidly going out of print--even Gilberto Freyre's
Masters and the Slaves became unavailable for classroom
use in early 1978. The bibliography, which contains more
than nine hundred entries in English, should be used as a
point for further investigation. Some of the texts and general works in Section III of the bibliography will be useful
for tracing the context of isolated entries and for additional
background and explanatory detail.

Entries are arranged in alphabetical order, and are
cross-referenced where confusion might occur. When Brazilians themselves preferred traditional spelling of their names,
they are used: thus Gilberto Freyre but Paulo Freire. Al-
phabetization of names follows the conventional Brazilian
style: Francisco de Assis Rosa e Silva but Alfredo de Escragnolle Taunay.

I have tried to add entries which illustrate my view
of Brazilian society as multi-dimensional. Texts as well as
standard reference works tend to concentrate on a historical
perspective which views events only from the top: the Establishment and its world outlook. Thus I have included such
entries as "Popular Music," "Sugismundo," "Rouba Mas Faz,"
and "Abraço." In fact, "um abraço" to all of you!

                                    Robert M. Levine
                                    January 15, 1978
                                    Port Jefferson, New York

THE DICTIONARY

ABACAXI. 1) Pineapple. 2) (slang) A mess, a confused state of things. See also BAGUNÇA.

ABARÁ. Afro-Brazilian dish prepared by cooking beans in peppers and dendê (palm) oil; a prime example of Bahian cuisine.

ABORIGINAL POPULATION. Although the Jesuits who first arrived in Brazil divided the indigenous tribes into two groups--Tapuias and Tupís--the lands of Brazil supported between one and one-and-a-half million aboriginal inhabitants divided into hundreds of tribes and speaking several languages. Chief among them were the coastal Tupís, centered in the Paraguay and Paraná River valleys; the Tapuias, or Jés, less advanced in economic development and organization; the Aruaques of the high Amazon, known for their ceramics and riverine navigational skills; and the Caraíbas, cannibals, in the region of the Xingú River. None of the indigenous peoples were as socially organized as the Incas or Aztecs. The tropical forest tribes were primarily horticulturists and fishermen, and the others were migrants who depended on hunting and food gathering. Lack of unity among the tribes and peoples is one of factors frequently cited for their lack of resistance to European incursions into their midst.

   With the advent of plantation agriculture, the Portuguese turned to imported African slaves rather than to use indigenous labor, since the latter lacked a tradition of sedentary agriculture, and resisted enslavement. By the nineteenth century, most coastal aboriginal groups had disappeared, their numbers decimated by disease, brutality, and miscegenation (see CABOCLOS). Other, more primitive tribes continued to live free from European influence in the interior, beyond the reach of urbanizing centers. Oddly, the birth of uniquely Brazilian literature in the mid-nineteenth century coincided with a

1

romanticized vogue for Indian life; the principal novelist of this genre, José de Alencar, idealized and glorified the Indian characters in his Iracema and The Guaraní to the extent that they are portrayed as Athenian. Few literate Brazilians had even seen an Indian; fewer cared about how they really lived. The romantic Indian vogue survived through the early twentieth century, when it was adopted by nationalistic groups which were emerging in search of a truly "Brazilian" past. See also INDIAN PROTECTIVE ASSOCIATION; VILAS BOAS BROTHERS; TRANSAMAZON HIGHWAY.

ABRAÇO. A hug, the ritual greeting and leave-taking among friends, especially between males.

ABRAÇO DE TAMANDUÁ. (slang) Treachery or disloyalty.

ABRANTES, MARQUÉS DE (1794-1865). Miguel Calmon du Pin e Almeida, an Imperial-era statesman and cabinet minister. The holder of a law degree from Coimbra, Abrantes helped negotiate various accords with the British including one which revoked an act of the English parliament prohibiting the importation of sugar produced on plantations using slave labor.

ABREU, CASEMIRO DE (1839-1960). Poet from Rio de Janeiro state whose death at the age of 21 left only one book of verse, As Primaveiras (Spring), considered nonetheless a major contribution to Brazilian literature.

ABROLHOS, BATTLE OF. Dutch defeat, at Bahia, on September 12, 1631, by D. Antônio de Oquendo.

ACABOCLAR. Literally, "to appear like or behave like a caboclo, or peasant." The word is also defined in Brazilian dictionaries as meaning "rustic, rural, churlish, boorish."

ACABRALHADO. A person with one mulatto and one black parent; mixed breed.

ACADEMIA BRASILEIRA DE CIÊNCIAS. The Brazilian Academy of Sciences was founded in Rio de Janeiro in 1916. Five years later it changed its name to the "Sociedade Brasileira de Ciências." It spans three scientific areas: mathematics, physical chemistry, and biology.

ACADEMIA BRASILEIRA DE LETRAS. The Brazilian Academy of Letters was established in 1897 on the model of the French Academy, complete with 40 chairs for cultural and intellectual "immortals." After the initial selection of members, new places are filled only on the death of an incumbent. Tradition required that would-be members demonstrate their interest by exchanging pleasantries with academicians and otherwise paying their respects. As such, some intellectuals--notably Gilberto Freyre--refused to do so, and was never admitted. The Academy generally courted writers and other intellectuals whose works were ideologically "safe"; in 1941 it accepted dictator Getúlio Vargas, and military officers have been disproportionately represented in later years. In 1977 the first woman, Rachel de Queiroz, was elected.

ACADEMIA DOS ESQUECIDOS. The Brazilian "Academy of the Forgotten," founded in Salvador in 1724, the first academy of intellectual activity in the colony.

ACADEMIA MILITAR DAS AGULHAS NEGRAS. Established in 1810 as the Academia Real Militar (the Royal Military Academy), the school trained generations of military officers; in 1943 it was renamed after its location in Rezende, Rio de Janeiro state, and in 1951 to its current name, the Agulhas Negras Military Academy.

ACADEMIA MILITAR E NAVAL. The first military and naval academies, founded in 1832 as a single institution but separated in the same year.

ACADEMIA REAL MILITAR   see   ACADEMIA MILITAR DAS AGULHAS NEGRAS

ACADEMIA SUASSUNA. Pre-masonic secret organization existing in Pernambuco at the end of the eighteenth century, supplanted in 1814 by the first formal masonic chapter in Brazil, the Loja Maçonica Patriotismo.

AÇÃO CATOLICA. Catholic Action, organized in 1935 under the supervision of Cardinal Sebastião Leme, a part of the larger, international movement intending to organize laymen in an effort to achieve Church goals through political and social activity. Under Leme, Brazil adopted the Italian (corporatist and authoritarian) model for Catholic Action, but it never succeeded. Bruneau notes the probable reasons for its failure: with the move of the Vargas regime to the right and the suppression of the left, the movement's goals were co-opted and its seeming urgency reduced.

AÇÃO IMPERIAL PATRONOVISTA BRASILEIRA. A neo-monarchical, corporatist, and Catholic movement organized in 1928 with the goal of restoration of the monarchy and medieval corporations linking Church and State. Its members rejected the example of the Empire as excessively liberal, since it was neither Catholic nor corporatist.

AÇÃO INTEGRALISTA BRASILEIRA (AIB)   see   INTEGRALISM

AÇÃO SOCIAL BRASILEIRA. A pre-Integralist party of the far right, founded by J. Fabrino, and openly fascist and given to demands for rigid discipline.

AÇÃO SOCIAL NACIONALISTA. A cultural-nationalistic organization led by Afonso Celso and based in Rio de Janeiro after World War I. It advocated such measures as the transfer of the national capital to the interior, limits on profit remission by foreign firms, closer relations with other Latin American countries, and a stronger federal government given to regulation of the economy and protection of domestic interests.

AÇOMINAS. State-run steel company which in 1977 successfully borrowed one billion dollars from a consortium of foreign syndicates including Chase Manhattan, Morgan Grefell, Banque de Paris et des Pays Bas, and Dresdner Bank, matched by an equal quantity of export credits.

ACRE. State, formerly territory, bordering Peru and Bolivia at the southern most boundary of Amazonas, with its capital at Rio Branco.

ACRE WAR. Fought as a successionist venture with Bolivia after the advent of the rubber boom there. After Bolivian officials attempted to establish a custom's post there, the Brazilians revolted and were victorious militarily. Under the 1903 Petropolis Treaty, Acre was ceded to Brazil in exchange for £2,000,000 and a pledge, never fulfilled, to build a railroad from Marmoré to Madeira. See MAMORÉ-MEDEIRA RAILROAD.

AÇUDES. Storage dams, or reservoirs, constructed in the

drought-ridden Northeast from the mid-nineteenth century
to the 1920's, during which time the drought was seen
mainly as an engineering problem, not one needful of
social solutions (e. g. relocating populations, or introducing new forms of economic endeavor).

AGASSIZ, LOUIS (1807-1873). Swiss-born American zoologist
who led an expedition to the Amazon in 1865-66. As a
result of his trip he published A Journey in Brazil,
which chided Brazilian scientists for lacking an interest
in experimentation, being theoreticians instead.

AGOGÔ. A bell-like instrument struck with a piece of metal,
used in candomblé and macumba (qq. v.) ceremonies to
encourage the descent of the gods when they seem to be
delaying their appearance.

AGREGADOS. Generic name for landless tenants who pay
rent by working for the landowner a specified number of
days per week. See also MORADORES.

AGRESTE. A narrow climatic zone stretching north and
south along the northern coast of the country, separating
the more arid sertão from the humid, mostly forested
zona da mata of the littoral. / The agreste is the only
northeastern zone where family farms have been established, dating back to the eighteenth century. See
SERTÃO; ZONA DA MATA.

AGROVILAS. Planned villages of settlement along the Trans-
Amazonian highway, some of which failed during the first
years the highway was opened, opening government officials to charges of failing to prepare migrants for the
rigors of Amazonian life and for the differences in climate and other environmental factors. Agrovilas were
generally settled with destitute northeastern migrants
from the overcrowded zona da mata.

AGUARDENTE. A raw sugar-cane rum, usually known as
cachaça, or, more colloquially, pinga. Bottled in liter-
sized containers with throw-away metal caps (Coca-Cola-
like) rather than corks, this traditionally is the alcoholic
drink of the poor. Affluent Brazilians mix aguardente to
make caipiras, mellower drinks flavored by lemon juice,
peanuts, maracujá, or cajú. The fiery liquid is also
known as a-do-ó, água bruta, aninha, cachorro-de-engenho,
filha-de-senhor-de-engenho, gás, mata-bicho, meu-consôlo,

mamaē-de-luanda, and xinapre, among hundreds of other
slang names guaranteed to send anthropologists for their
notebooks.

AIPIM.   Sweet cassava root, known by the name macaxeira
in the Northeast.

AJOUJOS.   Canoes lashed together to transport cattle down-
river in the colonial-era Amazon.   The method of shipment was especially widespread on the Rio Negro.

ALA VERMELHA ("Red Wing").   A branch of the Maoist
Partido Comunista of Brasil (PC do B), crushed by the
government after 1973.

ALAGADO.   Area or district occupied predominantly by
mocambos, or ground-level mud hovels of the poor in
northeastern coastal cities.

ALAGBE.   The person responsible for playing the drums
during a candomblé or macumba ceremony.

ALBUQUERQUE, LUCÍLIO DE (1877-1939).   Artist connected
to the Impressionist school, whose revolutionary style
paralleled the shift of Brazilian painting from fixed to
varied themes.

ALCÂNTARA MACHADO, JOSÉ DE (1875-1941).   Historian
whose research into Paulista records and wills proved
that the bandeirantes lived lives of relative poverty, in
contrast to the earlier assumptions that they lived in
wealth and aristocratic refinement in the manner of the
northeastern senhores de engenho.   See also OLIVEIRA
VIANNA, F. J. DE.

ALDEIA.   A village.   During the colonial period, the word
referred to Indian settlements established by religious
orders like the Jesuits and Franciscans.

ALEIJADINHO   see   LISBOA, ANTONIO FRANCISCO

ALENCAR, JOSÉ DE (1829-1877).   Leading proponent of the
Indianist school of the mid-nineteenth century.   His four
novels, O Guaraní, Iracema, Ubirajara, and As Minas
de Prata, all glorified the Indian and invented noble and
lofty characterizations of Indian life.   In contrast, Alencar
deprecated Portuguese life and encouraged the use of
Tupí as the Brazilian language and the future basis for
Brazilian culture.

ALENCAR, MÁRIO COKRANE DE (1872-1925). Novelist,
  poet, and critic. Alencar was the son of romanticist
  José de Alencar; after a degree in law from São Paulo,
  he switched to letters. He earned his living as librarian
  of the Chamber of Deputies.

ALENCAR FURTADO, JOSÉ DE (1926-   ). Ceará-born deputy
  from Paraná, and a leader of the MDB opposition party,
  he was stripped of his political rights in August 1977 for
  having made a television speech in which he was considered
  to have provoked the Geisel administration unnecessarily
  on the issue of permitting free elections for the presidency.

ALFERES. Colonial period military rank, corresponding to
  today's second lieutenant.

ALIANÇA LIBERAL. The "Liberal Alliance," the coalition
  of the incumbent parties of three states--Minas Gerais,
  Rio Grande do Sul, and Paraíba--during the electoral
  campaign for the presidency in 1930. The Alliance backed
  the candidacy of Getúlio Vargas, and despite defeat at
  the polls, took power in the wake of the military revolt
  launched in October. See also REVOLUTION OF 1930;
  VARGAS, GETÚLIO.

ALIANÇA LIBERAL, PLATFORM. As presidential candidate
  in 1930, Vargas called for the following: a general
  amnesty for all persons exiled in consequence of the 1922
  and 1924 military uprisings; the right to choose the president without interference from politicians; compulsory
  voting; a secret ballot, without fraud; improved public
  education; improved public health; legalization of labor
  unions; new social legislation; an independent judiciary;
  aid to all areas of agriculture, not just coffee; cheaper
  transportation; measures to protect industry; a balanced
  budget; an end to indirect taxes weighing heaviest on the
  poor; autonomy for the Federal District; new equipment
  for the armed forces; a revival of irrigation projects in
  the North-East.

ALIANÇA LIBERTADORA. The coalition of the Partido
  Federalista and Partido Democrático in Rio Grande do
  Sul which was created in support of the candidacy of
  Joaquim Francisco Assis Brasil for the governorship in
  1922. The Democrats (PD) had been inactive since Rui
  Barbosa's defeat in 1910. Realizing that the chances of

overthrowing state political chieftain Borges de Medeiros
was the greatest in perhaps thirty years, the two groups
merged in opposition to the incumbent Republican Party,
the PRP.

The 1922 election was the first contested contest
in the state since 1907, and both camps charged fraud.
The legislative electoral commission declared Borges
the overwhelming victor. In the light of this
affront, the Libertadores revolted; on Borges's inauguration day, January 25, 1923, regional insurrections erupted
across the state. In the end, the insurgents were out-
manned and the revolt was put down. They did, however, force Borges to curtail his authority by promulgat-
ing a constitutional amendment which proscribed gubernatorial re-election. See also BORGES DE MEDEIROS.

ALIANÇA NACIONAL LIBERTADORA (ANL). National Liberation Alliance, a popular-front mass movement organized
in early 1935 by anti-fascists with the backing and support
of the underground Brazilian Communist Party. Suppressed after only a few months, the ANL disintegrated as a
popular movement but was used by PCB and some ANL
leaders as the spearhead of a futile anti-Vargas insurrection in November among military enlisted men and cadets
in Natal, Recife, and in Rio de Janeiro.

ALIANÇA RENOVADORA NACIONAL (ARENA). The official
party of the 1964 revolution.

ALLIATA-BRONNER, CESARE. An agent of the Italian
secret police, assigned to the São Paulo consulate to
keep anarchists, syndicalists, and other presumed agita-
tors under surveillance. His letters to his superiors
are available in the Italian state archives and they provide an invaluable glimpse of incipient trade union militancy in Brazil at the turn of the century. See LABOR
ORGANIZATION.

ALMANAQUE DO PESSOAL MILITAR DO EXÉRCITO. An-
nually-published list of promotions and assignments within
all branches of the armed forces at the officer level,
dating back to 1829, issued in limited editions (3,800
copies in 1977), and the leading manual for Brazil-watch-
ers seeking to decipher patterns of influence and power
in the military.

ALMEIDA, CÂNDIDO MENDES DE (1818-1881). Politician
and jurist, a graduate of the Olinda (later Recife) Law

School (1839), and a defender of the two imprisoned bish-
ops--Dom Vital and D. Antônio de Macedo Costa--during
the so-called Religious Question of the 1870's.

ALMEIDA, CIPRIANO JOSÉ BARATA (1762-1838).   A journalist, deputy and political figure of the early monarchy.
In Recife, the Bahia-born, Coimbra-trained physician
edited an opposition newspaper, Sentinela da Liberdade,
from 1823 to 1832.   Implicated in several republican
conspiracies, he was imprisoned during several years.
Freed in 1829, he helped lead the campaign against Pedro
I.   After Pedro's abdication in 1831, he returned to Rio
de Janeiro; after further political intrigues, he retired
to Natal, Rio Grande do Norte, where he operated a
pharmacy.

ALMOCREVE.   A muleteer; there were thousands of almo-
creves in the backlands of the northeast before giving
way to motorized trucks in the 1920's and 1930's.

ALQUEIRE.   Land measure used during the colonial period,
varying in size from region to region between about 6
to 12 acres (24,200 to 48,400 square meters).

ALVARES, DIOGO.   Known as Caramurú, he was a Portuguese sailor shipwrecked off the Bahian coast whose
timely use of his rifle caused the local aborigines to
treat him as a god (and eschew plans to eat him, as
they had done to his shipwrecked comrades).   He produced dozens of progeny, and his influence over the local
population greatly aided the Portuguese efforts to establish a settlement at Salvador.

ÁLVES, MARCIO MOREIRA (1936-   ).   A journalist elected
to Congress in 1966, two years after the military coup,
who rose to denounce the dictatorship from his congressional seat and, in consequence, was deprived of his
political rights and ultimately exiled to France.   Álves
demonstrated a flair for the dramatic, attacking the
machismo of the armed forces by urging what he termed
Operations Lysistrata--the wives and lovers of military
men would refuse the advances of their men until the
regime's use of violence was curtailed.

ÁLVIM, DANILO (1921-).   Soccer idol of the 1940's and
early 1950's; a member of the World Cup squad favored
to beat Uruguay in 1950 but losers, and known in the
press either as Danilo or "Príncipe" ("The Prince").

Amado   10

AMADO, GILBERTO (1887-1969). Writer and diplomat, a
  neoparnassian poet, and member of Congress from his
  native Sergipe although he spent most of his life in Rio
  de Janeiro and in Europe. Amado represented Brazil
  on the United Nations Commission on International Law
  and was elected in 1963 to the Academy of Letters.

AMADO, JORGE (1912-   ). Major novelist, and the Brazilian
  author most frequently translated into English for his
  colorful portrayal of Bahian life. From the early 1930's,
  when his O País do Carvaval (Carnival Land) became a
  best-seller, through the 1970's, Amado's charm and wit
  in spinning gossipy and delightfully original tales of everyday life made him immensely popular. His Gabriela:
  Cravo e Canela (Gabriela: Clove and Cinnamon), a tale
  based on a mythological characterization of a mulata who
  comes to the bustling Bahian port town of Ilhéus, was
  turned into a successful television serial. During the
  early Vargas period Amado sympathized with the popular
  front Aliança Nacional Libertadora, and wrote a laudatory
  biography of Luis Carlos Prestes which officials later
  suppressed. Most of his later works have been apolitical.

AMAPÁ. Federal territory in the northern Amazon, bordered
  by French Guiana and the state of Pará. Its capital,
  Macapá, lies directly across from the large Ilha de
  Marajó, in Pará. The territory's major exports are
  timber, minerals, and skins.

AMAPÁ ATROCITIES. The reported massacre of 38 inhabitants of the frontier province of Amapá, in the main
  women and children, by invading forces from French
  Guiana. Failure of the Prudente de Morais government
  to react militarily brought derision to the administration.

AMARAÇÕES. Indian-hunting expeditions in the captaincy of
  Rio Negro, given the name from the verb "ammarar,"
  meaning, to bind or tie up. Prohibited for half a century, under the Pombaline reforms, they were resumed
  after the laws were revoked in 1798.

AMARAL, TARSILA DO (1886-1973). São Paulo-born artist
  who studied in Paris after the First World War with
  Léger and others, painting in the cubist style and adapt-
  ing it to Anthropophagism (iconoclastic, surprising, almost surrealistic forms), and developing a uniquely
  national style grounded in lavish color and plastic figures.

AMAZON BASIN. The Amazon River is fed by more than
one thousand tributaries, forming a basin of approximately
4,800,000 square kilometers--the largest in the world.
The major tributaries include, on the northern side, the
Javari, Jundiaí, Jutaí, Juruá, Tefé, Coari, Purus,
Madeira, Tapajós, Xingu, Anapú, and Tocantins; to the
south, Içá (or Putamaio), Japurá, Negro, Atumã, Ja-
mundá, Trombetas, Maicurú, Parú, Jari, Maracá, and
the Araguaia. See also PARANÁ BASIN.

AMAZON VALLEY. The Brazilian part encompasses the
enormous reaches of the states of Acre, Amazonas,
Pará, northern Maranhão, and the federal territories of
Amapá, Rondônia, and Roraima. Ninety percent of the
area lies above flood level; on the Venezuelan border
mountains rise above 8,000 feet. Humidity is high,
making the climate uncomfortable; temperatures are, by
comparison, relatively moderate. Rainfall, often ex-
ceeding 100 inches a year, falls mainly in the months
between January and June. Transportation is dependent
upon riverboats, military and commercial aircraft, and
the Trans-Amazon Highway, opened in the late 1960's,
and, according to popular belief, visible with the naked
eye from the surface of the moon.

AMAZONAS. Brazil's largest state, it borders Colombia,
Venezuela, Peru; the federal territories of Roraima
and Rondônia; and the states of Pará, Acre, and Mato
Grosso. Larger than most countries, it covers 1,564,445
square kilometers and comprises seven geographic sub-
regions. Its capital is Manaos.

AMAZONIAN REVOLUTION OF 1924. A brief-lived insurrection, successful for thirty days, in sympathy with
the 1924 tenente revolt in São Paulo, led by Ten. Alfredo
Augusto Ribeiro Júnior.

AMÉLIA, IMPERATRIZ. Wife to Pedro I and mother of the
future Pedro II, left behind with tutors when the royal
couple returned to Portugal after Pedro I abdicated.
On her departure, she wrote a sentimental, if platitudi-
nous letter to the young "órfão-imperador" (orphan-Em-
peror), asking that the "mothers of Brazil" adopt the
boy in their hearts.

AMÉRICO, PEDRO (1843-1905). Artist of the nineteenth
century whose works included celebrations of national
history. His most renowned work is the "Battle of Avahy."

AMÉRICO DE ALMEIDA, JOSÉ (1887-   ). Paraibano writer
and politician named federal interventor in his state in
1930, a cabinet minister (Viação) in 1935, and the "official" candidate to succeed Vargas in 1937. In part as
a result of his fiery campaign rhetoric (which made him
seem reckless), Vargas revoked his support of José
Américo's candidacy and cancelled the elections with the
promulgation of the Estado Novo in November 1937.
His novel A Bagaceira (1928) is considered a major
representative of regional literature.

AMOROSO LIMA, ALCEU   see   CENTRO DOM VITAL

"ANAUÉ!" The Integralist salutation, taken from the Tupí,
and used by Plinio Salgado's followers in place of the
Nazi "Heil!"

ANDRADA, GOMES FREIRE DE(? - 1763). The Count of
Bobadela, governor-general of Rio de Janeiro for thirty
years, from 1733 until his death. He governed more or
less as if he were head of a southern state, cut off, as
it were, from the economic life of the Northeast. In
the year of his death Rio de Janeiro became the capital
of Brazil, a change brought about by the shift of prosperity from the Northeast to the Center-South with the
opening of Minas Gerais to gold mining.

ANDRADA E SILVA, ANTÔNIO CARLOS RIBEIRO DE (1773-
1845). José Bonifácio's brother, and one of the leading
orators of his time. As spokesman for the Brazilian
delegation to the Portuguese Cortes, he helped pave the
way for the break which would take place in 1822. He
was deported in 1823 for his opposition to Pedro I, and
only returned in 1828. In 1831, again taking an active
role in national politics, he was accused of supporting
a restoration faction and again was forced into European
exile. After Pedro's death he returned and entered the
Chamber of Deputies, representing São Paulo.

ANDRADA E SILVA, ANTÔNIO CARLOS IV DE (1870-1945).
Barbacena (Minas Gerais)-born politician who, as head
of the Mineiro state administration in 1926, expected to
win the nomination to succeed Paulista Washington Luís
in the presidency. When the Mineiros were ignored,
Antônio Carlos led his state into the opposition Liberal
Alliance. After Vargas's victory he was rewarded with
a cabinet post (Treasury) and in 1935 was elected president of the Chamber of Deputies.

ANDRADA E SILVA, JOSÉ BONIFÁCIO (1763-1838). Chief advisor to Pedro I and considered in Brazilian historiography to be one of the precursors of independence, owing to his great personal influence on the young monarch as well as on his son, Pedro II. Andrada was São Paulo-born but took a law degree at Coimbra and studied natural science in Saxony, Bohemia, Prussia, Denmark, Sweden, Norway, Scotland, and Spain. When the French invaded Portugal he fought in the resistance; in 1819, after thirty-six years, he returned to Brazil where he became Pedro's minister of kingdom and foreign relations. Following Pedro's dissolution of the Constituent Assembly in 1823, he was imprisoned and deported to France, where he spent an additional six years. In 1831, with the abdication of Pedro, José Bonifácio was named tutor of the monarch's four children who remained in Brazil.

ANDRADE, CARLOS DRUMMOND DE (1902-   ). Contemporary poet, born in Itabira, Minas Gerais, and the author of nearly a dozen major works of poetry. Drummond's poetry conveys harsh, classical visions of reality, and avoids what has been called the "Condoric Latin eloquence of the tropics." Socially conscious, Drummond does not expect secular redemption of injustice.

ANDREONI, GIOVANNI ANTÔNIO (1650-1716). Italian Jesuit author (under the pseudonym of André Antonil) of Cultura e Opulência do Brasil por Suas Drogas e Minas, published in 1711 but immediately suppressed for being too informative to foreigners. It was reprinted in 1837; Antonil's identity was revealed only in 1886 by Capistrano de Abreu.

ANDRÓFAGO. Cannibal who eats only male flesh. "Androphagy" is practiced among those Brazilian Amerindian tribes which follow cannibalistic behavior only as a byproduct of warfare--eating, as it were, male prisoners taken in battle.

ANGÉLICA, SOROR JOANA (1761-1822). Abbess of the Convent of Lapa in Salvador, and killed by a Portuguese soldier during the struggle in that city between loyalist and pro-Independence forces. She has been made into one of the major heroines in Brazilian history.

ANHANGÜERA see BUENO DA SILVA, BARTOLOMEU

ANHEMBI PARK. Exhibition and commercial center in the city of São Paulo.

ANTARCTIC FRANCE.   Fortified French settlement on an
island in the Bay of Guanabara in 1555 under the leadership of Nicolas de Villegaignon.   The European settlers
included both Catholics and Protestants, leading to rivalry
and ultimate internal conflict.   At one point Villegaignon
expelled the colony's Huguenots.   In 1559, pessimistic
about the future of the colony, he returned to France.
A year later the French settlement was taken by forces
led by Mem de Sá, Brazilian governor-general, driving
the remaining French and their Amerindian allies into
the interior.   The conquest was completed in 1567.

ANTI-PUBLIC WHIPPING LAW.   Passed in 1886, as pressure
for abolition mounted and the Imperial legislature found
itself obligated to show progress toward that ultimate
goal, finally achieved two years later.

ANTI-ROSAS INTERVENTION.   Incursion, in 1852, by several
thousand Brazilian troops as part of the movement to
overthrow the dictator Juan Manuel de Rosas.

ANTONIL, ANDRÉ JÕAO   see   ANDREONI, GIOVANNI AN-
TÔNIO

ANUÁRIO ESTATÍSTICO.   Annual statistical report of census
bureau, issued nationally and by most states.

ANÚNCIOS DOS ESCRAVOS FUGIDOS.   Fugitive-slave advertisements, placed by owners in newspapers around Brazil.
These advertisements offer valuable insight into the nature of the slave system, and have been studied by
Gilberto Freyre and others.

ARACAJÚ.   Capital of the northeastern state of Sergipe,
five kilometers from the coast on the right bank of the
Sergipe River, a sleepy city whose commerce falls within
the economic orbit of Salvador.

ARAGÃO, MONIZ DE.   Brazilian ambassador to Berlin during
the mid- and late 1930's, recalled when Vargas expelled
German chargé Karl Ritter in 1938 for interference in
domestic affairs, at the request of the Reich.

ARANHA, BENTO DE FIGUEIREDO TENREIRO (1769-1811).
Belém-born author with a rudimentary formal education
who wrote poems, orations, and plays; his theater piece,
A Felicidade no Brasil (a nativist drama), was presented
in Belém's Teatro Público in 1808.

ARANHA, GRAÇA (1868-1931). A student of Tobias Barreto
at the Recife Law School and a native of Maranhão,
Aranha published a novel, Canaan, the story of a German
immigrant settling in the Brazilian backlands. His second
romance, Viagem Maravilhosa (Marvelous Journey), appeared twenty years later.

ARANHA, OSWALDO (1894-1960). Gaúcho political figure
and confidant of Getúlio Vargas, Aranha was one of the
principal civilian actors in the tenente-led Liberal Alliance. After the successful 1930 Revolution he held
various cabinet-level posts and was sent to Washington
as Ambassador. A liberal democrat, Aranha was ex-
tremely popular in the United States, but broke with
Vargas over the imposition of the authoritarian Estado
Novo constitution in 1937. Reconciled, he served as
Foreign Minister (1938-1944) and Ambassador to the
United Nations under Dutra (1945-1947) and served as
the President of the General Assembly in 1947. A hand-
some man and somewhat of a bon-vivant, Aranha helped
soothe relations between Brazil and the United States,
and before the Second World War was one of the few
advocates in high circles of entry on the side of the
Allies.

ARARIPE, TRISTÃO GONÇALVES PEREIRA DE ALENCAR.
Leader of the Confederation of the Equator from Ceará,
a province in which the insurrection was strongly supported. The municipal councils of Quixeramobim and
Icó were the first to break with D. Pedro, communicating
their decision to Fortaleza, where Tristão de Alencar
and others led a coup against the loyalist government.
Ceará was ultimately restored to Imperial control after
the suppression of the revolt in Pernambuco.

ARATÚ INDUSTRIAL CENTER. A new (1960's) zone designed
to accommodate heavy and light industry outside of the
city of Salvador on the Bahia de Todos os Santos.

ARAUCÁRIA PINE. A lovely, distinctive evergreen, native
to Paraná, found at altitudes between 600 and 900 meters.

ARAÚJO LIMA, PEDRO DE (1793-1870). Regent of the Empire after the resignation of Father Feijó in 1837, the
Conservative Party leader and a prominent congressional
figure popular with the Portuguese elements who had been
pushed into the background with Pedro's proclamation of

independence in 1822.   Araújo's three years as regent
saw economic gains but his inability to control successionist movements on the periphery--especially in the
South--created a constitutional crisis and led to the early
accession of Pedro II, at the age of fourteen, to the
throne in 1840.

ARCHIVOS DO MUSEU NACIONAL.   Established in 1876 as
the journal of the National Museum, and the first significant scientific journal in the country.

ARCO-VERDE.   Tabajara cacique who fought alongside Duarte
Coelho in the donatary's campaigns against the Cateé
Indians in Pernambuco.   In the nineteenth century a
sertão village to the west of Pesqueira was named for
the chieftain.

ARCOVERDE, CARDEAL (1850-1930).   Born Joaquim Arco-
verde de Albuquerque Cavalcanti in Cimbres, Pernambuco,
Arcoverde studied at Rome at the Gregorian University;
he returned in 1876 as a priest and was named bishop
of São Paulo in 1894.   In 1905 Pope Pius X named him
the first Latin American cardinal.

AREA.   Brazil's land mass comprises 8,456,000 square
kilometers.

ARGOLLO, FRANCISCO DE PAULA (1837-1930).   War Minister in 1904, Argollo argued for expanded military expenditures (and universal conscription) in order to protect
Brazil's frontiers and back up Brazil's diplomatic negotiating position.

ARINOS, AFONSO (1868-1916).   Journalist and short story
writer, born in the sertão of Minas Gerais (Paracatú),
a bacharel in law, and world traveler although his writing
reflected his memories of the pastoral hinterland.

ARMADOR.   Urban-based supplier of arms, especially to
bandeirante expeditions.   See BANDEIRAS.

ARMAZÉN.   A storehouse on a fazenda.

ARMITAGE, JOHN (1807-1856).   English-born historian and
writer who lived in Rio de Janeiro from 1828 to 1835,
and the author of an important history of Brazil from
the arrival of the royal family to the abdication of Pedro
I in 1831.   Armitage was a close friend of Evaristo da
Veiga.

ARMY MEDICAL CORPS. Formally organized in 1915, although the armed forces maintained some treatment centers, such as the Asilo de Inválidos da Pátria, a soldier's
home, during the late nineteenth century. On the whole,
the system was deficient, and did not meet the service's
needs; Army post infirmaries often lacked even indoor
plumbing. As McCann notes, the army's health mirrored
the paradoxical state of health care in civilian society:
while Oswaldo Cruz and others labored to carry out
elaborate programs in experimental medicine and to eradi-
cate epidemic disease, there was a lack of hospitals,
physicians, and nurses; many municípios did not have
even one health care professional.

ARMY STRENGTH. In 1976, Brazil's standing army contained 182,808 soldiers, including 129 general officers,
15,308 commissioned officers, and 118,466 conscripts
and volunteers (the remainder being career soldiers in
non-commissioned ranks).

ARRAES, MIGUEL (1916-). Governor of Pernambuco in
the heady Goulart period, and one of the more socially
militant political figures of the day. With the 1964 coup
he took refuge in Algeria, dividing his residence in exile
between Algiers and France. Prior to his election as
governor he served as Recife's mayor; he was the first
socialist to hold either office. He published an angry
book-length essay: Brazil: The People and the Power,
in Paris and London in 1969.

ARRAIAIS. Mining camps established by the bandeirantes
in the hinterland beyond São Vicente.

ARRAIAL DO TIJUCO see DIAMANTINA

ARROBA. Portuguese measure of weight equivalent to thirty-
three pounds. The Spanish arroba was only twenty-five
pounds.

ARRUDA CÂMARA, MANUEL DE (1752-1810). The "father
of Brazilian agronomy," one of the best-informed men
in the late eighteenth century, but whose memoirs reveal
no knowledge of the cotton gin seven years after its in-
vention by Eli Whitney. In 1813, a Rio de Janeiro
journal published Arruda Câmara's Memória in three
issues, without a single mention of the significant developments which had occurred in cotton agriculture since
1792. As late as 1817, Martius noted the use of old-

fashioned methods in Brazilian cotton production, as did
St. Hilaire two years later.   Arruda Câmara experimented
with possible improvements on the old cotton milling
procedures, but he remained ignorant of the advances
made outside the country.

ASAS.   The "wings" of the city of Brasília, designed by
urban planner Lúcio Costa to look, on a map or from
the sky, like a giant airplane.

ASHOGOUN.   The person responsible for attending to the
animal sacrifice--often a chicken--during the macumba
or candomblé ceremony.

ASKI MARKS   see   COMPENSATION MARKS

ASSEMBLIES OF GOD.   The oldest and largest Pentecostal
sect in Brazil, arriving through missionaries about 1910.

ASSESSORIA DE RELAÇÕES PÚBLICAS DA PRESIDÊNCIA
DA REPÚBLICA (ARP).   The public relations agency of
the federal government, created after the 1964 Revolution,
and highly acclaimed for its cleverness in the use of
radio, television, advertising, and other forms of raising
public awareness in the area of civic responsibility and
patriotic pride.   The ARP, a historical descendant of
Vargas's DIP--the Estado Novo's Departamento de Imprensa e Propaganda (q. v.)--has enjoyed large budgetary
resources, nearly one million cruzeiros during the Semana
da Pátria (a patriotic week-long celebration in February)
in 1977.

ASSIM MARCHA A FAMÍLIA.   A collection of essays (1965)
edited by Carlos Heitor Cony, titled Thus Goes the
Family, and one of the only books ever published in
Brazil on what might be called the underside of urban
life: prostitution, homosexuality, crime, transvestism,
and poverty.   The book was allowed to be published although copies were seized from time to time by individual
police officials, and within a few years harassment of the
publisher, Editôra Civilização Brasileira of Rio de Janeiro, had virtually led to its bankruptcy.

ASSIS, MACHADO DE (1839-1908).   Brazil's major literary
figure, a mulatto whose works reveal nothing of racial
awareness or concern, and a modernist of unequalled
skill in imagery whether as a Parnassian poet or as a
novelist and short story writer.

ASSIS BRASIL, JOAQUIM FRANCISCO DE (1857-1938).
Gaucho diplomat, writer, and politician, and leader of
the state Aliança Libertadora; governor of Rio Grande
do Sul, and historical republican.

ASSIS CHATEAUBRIAND, FRANCISCO (1891-1968). Born
Francisco Bandeira de Melo in Umbuzeiro, Paraíba.
His father founded a school in Recife named after Vicomte
François René de Chateaubriand, and, as was somewhat
usual for the period, changed his own name and adopted
that of his savant. After a degree in law in Recife,
young Francisco became a journalist, working for various
leading Rio de Janeiro newspapers before founding his
own, O Jornal, which was to become the cornerstone of
a journalistic empire. He was a federal senator during
the Republic, and participated in the Liberal Alliance
coup of 1930. Known to Brazilians as Chatô, he built,
by the time of his death, a chain of 32 newspapers, 18
television stations, 24 radio stations, 4 magazines and
a news agency. He aided domestic aviation in the 1930's,
built child-care centers, and donated art valued more
than $25 million to the São Paulo Art Museum, which he
helped build. Suffering a stroke in 1960, he nonetheless
directed his empire from his hospital bed.

ASSOCIAÇÃO CULTURAL DO NEGRO. Negro Cultural Association, an organization formed in the 1950's in the image
of the old Frente Negro Brasileiro. It located its headquarters in São Paulo, and incorporated much of the old
Frente's library and archives. The association never
succeeded and disappeared by the end of the decade.

ASSUMPÇÃO, CARLOS DE (1833-1912). Afro-Brazilian poet
of the 1960's, from São Paulo.

A ASTRÉIA see AURORA, A.

ATABAQUE. A conical drum with a single head at the wide
end, invariably played in sets of three. Sudanese and
Bantu in origin, they are used in Afro-Brazilian religious
ritual.

ATAÍDE E MELO, PEDRO MARIA XAVIER DE. Governor
of Minas Gerais in 1803, and the official responsible
for a systematic campaign against the Botocudo (Aimoré)
tribe, dividing the "infested area" of the province into
military districts and declaring war against the "savages."

ATHAÍDE, AUSTREGÉSILO DE (1898-   ).   Pernambuco-born
Athaíde rose through the Assis Chateaubriand chain of
newspapers and became an editor of Rio's O Jornal.   An
adversary of the 1930 Revolution, he participated in the
1932 São Paulo uprising and was jailed and exiled in
consequence.   He rejoined the Chateaubriand organization
on his return in 1934; in 1951 he was elected to the
Academy of Letters, ostensibly for his belletristic merit,
and rose to be its president during the 1960's and 1970's.
Athaíde won decorations from several foreign governments,
including Chile, Peru, France, Great Britain, and the
Vatican.

ATIRADORES.   Marksmen; refers to members of the civilian
Tiros da Guerra.   See LINHAS DO TIRO.

ATO ADICIONAL (1834).   Act reforming the political structure of the Empire by giving more autonomy to provincial
legislatures, and substituting an elected regent for the
triumvirate governing Brazil in the name of the young
Emperor Pedro II.

ATO ADICIONAL (1961).   Act substituting a parliamentary
form of presidential selection, occasioned by the renunciation of the presidency by Jânio Quadros in the absence
of Vice-President João Goulart.   The parliamentary experiment was ended in 1963 when it was defeated by
plebiscite (Jan. 6).

ATO INSTITUCIONAL No. 1 (1964).   Decree of the Revolutionary military government suspending the political
rights of the last three presidents of the Republic--Kubit-
schek, Quadros, and Goulart--as well as hundreds of
other public officials, civilian and military.

ATO INSTITUCIONAL No. 5 see CONSTITUTION OF 1967.

ATURIÁ.   A bird of the bindoree family, commonly called
"stinkbird."   The term is also applied to gypsies (aturiá
cigana).

AURORA, A.   Newspaper of the Moderado faction during the
Regency era, published in Rio de Janeiro, along with O
Independente and A Astréia.

AURORA FLUMINENSE.   Rio de Janeiro newspaper established
in 1827 by Evaristo da Veiga.

"AVANTE. " The Integralist anthem, used during the 1930's
in tandem with the Brazilian national anthem at gatherings
of the Ação Integralista Brasileira.

AVANTI! Brazil's first socialist newspaper, published in
Italian in São Paulo in 1902, by immigrant dockworkers.
It was discontinued in the same year, but followed ten
years later by a second Italian-language socialist paper,
Il Progresso.

-B-

BABÁ. A nursemaid, traditionally African or Afro-Brazilian.
In the 1970's, some upper-class families in the South,
especially São Paulo and Rio Grande do Sul, began to
hire European (even Scandinavian) au pair girls as nurse-
maids and governesses.

BABA SUJA. A scum formed in the process of boiling raw
sugar cane juices, when making rapadura, which must be
skimmed off. The discard has a high molasses content,
and can be used either as a cattle feed or for distillation
into cachaça.

BABOSA. Plant whose leaf is used to make a bitter paste
to apply to a rural nursing mother's nipple to aid in
weaning. In towns, children who resist weaning are
sent away to live with their grandmothers.

BACALHÃO. 1) Dried codfish, usually consumed by the poor
as a substitute for meat; 2) Slang for a whip. See also
CHARQUE.

BACHAREL, BACHARÉIS. University graduate(s). In the
nineteenth century, until the advent of the federal republic,
there were only four university-level institutions in Brazil:
law schools in São Paulo and Recife, and medical schools
in Rio de Janeiro and Salvador. Graduates of these universities, and from the newer institutions established in
the states after 1889, were virtually guaranteed public
posts if they sought them. During the Republic, the
"bacharel" became the symbol of the bureaucratically-
oriented state-level political elites. From 70 to 85 percent of all officeholders at the highest state and federal
levels were bacharéis through the 1930 Revolution.

BACHARELADO. Degree awarded after four years of study

(after three years before 1962) in a Faculty of Philosophy
and Letters, or after five years in a Law Faculty.

BACHARELANDO.   Literally, "in the process of attaining a
bacharel degree." The term was used to designate law
students in their last year of study during the Empire
and Old Republic.

"BACHIANAS BRASILEIRAS." Nine recreations of the con-
trapuntal canons of J. S. Bach, by the native composer
Heitor Villa-Lobos, who adapted the Bachian form to
Brazilian folk themes to produce an audacious yet brilliant set of compositions.

BAETA.   A cotton flannel cloth used to fashion outergarments
for slaves during the cool nights of the dry season in
the Paraíba Valley.

BAGASSE.   Sugarcane pressed until it is sufficiently dry to
be burned as a low-grade kind of fuel in engenho boilers.
See also ENGENHO.

BAGUNÇA.   A mess, confusion, disorder.   See also ABACAXI.

BAHIA.   The major state of the East-Northeast south of
Pernambuco, and, through its capital, Salvador, the
gateway to much of the rural interior of Pernambuco,
Piauí, Goiás, and Minas Gerais.   Rich in architecture
and history, Bahia played a major role in political affairs
through the end of the Empire but then, with Pernambuco,
was eclipsed by the rising states of the Center-South:
São Paulo, Minas Gerais and Rio Grande do Sul.   Bahia
is primarily agricultural although an industrial zone has
been constructed under federal auspices to attract capital
investment from the South and from abroad.   Its 1970
population was 7,195,000, half a million of which live
in Salvador.

BAHIA, ARCHBISHOPRIC OF.   Brazil's only archbishopric
until the late eighteenth century, with jurisdiction over
the captaincies of Bahia and Sergipe, and supremacy over
Brazil and Angola.   There were six bishoprics: Pará,
Maranhão, Olinda (Pernambuco), Rio de Janeiro, São
Paulo, and Mariana (Minas Gerais).

BAHIA DE TODOS OS SANTOS.   One of the original captaincies, the territory deeded to the noble Francisco Pereira

Coutinho. The captaincy was the first to revert to Crown control, and in 1549 it became the site of the Brazilian capital.

BAHIAN IMMIGRATION SOCIETY. A group organized in the 1880's to attract European settlers through methods like those employed by the Paulistas, by subsidizing ship passages and otherwise recruiting in European port cities. The society never accomplished very much, although it cleared the air about Bahian planters' preferences for "intelligent" Europeans over "boorish" slaves.

BAHIAN SEMINARY. Also known as the Seminary of Todos os Santos, a Jesuit academy which, in 1575, became the first institution to award the bachelor of arts degree; in 1576 it offered its first master's degree. Its most famous graduate was Father Antônio Vieira, who later earned fame as an eloquent spokesman against enslavement of the aboriginal population. See also ANTÔNIO VIEIRA.

BAHIANO. Resident or inhabitant of the state of Bahia, portrayed popularly as eloquent and (superficially) verbose and learned. The stereotype probably derives from the reputation of Rui Barbosa, a famous Bahiano statesman and politician of the early Republic. In São Paulo, the term has another, more pejorative, meaning--that of any migrant from the rural Northeast.

BAÍA CABRÁLIA. The site on the Bahias coast where Cabral landed in 1500, and later named after the explorer.

BAIÃO. Story-telling variety of popular music, popularized in the mid-1940's by Luiz Gonzaga and Humberto Teixeira; generally nationalistic.

BAIXADA FLUMINENSE. Coastal lowlands interrupted only by low rounded hills and isolated hillocks, one of the colony's principal population centers, and the location of the settlements in and around Rio de Janeiro.

BALA E ONÇA. "Rough and ready," a term applied to Paulistas. The name originated from the Bandeirante (q. v.) legends.

BALAIADA REVOLT. Regionalist insurrection in the province of Maranhão during the Araújo Lima regency from

1838 to 1841. Among the 11,000 rebel forces, 3,000
were escaped slaves who were recruited to the revolutionary banner. The rebellion was suppressed by troops
under General Luís Alves de Lima, who was awarded
the title "Baron of Caxias" for his service. See also
FARROUPILHA REVOLT.

BALSAS. Flat, shuttle ferries propelled by outboard motors
used to convey passengers (and even automobiles) back
and forth across riverbanks in the Amazon.

BANCADA. A state's delegation of deputies or congressmen.

BANCO ALEMÃO TRANSATLÂNTICO. One of the two German
banks operating in Brazil in the 1930's, with branches
in six cities. There was only one American bank, First
National City of New York.

BANCO DO BRASIL. Established under the auspices of the
Prince-Regent D. João in 1808, it was liquidated in 1829
but revived in 1853, when the accompanying period of
prosperity necessitated new sources of credit. The
Banco do Brasil played a major role in the economic
development of the interior by opening small agencies in
rural municípios across Brazil during the Old Republic.
The majority of its shares are held by the federal government, for which it acts as fiscal agent.

BANCO NACIONAL DE HABITAÇÃO (BNH). The National
Housing Bank, established in 1964 by the military government. The Bank received approximately one percent of
the national industrial payroll in the form of unemploy-
ment compensation; in turn, it was obliged to invest the
funds in housing.

BANDEIRA. In colonial times, an armed expedition, usually
from the settlement of São Vicente (São Paulo) which
penetrated the hinterland to capture Amerindian slaves
or to search for gold. The bandeiras reached their
height during the period between 1650 and 1750. See
also BANDEIRANTE.

BANDEIRA DE MELLO, FELIPE. Head of FUNAI, and a
leading exponent of the "Integration" approach--that
indigenous   tribes   should   be   brought   into   Brazilian
life.

BANDEIRANTE. A participant in the bandeiras, usually a

Brazilian-born Portuguese who adapted to indigenous customs and who took indigenous wives or concubines.   See also LINGUA GERAL.

BANGÜÊ.   Literally, the brick-lined trough through which the cane mash flowed.   The term was also applied to sugar engenhos (q. v.), especially to smaller ones where the mill fires were stilled after the advent of the usinas (q. v.), when the engenhos became simple suppliers of cane.

BARATA RIBEIRO, CÂNDIDO (1843-1910).   Physician and federal judge, Barata Ribeiro fought ardently for a republic and was a leading abolitionist.   One of the four principal avenues in Rio's Copacabana was named after him in the 1920's.

BARBALHO DE UCHOA CAVALCANTI, JOÃO (1846-1909).   Son of a Pernambuco planter, João Barbalho distinguished himself as a jurist, director of public education, and the author of a major study (1902) on the 1891 federal constitution.

BARBEIRO.   Blood-sucking tick infesting unsanitary housing of the poor in central Brazil, and identified as a disease-carrier by Carlos Chagas in 1912.   Chagas's call for sanitary prophylaxis was opposed by conservative physicians who questioned his experiments.

BARBEIROS.   Slave musical groups, usually made up in the eighteenth and nineteenth centuries by barbers, from whose name the word barbeiro was taken.

BARBOSA, DOMINGOS CALDAS (1738-1800).   A mulatto, and the first Brazilian to pursue a musical career abroad. He became a sensation singing Brazilian songs in Portugal.

BARBOSA, RUI (1840-1923).   Diminutive jurist, orator, diplomat, and would-be president of the republic.   Barbosa was born in Salvador, studied law at Recife and São Paulo, and practiced law while he built a reputation as an abolitionist.   A cabinet minister in the first Republican government, he helped establish the separation of Church and State.   Barbosa flitted between government and journalism, and in 1907 was sent as Brazilian representative to the Hague Peace meeting, where he gained fame as defender of the concept of an International Court.

In 1910 he ran unsuccessfully for the presidency, being defeated by War Minister Hermes da Fonseca.

BARBOSA LIMA, ALEXANDRÉ JOSÉ (1862-1931). Positivist and career army officer chosen by Floriano Peixoto to govern his home state of Pernambuco in 1892, which was proving itself ungovernable. An iron-fisted administrator, Barbosa Lima so alienated the state's political elite that he was unable to seek a second term, leaving for a federal senatorship in Rio and letting political control fall to the former head of the Imperial Conservative party, Francisco de Assis Rosa e Silva. Barbosa Lima's career in the Senate was long and distinguished, but he never returned to Pernambuco.

BARCELOS, PERO DE. An early Portuguese explorer, who, with João Fernandes Lavrador, discovered, or re-discovered, Greenland in 1495. See also LAVRADOR.

BARON, VICTOR ALLAN (1902-1936). A young American and member of the Comintern sent to Brazil during the period of the Communist Party-backed Aliança Nacional Libertadora, arrested, and allegedly murdered by the police (officially he committed suicide in jail).

BARRACÃO. A trading post or company store, a major fixture in rural Brazil, and the bane of the poor and the isolated. The barracão sells on credit; in the Amazon they serve as depots at which trappers and other sellers deposit and merchandise their goods. The barracão rarely if ever faces competition; many peasants soon run up bills which, owing to compound interest, can never be paid off in the lifetime of the borrower.

BARRACO. A shack, of wood or mud brick, typical of squatter settlements in São Paulo and outside the city of Brasília. See also MOCAMBO; ALAGADO.

BARRAVENTO. "The turning wind," the point of violence at which the sea and earth become transformed, and the title of a 1962 Cinema Nôvo film by Glauber Rocha. The director's first full-length movie, it calls for violent social change. It is set in a coastal Bahian fishing village.

BARRETO, AFONSO HENRIQUES DE LIMA (1881-1922). A mulatto novelist who, unlike Machado de Assis, was conscious of the existence of racial discrimination and whose

books reflect an anguished call for justice. Lima Barreto's own life was unhappy; he refused to bow to the
"comportment line" set by white society, and his death
in Rio de Janeiro after a life of poverty and alcoholism
may be attributed in part to his frankness on the subject
during a period--the 1920's--when such feelings were
tacitly forbidden.

BARRETO, EDMUNDO MUNIZ (1864-1934). Commander of
the Luso-Brazilian forces at the decisive Battle of Guararapes, won after five hours of armed combat. The
fighting took place on April 19, 1648. The final Dutch
stand took place at the second battle of Guararapes, on
February 19, 1649.

BARRETO, EMÍDIO DANTAS (1850-1931). A career military
officer who entered the army as a volunteer in the
Paraguayan War and who rose to be War Minister in
1910. Named opposition candidate for the governorship
of Pernambuco as part of the salvacionista campaign to
unseat state oligarchies, he defeated political boss Rosa
e Silva in a violent electoral campaign marked by fraud
on both sides. After one term as governor the state
passed into the hands of Manoel Borba, a Dantista who
soon broke with his mentor; by 1918 control of the state
machine had passed back into the hands of the old elite.

BARROS, ADHEMAR DE (1901-1969). Paulista politician and
governor from 1947 to 1951 and again from 1962 to 1966,
when he broke with the military government and was removed from office. A consummate politician who ex-
ploited his Catholicism, he was known to be personally
corrupt in spite of his popularity. See also "ROUBA
MAS FAZ."

BARROSO, ALMIRANTE (1804-1882). Portuguese-born admiral and hero of the Paraguayan War. At the age of
four his family came to Brazil; he was one of the first
graduates of the new Naval Academy in Rio de Janeiro,
and served in every major naval action of the early Empire: the Cisplatine War (1826-28), the Pará rebellion
(1836), and the War with Paraguay, where he commanded
the victorious fleet at the Battle of Riachuelo, in the
River Plate.

BARROSO, GUSTAVO DODT (1888-1959). Writer, member
of the Brazilian delegation to Versailles in 1919, and
intellectual chefe of the fascist Integralist party in the

1930's. Despite protests from the supreme chefe, Plínio
Salgado, who maintained his movement's neutrality on
race, Barroso was a vicious racist and anti-Semite
who used even his position in the Academy of Letters
(to whose meetings he carried a pistol) as a soapbox.
Barroso was a regionalist and an author of various histories and commentaries on folk-culture.

BASBAUM, LEÓNCIO (1907-1969). A stalwart member of
the Brazilian Communist Party from 1926 until his expulsion in the late 1950's over a sectarian disagreement;
a humane man from a wealthy family based in São Paulo;
and a Marxist historian, author of the multi-volume
História Sincera da República. A member of the intellectual, non-violent faction of the Party, Basbaum was
influenced by such figures as Solzhenitsyn and Milovan
Djilas.

BASTANI, TANUS JORGE. Writer of Arab extraction whose
book, Memorias de um Mascate (1939?), speaks to the
problems faced by this immigrant group.

BASTOS, ABGUAR. Deputy from Goiás to the Vargas-era
Congress of 1934 and 1935, and one of the few of "radical" persuasion. His support of the National Liberation
Alliance (ANL) in 1935 saw him harassed, arrested, and
finally jailed in spite of parliamentary immunity. Bastos
wrote one of the first biographies of Luís Carlos Prestes,
one of the few, in fact, to be allowed to be published in
Brazil over the years.

BASTOS, JOSE TAVARES (1813-1893). Mid-nineteenth century advocate of Imperial political reform, holding the
centralized parliamentary system to be artificial in a
nation as diverse as Brazil, and favoring progress
towards representative liberal democracy. Bastos also
favored a gradual phase-out of slavery, although not its
immediate abolition.

BATÁ-COTÔ. A Yoruba war drum which produced such
stirring effects on slaves that its importation was banned
in 1835 after it figured prominently in a major slave
revolt of that year.

BATALHÕES. Cooperative labor groups in the Bahian Recôncavo, in which neighbors and friends aid in building
or repairing a house. The batalhões are akin to the

system of <u>mutirão</u> (q. v.), the agricultural labor battalions
of the Northeast.

BATEIA. A batell, a concave pan used by <u>garimpeiros</u> to
filter out sediment from river water, separating it from
gold nuggets or other minerals.

BATISTA, PEDRO ERNESTO (1885-1942). Popular Pernambuco-born physician who briefly served as mayor of the
Federal District (1931-1936) and who was reviled for
his left leanings and social views. He established a
major hospital in Rio which today bears his name, although he was driven out of office in 1939 for his associations with suspected communists. Pedro Ernesto
treated Vargas and his wife when they suffered an auto-
mobile accident and may have saved the president's life.

BATUQUE. 1) Hammering, drumming, noisiness. 2) Afro-
Brazilian dance. 3) Ball or carnaval gathering of blacks.
See also CARNAVAL.

B E A O. Third-largest consortium of banks in West Africa,
acquired in 1977 by the Bank of Brazil through purchase
of majority shareholdings in order to facilitate Brazil's
foreign policy objectives of improving trade relations
with African nations.

BEBIDA DIVINA. Sarcastic Amazon-region term, "divine
beverage," for <u>cachaça</u>, the raw rum used by traders
and adventurers in dealing with aboriginal populations.
The poor quality of the region's sugar cane, in fact,
had helped encourage the growth of the rum industry.

BECKMAN, MANUEL (1630-1685). Known as "O Bequimão,"
Beckman led the first revolt against the Crown for reasons of economic oppression caused by the Portuguese
system. Beckman, a Maranhense, spoke out against the
Jesuits and the monopoly of the Companhia do Comércio
do Estado do Maranhão, in 1684. In the absence of the
governor, Beckman and his fellow conspirators seized
control of the city and established a provisional government. In the end, the rebellion failed and Beckman
fled; he was deported to Pernambuco, where he remained
until pardoned by the Crown twenty years later.

BELÉM. Capital of Pará State, on the shores of Guajará
bay, and Brazil's eighth largest city. It is the economic
gateway to the Amazon Valley.

BELÉM-BRASÍLIA HIGHWAY. The famous BR-14, opened
in 1962 after a decade of construction, linking Belém on
the northern coast to the new federal capital. From
1962 to 1972 the number of inhabited towns along the
road grew from 10 to 120; population along the road
numbered two million. The road has become a major
route for migrants from the impoverished North into
the Brasília region.

BELO HORIZONTE. The capital city of Minas Gerais, built
according to predesigned plan, like Washington, D. C. ,
and inaugurated in 1896. In 1967 its population surpassed
one million: it is noted for its commercial activity,
banks, and Federal University. On the debit side, its
Political and Social Police (DOPS) have earned notoriety
for brutality and use of torture during the years following
the 1964 Revolution.

BENTO, ANTÔNIO (1843-19??). A radical abolitionist, born
in São Paulo, and even as a youth a non-conformist who
jeopardized his career in public service by taking uncon-
ventional stands. A lawyer, he was close to antislavery
leader Luís Gama, and became the de facto leader of
the activist faction when Gama died in 1882. He was
known to be inspiring, indefatigable, but severe, cold,
and intimidating; his personality was bizarre, made to
seem even more mysterious by the underground nature
of the work he undertook, helping slaves to escape from
their owners and otherwise aiding the cause.

BENTO GONÇALVES DA SILVA (1788-1847). Early nineteenth-century gaucho revolutionary leader, and chieftain
of the republican forces in the War of the Farrapos, or
Farroupilhas, in 1835-37. The self-proclaimed president
of the Rio Grandense Republic, he was defeated at the
battle of Cangaçú in 1843 and finally subdued by Caxias
and Canabarro in 1845.

BEQUIMÃO, O. see BECKMAN, MANUEL

BERLINDA. The canopied sedan chairs used to carry the
affluent--on the shoulders of slaves--during the late
colonial period.

BERNARDES, ARTUR (1875-1955). Mineiro lawyer and
politician elected president of the republic in 1922, after
he had headed the state government of Minas since 1918.
A civilian, Bernardes used the force of military inter-

vention to punish the supporters of opposition candidate
Nilo Peçanha; he also instituted a policy of financial
austerity, cancelling most of the programs initiated by
his predecessor, Epitácio Pessoa, to send federal monies
for anti-drought public works. In 1932 he supported the
São Paulo constitutionalist rebellion and as a result was
exiled until 1935. In 1945 he joined the new U. D. N. but
later left to found his own party, the Partido Republicano.

BETHELEM, HUGO. General and former Ambassador to
    Bolivia arrested in La Paz in January 1971, and con-
    victed on financing a plot against the Torres government.
    Torres was overthrown eight months later and replaced
    by a regime friendly to Brazil. The episode is taken
    as evidence by those who see Brazil as a future hemi-
    spheric power that Brazil is actively attempting to set
    up a circle of "client" states on its borders--Bolivia,
    Paraguay, perhaps Guyana. General Bethelem himself
    stated to the press that protectorates should be established
    by Brazil over countries like Bolivia which maintained
    relations with countries outside the hemisphere which
    might pose a threat to hemispheric security.

BEVILAQUA, CLÓVIS (1859-1944). Ceará-born jurist and
    writer, and a graduate of the Recife Law School at its
    height (1882), Bevilaqua helped write the Brazilian Civil
    Code.

BIAS FORTES, CRISPIM JACQUES (1847-1917). Political
    boss and former governor of Minas Gerais, Bias Fortes,
    born in the town of Barbacena, never in his life visited
    Rio de Janeiro out of fear, as it was said, that he would
    be ridiculed as a rube by the Cariocas.

BICHOS. Insects or vermin.

BICO. Literally, a "faucet. " The term refers to supple-
    mental jobs or sources of income for workers.

BILAC, OLAVO (1865-1918). Poet and medical student who
    left his studies in the fifth year to study law and who left
    law school to write. An outspoken critic of Floriano
    Peixoto, he was imprisoned in 1892 but amnestied; in
    1910 he represented Brazil at the Buenos Aires Pan
    American Congress. Bilac dedicated the later years of
    his life to the campaign for universal military service.

BLUMENAU, HERMANN (1819-1899). Founder of an all-

German settlement in the region of the Itajahy-Assú
River in Santa Catarina, in 1848, which was named after
him.   Blumenau grew to become the most important
municipality in the province, spawning, as well, other
satellite settlements: Joinville, in 1849; Santa Thereza
and Terezopolis in 1853; Angelina in 1860; São Bento in
1870.   Following Blumenau's lead, Hanseatic agrarian
colonies were established in various places in 1897, including Hansa-Harmonia, Natal, Sertão, Hansa-Humboldt,
and Jaraguá.

BLUMENAU ZEITUNG.   Integralist German-language daily
newspaper published in the Santa Catarina city in the
mid-1930's.

BLUNTSCHLI, HANS.   Swiss scientist and naturalist who
travelled extensively through the Amazon in 1912 and
whose description of the region's water cycle--from sea
to air to ground, returning to the sea through the fluvial
plain--has been widely commented upon in the literature.

BOA ESPERANÇA.   Major hydro-electric plant serving the
North-Northeast, located on the Maranhão-Piauí border.
With the larger plant at Paulo Afonso (Bahia), most of
the needs of the region are met.

BOA VIAGEM.   The beach-front district of Recife, opened
to urbanization after the construction of a road along the
shore during the 1920's (at great expense) and the appli-
cation of prophylactic measures to curb malarial mosquitos
in the swamps at its rear.   Boa Viagem, since the early
1960's, has become an elegant and high-priced neighborhood, resembling Rio de Janeiro's Copacabana.

BOA VISTA.   Capital of the federal territory of Roraima,
about fifty kilometers from the border of Guiana.

BOAL, AUGUSTO.   Founder of the experimental Teatro
Arena of São Paulo, Boal was exiled by the post-1964
military regime and resides in Portugal.   Ironically, his
father came to Brazil as an exile from Portugal's fascist
government.

BOBADELA, CONDE DE   see   ANDRADA, GOMES FREIRE DE

BÔCA DO MONTE-SANTA MARIA TRAIL.   Newer cattle route
from Rio Grande do Sul to Sao Paulo, which cut westward

across the serra after the Viamão region's decline ren-
dered the trail from that region obsolete by the early
nineteenth century. A century after the Bôca do Monte-
Santa Maria trail opened it became "fixed," as it were,
by the construction of a railroad line which replaced
the need for cattle drives.

BOCAIÚVA, QUINTINO (1836-1912). Journalist and political
figure, born Quintino Ferreira de Sousa, Bocaiúva was
a founder of the Brazilian Republican Party in 1870. In
1890 he was named Minister of Foreign Affairs and later
Senator from Rio de Janeiro; in 1891 he was arrested
and imprisoned as a suspected conspirator against Marshal
Deodoro. He returned to the Senate until before his
death.

BÔDE. 1) Billy-goat. 2) Mulatto.

BODEGA. A rural or small town shop for staple foodstuffs
and supplies.

BOLETINS DE EFICIÊNCIA. "Efficiency bulletins," issued
by administrative supervisors in federal agencies to rate
employees under the merit civil service system, and
criticized, by the late 1940's, for their mechanical (and
predictable) endorsements without genuine scrutiny.

"BOM BURGUÊS" see VALE, JORGE MEDEIROS

BOMILCAR, ÁLVARO (1874-1957). Author of a forthright
pamphlet, "Race Prejudice in Brazil" (1916), which actually was written in 1911 but withheld from publication
for several years in the hopes of finding a more
welcome climate for its reception. Bomilcar attacked the
racist conditions which precipitated the naval revolt of
1910; in 1917 he helped found the nationalist journal
Brazilea and the "Nativist Propaganda Association,"
which was renamed "Social Nationalist Action" in 1920,
a group seeking to work for equality among the races
as one of its goals.

BONDE. A streetcar. The last bondes ran in Rio de Janeiro
in the early 1960's (although one line, to Santa Thereza,
still operated later). The open cars, frequently breaking
down when their guide wires broke contact with the over-
head electrical circuits, replaced the horse-drawn trolleys
of the early twentieth century; they are being replaced,

in turn, by diesel buses and, in Rio de Janeiro and São Paulo, with subways.

"BONZINHOS. " A pejorative term for the "good little people," who filled public jobs at the local level in the Northeast after the 1964 coup and the demise of Francisco Juliao's Peasant Leagues. These people respect the power structure, following orders even if personally distasteful, and overlooking the frustrations that fueled social unrest before the end of the old order.

BOQUEIRÕES. Narrow gorges in the hilly regions of the Northeast frequently filled by intermittent rivers, and thereby considered excellent locations for dam construction.

BORBA DE MORAES, RUBENS   see   MORAES, RUBENS BORBA DE

BORBOREMA PLATEAU. A broad mountain system rising to a maximum elevation of about 1,000 meters, dominating the northeastern states of Paraíba and Pernambuco.

BORGES DA FONSECA, ANTÔNIO (1810?-1872). Nineteenth-century "republican" revolutionary, beginning with a career as "Jacobin" editor in Rio de Janeiro in 1830 and continuing through the Praieira revolt and until his death.

BORGES DE MEDEIROS, ANTÔNIO AUGUSTO (1863-1961). The major political boss of the state of Rio Grande do Sul during the second part of the Old Republic, and the successor to Júlio de Castilhos as chief of the Riograndense Republican Party (PRP).

BOSSA NOVA. The musical successor to the samba, becoming highly popular in the late 1950's and 1960's, with its roots in samba, modern jazz, and in classical music.

BOTOCUDOS. Name commonly given to the Aimoré tribe, a ferocious and warlike people whose men ornamented themselves by driving wooden pegs, or botoques, through their lower lips. The most frequent "visitors" to coastal settlements, they also were the most likely to attack both white villages and neighboring aboriginal tribes. The "Botocudos" inhabited the coastal strip separating

Minas Gerais from Espirito Santo and Rio de Janeiro.

BOUÇAS, VALENTIM F. (1891-1964). Son of a Spanish immigrant, Bouças made a fortune in business, won the Brazilian franchise for the Hollerith Company (later I. B. M.), and became a close crony to Vargas, with whom he played golf and cards and to whom he constantly gave personal advice.

BRAÇA. A measurement of 2.2 meters.

BRAGA, CINCINATO (1864-1953). Lawyer and economist who entered republican politics in 1890 on the strength of his membership in republican and abolitionist groups in São Paulo in the 1880's. Braga wrote several books on Brazilian history and was the president of the Bank of Brazil in 1924.

BRANCARRÕES. Light-skinned mulattos, who, by virtue of their light pigmentation managed to rise in the colonial social environment. Dark-skinned mulattos, as Caio Prado observes, and Negroes found the color bar too strong; they were indelibly marked with the stigma of race.

BRANCO. A white person.

BRANCOS DA BAHIA. Near-whites, with some Negroid ancestry, literally "whites from Bahia." Most would be able to pass for white in the United States if so inclined.

BRANDÃO, AMBRÓSIO FERNANDES. Author of Diálogos das Grandezas do Brasil (Dialogues of Brazil's Greatness), written in 1618, the first effort to speculate on Brazil's place in the Portuguese Empire and the world.

BRANDÃO, OCTÁVIO (1896- ?). Labor leader, anarchist leader, and, in the 1930's, a leader of the PCB, the Communist Party. Brandão appealed to the heros of the Brazilian past to develop the consciousness of the urban worker, but only immigrants seemed attracted to the trade unionists' message, and not nearly in as much force as in Argentina. Brandão failed to overcome the nativistic campaign which identified labor militancy with foreign ideas and therefore non-Brazilian values. See also LABOR ORGANIZATION.

BRANQUEAMENTO. The process of "whitening" whereby--

to many Brazilians, especially in the twentieth century--
miscegenation would erase the more pronouncedly Negroid
traits of the Brazilian population. The concept runs
counter to that of the so-called "mulatto escape hatch,"
and, if accepted, may contribute to rejection of Afro-
Brazilian values and even to self-hatred by blacks.

BRÁS, VENCESLAU (1868-1962). President from 1914 to
1918, prior to which time he headed the state government
of Minas Gerais. His administration's greatest achievement was the promulgation of the Civil Code in 1917.

BRASÍLIA. A planned city built on the planalto central in
the state of Goiás, Brasília was inaugurated as the federal capital (and new Federal District) by President
Juscelino Kubitschek on April 4, 1960. Urban planner
Lúcio Costa, together with architect Oscar Niemeyer,
executed most of the design for the modern city.

BRAZIL, ZEFERINO (1870-1942). Poet from Rio Grande do
Sul, considered a "bohemian" in his day, and the author
of "Vovó Musa," a compilation of poems reflecting gaúcho
culture.

BRAZILÉA. Journal founded in 1917 by the nationalist and
crusader for rights for non-whites, Álvaro Bomilcar.

BRAZILIAN ACADEMY OF LETTERS see ACADEMIA
BRASILEIRA DE LETRAS

BRENNAND, FRANCISCO (1927-   ). Recife-born ceramicist
and artist, who has adapted the folklore and flora of the
Northeast to his hand-made tiles in strikingly original
ways. Brennand's efforts have resulted in a revival of
traditional forms of tile and pottery manufacture.

BRETOA. First merchant ship to carry brasilwood to Portugal, in 1511. Wood was gathered from along the coast
of Cabo Frio, near Rio de Janeiro.

BRISE-SOLEIL. Architectural innovation by Le Corbusier,
used in his design (1936) for Rio de Janeiro's Ministry
of Education and Culture (MEC). The brise-soleil is a
vertical series of adjustable slots used instead of win-
dows to allow for improved ventilation in the tropical
environment.

BROCA. A coffee pest, scientifically H. Lampei F., which
after 1940 became controllable through insecticide.

BUARQUE DE HOLANDA, CHICO (1946-). Major composer
of popular songs during the mid-1960's and after, some
of which, like his "A Banda" (The Band) were banned or
otherwise suppressed by authorities for alleged subversive
tendencies. He is the son of historian Sérgio Buarque
de Holanda.

BUENO DA SILVA, BARTOLOMEU. Nicknamed "Anhangüera,"
from the Tupi word for "devil" or "evil spirit." He
was a bandeirante from São Paulo who discovered gold
in Goiás in 1725. He is known for having pioneered the
first major trail into Goiás the "Guaiases Trail," which
is followed by the present-day railroad lines of Mojiana
and São Paulo-Goiás.

BUGRES. Literally, "buggers," the name given by the
Portuguese to the aboriginal population, who were believed to practice sodomy.

BUGRISMO. Refers to one of Amerindian ancestry and used
as an insult.

BUMBA-MEU-BOI. A popular pageant-like dance in the
rural Northeast, with characters dressed as vaqueiros
and bois, or oxen. Also known as boi-surubi, the pro-
cession winds through the streets, especially at Carnival-
time. See also CARNAVAL.

BURLE MARX, ROBERTO (1909-). Trained as a painter,
Burle Marx turned to landscape architecture, creating
a major genre of tropical landscape design unsurpassed
anywhere in the world. Burle Marx's gardens in downtown Rio de Janeiro, at Petropolis, and elsewhere integrate luxurious nature with creative and innovative treat-
ments of overall environments.

BUTANTÃ INSTITUTE. São Paulo-based center of study of
serum-development for snakebite, long considered a
major Brazilian scientific institute but, as Nancy Stepan
points out, much in the mold of "colonial" medical and
scientific institutes for its reliance on foreign techniques
and traditions, with no independent research component.
See also OSWALDO CRUZ INSTITUTE.

-C-

CAATINGA. Stunted, scrub forest found in part of the north-

eastern sertão and the western agreste. The stunted,
thorny vegetation of the region forced local cowboys
(vaqueiros) to adopt leather coverings from head to foot,
giving him, in the words of Euclides da Cunha, the
leathery visage of a medieval knight of armor. See
also SERTÃO; VAQUEIRO; AGRESTE.

CAATINGUEIROS. Transient workers who migrate to the
sugar cane plantations of the northeastern zona da mata
for the harvest season and then return to the caatinga--
the land beyond the agreste--to tend their own subsistence
crops.

CABANADA. A localized insurrection in the province of
Pará, between 1835 and 1840, expressedly for the restoration of the abdicated monarch, Pedro I. One of
several regional revolts (see SABINADA; BALAIADA;
FARROUPILHA) during the early nineteenth century reflecting local frustration at the centralized form of government based at the Court in Rio de Janeiro and demonstrating the weakness of the Regency.

CABIDE DE EMPRÊGOS. A person who holds several jobs,
usually in the bureaucracy. A cabide is literally a coat
hanger. The term was used widely during the 1950's.

CABO VERDE. From the name of the Cape Verde Islands,
a racial category designating blacks lighter than the
preto but still quite dark, but with straight hair, thin
lips, and a narrow, straight nose.

CABO-VERDIANO. Native or inhabitant of the Cape Verde
Islands, many of whom emigrated to the New World
(North America, especially New England, as well as
Brazil).

CABOCLADA. 1) Group or reunion of caboclos. 2) Action
or trait typical of caboclos. 3) Perfidy, treacherousness.
4) Vindictiveness.

CABOCLINO. Northeastern carnival dance form, akin to the
frevo and samba but performed by mostly male dancers
who wear grass skirts, bone necklaces and feathers, a
fantasy version of Indian costume. Each carries a wooden
bow and arrow, which is used to beat the rhythm of the
dance.

CABOCLO. Term (literally, "copper hued") applied to an

Amerindian or mestizo. In the Amazon and in the Northeast the term is applied indiscriminately to the rural poor (similar to "hillbilly"), even though many are poor whites. The same lower-class rural people in Bahia are called tabaréus; in São Paulo, jecas.

CABOCLO FOLK CULTURE. A term used by anthropologists and others to describe the culture of rural Brazilian communities, where religious practices more often follow folk patterns than orthodoxy, and where local vocabulary usage follows specialized usages not found in "coastal" or urban communities.

CABRA. Literally, a mestizo of African, Amerindian, and Caucasian origin. The term, like that of capanga, was applied to the personal bodyguards hired by coronéis and others.

CABRA-SÊCO. 1) Brute, bully, tough. 2) Aggressive black.

CABRAL, PEDRO ÁLVES (1467-1520). The head of the Portuguese fleet which, possibly blown off its course en route to India, sighted and landed on the Brazilian coast on April 22, 1500. Whether or not the discovery was accidental or whether Cabral was the first European to see Brazil, is irrelevant: the 1494 Treaty of Tordesillas had ceded all land east of a line 370 leagues from the Cape Verdes to the Portuguese crown; lands west fell to Spain. Cabral, who arrived in Calcutta three months after Brazil's discovery, called the new land "Vera Cruz" (or "Santa Cruz"); by 1503 it had come to be known as Brazil owing to the "pau brasil" (brazilwood) brought back by his ships, and valuable as a source of dye.

CABRAL DE MELLO NETO, JOÃO (1920-). Poet and diplomat from a leading Recife family, and author of the socially-conscious Vida e Morte de Severina (1965).

CABUNGUEIRO. A servant or worker relegated to the lowest sort of work, such as cleaning privies.

CABURÉ. A dark-skinned caboclo (q. v.).

CACHAÇA. Raw sugar-cane rum. See AGUARDENTE.

CACHOEIRA. The major town of the Bahian Recôncavo, and historically a tobacco-exporting center.

CADERNOS DO POVO BRASILEIRO. A series of paperback
books, no more than pamphlet-sized, issued by various
authors of intellectual stature (e. g. , Francisco Julião,
Nelson Werneck Sodré) in the early 1960's, in an effort
to bring to the working classes, normally too poor to
buy books, messages from the left. Some of the titles
were "Who Constitute the Brazilian People," "Why Don't
the Rich Strike?," "Who Are the Enemies of Brazil?"

CAFÉ FILHO, JOÃO (1899-1970). Rio Grande do Norte
politician who rose from a career of journalist and lawyer
to occupy the post of police chief of Natal after the 1930
Revolution, and, faintly identified with progressive causes,
was exiled after the Estado Novo coup in 1937.   In 1946
he was elected to the federal legislature and served as
Vargas's vice-president from 1951-54.   With Vargas's
suicide in 1954 he assumed the presidency of the Republic, which he held until November 1955.   His presidential administration followed policies which were generally more conservative than those of his predecessor.

CAFÉ-COM-LEITE.   The "coffee-with-milk" alliance between
coffee-producing São Paulo and dairy-cow-raising Minas
Gerais, during the Old Republic, an unwritten understanding which frequently led to Paulistas and Mineiros
alternating as presidential candidates for the official
slate.   The agreement broke down in 1930 when Paulista
Washington Luis Pereira de Sousa attempted to name a
fellow Paulista, Júlio Prestes, as his successor in the
presidency, thus precipitating, in part, the crisis which
led to the formation of the Aliança Liberal.

CAFÉZINHO.   A demitasse cup of black coffee, served heap-
ing with cane sugar, which is the Brazilian national
drink.   Up to six or eight or more cups are typically
consumed per day in urban centers.

CAFUSO.   Offspring of African and Amerindian parents.

CAIÇARA.   Bamboo fence surrounding Tupí-Guaraní settlements, to keep domesticated animals from wandering
and to offer protection from attack.

CAIRO DA SILVA, NILO.   Positivist and founder, in 1912,
of the University of Paraná; influenced by the National
Education Act of 1911, the Reforma Rivadávia.   See
CORREIA, RIVADÁVIA.

CALADO, JOÃO CRISÓSTOMO.   Commander of the loyalist

forces sent by the Regency to suppress the Sabinada revolt in Bahia in 1837.

CALÓGERAS, JOÃO PANDIÁ (1870-1934). The Republic's
only civilian minister of war, after the First World War,
and a historian and diplomat. Calógeras (whose name
is also spelled "Calógias") undertook a major expansion
of military facilities after an inspection trip around
Brazil which left him dismayed.

CALUNDÚ. First dance of African origin to be mentioned
in a book about Brazil, Nuno Marques Pereira's Com-
pêndio Narrativo do Peregrino na América (1728).

CÂMARA, DOM HELDER (1909-   ). Born in Fortaleza,
Câmara was ordained a priest in 1931 and joined, with
Severino Sombra, the corporatist labor group, the
Legiao Cearense. Later in the decade Câmara became
one of the most influential Integralists in Brazil, being
named to Plínio Salgado's Chamber of the 40. After
the war his views began to change. Made a bishop in
1952, in 1955 he was made auxiliary archbishop of Rio
de Janeiro, where he took the leadership of the socially
conscious National Conference of Bishops. In 1963 he
was made archbishop of Recife and Olinda, in the heart
of the impoverished Northeast. In 1964 Dom Helder was
isolated and removed from public view; newspapers were
forbidden to mention his name or print his photograph,
and his aides were kept under surveillance and harassed.
To his detractors Câmara is a demagogue and communist;
his defenders consider him a champion for civil rights
and human dignity. He was nominated for the Nobel
Peace Prize several times during the 1960's and 1970's.

CÂMARA CASCUDO, LUIS (1898-   ). Author, gadfly, former
Integralist, folklorist, and scourge of Rio Grande do Norte
intellectual society, the author of several serious books
on regional life, including a major study of the jangada.

CAMARÃO, FELIPE ANTÔNIO (1580-1648). Military leader
of the campaign against the Dutch, and an Amerindian of
the Potiguar tribe converted to Catholicism. Camarão was
his tribal name; Antônio his baptismal name; and Felipe
was taken in homage to the King of Spain, who awarded him
the title Dom.

CAMARGO, SÉRGIO DE (1930-   ). Leading sculptor, trained
in Europe and a resident of Paris for many years. He
presently mákes his home in Jacarepaguá, Rio de Janeiro.

CAMÕES, LUÍS DE (1524-1580). Portuguese epic poet, whose work, The Lusiads (1572) stands as the major expression of national prowess in Lusophonic literature. In another context, stanzas of the poem were used during the 1960's and 1970's by editors to fill in blank spaces in newspapers deleted by censors.

CAMPESINOS. Rural peasants or agricultural workers.

CAMPINA GRANDE. The "gateway to the sertão," a major commercial and trading center in the center of Paraíba, and the most important interior city in the Northeast.

CAMPO. A plot of land, rare in the rural interior, entirely cleared by a tractor or other means of tree stumps and rocks.

CAMPO CERRADO. Seasonally well-watered grasslands in the form of savannas, dominating the hinterland from the lowlands of Piauí and Maranhão across the plateaus of Goias and central Mato Grosso to the borders of Bolivia.

CAMPONÊS. A rural peasant, of whom Francisco Julião wrote, in his Que São as Ligas Camponesas? (What Are the Peasant Leagues?, 1962): he "acts like a vegetable, not a human being." The passivity of the camponês has frustrated would-be reformers and contributed to the Brazilian tradition of political docility at the lower end of the rural social scale.

CAMPOS, FRANCISCO LUIS DA SILVA (1891-1968). A young lawyer from Minas, allied with the right wing of the tenente movement as well as with the Integralist cause, Campos became Vargas's first Education Minister. He wrote the bulk of two Brazilian constitutions, the corporatist Estado Novo in 1937 and the 1967 document, incorporating the repressive Institutional Acts of 1964 and 1965, also partially his legal work.

CAMPOS, HUMBERTO DE (1886-1934). Poet and author of Poeira (Dust), in 1911, a eulogy to the fate of the Amerindian. See also RANGEL, ALBERTO.

CAMPOS, SIQUEIRA (1899-1930). The son of a coffee-plantation manager, he was sent to military school at Realengo because his family could not afford private educa-

tion.   He was commissioned in 1920 and stationed at
Fort Copacabana during the 1922 election campaign, the
one which precipitated the tenente revolt in which Campos
emerged as one of its leaders.   Of the 29 revolutionaries
in the Fort, Campos, a First Lieutenant, became the
leader of the mutineers when his commanding officer was
captured.   In the ensuing battle, Campos, Eduardo Gomes,
and one enlisted man survived; the other seven rebels
who remained in the fray died.   As they lay recuperating
in the army hospital, they suddenly were lionized by the
political opposition; even the President, Epitácio Pessoa,
visited him at bedside.   Romantics of every stripe, as
Macaulay notes, celebrated the Fort uprising as an au-
thentic act of patriotism.   Within a year he was released
on a writ of habeas corpus, angering President Bernardes;
at the ensuing trial, the rebels were formally charged
with attempting to overthrow the government.   Thus
threatened with long prison terms, six of the indicted
officers (including Juárez Távora) deserted the army
and went into hiding; Campos took up residence in Uruguay.   Campos and Távora returned secretly in 1924 to
rejoin the insurrection and ultimately participated in the
long guerrilla march known as the Prestes Column.   An
intense, driving man fired by revolutionary leanings, he
perished in an airplane crash in 1930.   If he had survived, he assuredly would have taken a major role in
the new Vargas administration, as did his fellow detachment commanders João Alberto, Miguel Costa, Cordeiro
de Farias, and Juárez Távora.

CAMPOS DE GOITACASES.   Plains of uniform relief, fertile
soil, and hospitable vegetation, outside of Rio de Janeiro,
in the present-day state of the same name.   Here centers
of settlement grew from the seventeenth century onward,
at first cattle raising, then sugar cane agriculture.   Its
river, the Paráiba, is navigable, offering simple transportation from the plain to the sea.   The principal town
of this region was São Salvador (now Campos); by 1799
there were 328 sugar engenhos as well as four distilleries
for rum and distilled alcohol.   Slavery played a major
role in the economic life of the area.

CAMPOS DO VIAMÃO.   The Viamão Plains, at the southernmost edge of the Brazilian plateau near the coast in the
present-day state of Rio Grande do Sul.   The plains
were used as grazing land by the first colonists, who
arrived from Laguna in 1719; but after a century of

slash-and-burn agriculture and heavy grazing the Viamão
grasslands were no longer as able to support pastoral
and agricultural life, driving, then, the cattle stations
westward.   By 1820 the cattle train from Viamão to São
Paulo had been for the most part abandoned.

CANABARRO, DAVI (1796-1867).   Military hero of the war
of the Farrapos; amnestied with other Farrapo leaders
in 1845, and Coronel of the National Guard of the province in 1851.   In 1845 he helped Caxias defeat his former
ally, Bento Gonçalves.

CANADA.   A measure of liquid, the equivalent of about three
English pints, used to aportion rations of wine and water
aboard ship during the voyages of discovery and exploration.

CANALHA.   A mob; ruffians.

CANANÉIA.   The name given to the land at the southernmost
extreme of Brazilian territory at the time D. João III
divided it into captaincies in 1534.

CANDOMBA.   A highly inflammable plant found in central
Brazil, used as kindling.

CANDOMBLÉ.   An African cult, related to Haitian vodun
(voodooism), strongest along the Northeastern coast of
Bahia and Sergipe.   In Pernambuco, the corresponding
cults are known as xangô; in Rio de Janeiro and environs
as candomblé.   They are highly organized and follow a
complex ritual blending West African and Portuguese
Catholic traditions.   Most followers of candomblé cults
are black, although it lately has become fashionable for
whites from the upper classes to join.   Jorge Amado's
novel Jubiabá (1935) is an accurate portrayal of Afro-
Brazilian life in Bahia and of the syncretism of the
African fetish cult with Roman Catholicism.

CANECA, FREI (1779-1825).   Priest and Recifense, and a
liberal defender of Pernambuco's secret societies, including Masonry, describing them as apolitical and praise-
worthy for their humanistic goals.   One of the leaders
of the regionalist insurrection in 1824, he was captured
and executed despite protests to the Emperor.   He was
born Joaquim do Amor Divino Rabelo.

CANGACEIRO.   A bandit of the northeastern backlands.   The

cangaceiros usually were rural caboclos who roamed the
sertão, looting and murdering, pursued by state and
federal troops.   Their heyday was the period between
the two world wars; rural banditry as an endemic phenomenon was ended by the systematic penetration of the
backlands by federal police after the Vargas Revolution
in 1930.   Some of the more famous cangaceiro bands,
led by men like Antônio Silvinho and Virgolino Ferreira
(Lampião), developed popular followings owing to their
Robin Hood-like exploits (mostly exaggerated) and their
success in avoiding their pursuers.   For some, the
cangaceiros symbolized the struggle for justice by the
inarticulate rural peasantry, but recent historical scholarship suggests that this interpretation is fanciful.   In
reality the peasants were squeezed between two violent
poles: the rural bandits on one side and the landowners
on the other.   The cangaceiro came to be romanticized
by outsiders as representative of unarticulated lower
class rage but little evidence exists to show that within
his own world the cangaceiro represented anything more
than a marauding form of terror.

CANINDÉ.   One of São Paulo's major favelas, the home of
Carolina Maria de Jesus, whose memoirs, Child of the
Dark, focused the attention of the world on the misery
of Brazil's urban slums during the early 1960's.

CANJICA.   Traditional Paulista dessert, made from green
corn meal, butter, coconut, milk, and sugar.   The use
of corn in the South was more widespread than in the
North, where manioc always has been the basic dietary
staple.   Martius suggests that fubá (corn meal) was
disdained in the North, while sulistas held the same low
opinion of manioc meal.

CANNIBALISM.   Practiced by some tribes, to the horror of
European arrivals.   An anthropologically accurate feature
film was made during the 1960's which depicted the rit-
ualistic aspects of cannibalism (translated as "How tasty
was my Frenchman"); it managed to pass through the
censor's net and received mild acclaim for its treatment
of the cannibalistic aborigines not as savages but as
human beings.

CANOAS.   Police sweeps of the city streets to round up
military recruits, through the advent of conscription in
1908, many of whom marched barefoot even after induc-
tion and military training.   See also MILITARY SERVICE.

CAPANGA. Personal bodyguard, usually a thug, retained by local men of influence especially during the Old Republic (1889-1930). See also CABRA.

CAPÃO DA TRAIÇÃO. Site of the massacre, on February 15, 1709, of defenseless Paulista soldiers who had come to Minas to help pacify the War of the Emboabas after they had laid down their arms and prepared to leave the region. In anger, the city of São Paulo sent 1,300 fresh troops to avenge the slaughter. The final result of the conflict was the separation of Minas from Rio de Janeiro and the formation of the Crown Captaincy of São Paulo, Minas do Ouro, in 1709.

CAPELÃO. A rural chaplain, one who organizes prayers and litanies in honor of local saints; he keeps the chapel and makes up the prayers for the saint of the neighborhood (bairro rural).

CAPISTRANO DE ABREU, JOÃO (1853-1927). Historian and critic whose writings in the 1870's complained of the lack of qualities native to Brazil in Brazilian art, literature and music; rather, he held, Brazilian culture amounted to a faint echo of European culture, deemed superior by most educated Brazilians. As a historian, he revolutionized Brazilian scholarship with his 1889 essay, "Os Caminhos Antigos e o Povoamento do Brasil," positing a thesis that the "real" Brazil lay in the interior, and that the coast was merely an extension of European civilization. José Honório Rodrígues and others have compared Capistrano's seminal work to that of Frederick Jackson Turner's writings on the frontier in the United States.

CAPITÃES MORES. In the early years of the Empire, the name given to agents of the provincial presidents who combed the streets of urban centers looking for recruits for military service--mostly unemployed caboclos, free blacks, vagabonds, beggars, and incorrigible slaves "donated" by their masters.

CAPITAL FEDERAL, A. Turn-of-the-century comedy by playright Artur de Azevedo, mocking the plight of small-town Mineiros adrift in urban Rio de Janeiro.

CAPITÃO-DE-MATA. A slave-hunter, employed by owners to pursue runaways and fugitives.

"CAPITÃO DE TRABUCO. " Name given popularly to cangaceiro Antônio Silvino, the military reference as result
of the fact that he affected army-like uniforms for himself and his men; he often dressed in officer garb appropriated from the National Guard.

CAPITÃO-MÔR. The military administrator of a captaincy
or municipality. Since he could draft men into military
service, he exercised great power; he was usually the
most influential landowner in the region, and held the
rank of regimental colonel.

CAPOEIRA. A stylized dance and form of self-defense,
brought to Brazil from Angola, and popular in the Bahian
region, the center of Afro-Brazilian culture. Capoeira
displays some of the elements of judo and the Chinese
tai chi. Youths are trained under the direction of capoeira mestres ("masters"), the most famous of whom
in recent years was the late Mestre Bimba.

CAPTAINCY SYSTEM. The method chosen by the Crown to
colonize Brazil, in which the entire land area of the New
World territory was divided into fifteen parallel strips
ranging from ten to a hundred leagues in width and
stretching indefinitely inward from the coast. The grant-
ees, or donatários (donatories), received the right to
exploit and develop their captaincy in perpetuity providing
certain stipulations were met. The system was ultimately
unsuccessful; by the 1540's the Crown began to reacquire
individual captaincies, the system itself was abrogated
under Pombal. See also FORAL; CARTA DE DOAÇÃO;
COELHO, DUARTE; POMBAL.

CARAÇÁ. An elite secondary school in the heart of mountainous Central Minas Gerais, run by the French Redemp-
tionist Fathers, and famous, as Wirth notes, during the
late 1800's and early 1900's for rigid discipline and very
bad food.

CARAMARÚ. Epic poem (1781). See RITA DURÃO, SANTA

CARAMURÚ see ALVARES, DIOGO

CARAMURÚS. Members of the faction which appeared late
in 1831 calling for the restoration of Pedro I to the
throne. José Bonifácio and the Viscount of Cairu supported the group, whose newspaper was called O Caramurú.

CARANGUEJOS.   Small crabs which infest the muddy rivers and swamps of Recife (and other coastal cities of the Northeast), and the main source of protein for the poor, although the crabs are frequently carriers of disease.

"CARCARÁ."   Hit song of 1965, a bossa nova lament of the poverty and hunger endemic to the Northeast.   In mid-song, the singer pauses to tell his audience (as Burns notes) that "in 1950 there were 2,000,000 northeasterners living outside their native states; 10 percent of the population of Ceará emigrated, 13 percent of Piauí; over 15 percent of Bahia, over 17 percent of Alagoas...."

"CARDEIAS, OS."   The "Cardinals," name given to the aging political elite of the Empire in the 1850's, many of whom entered government in the 1820's.

CARGOS PÚBLICOS.   Public positions, taken by members of the newly arrived Portuguese Court after 1808, and, as Douglas Graham remarks, served as an inauspicious symbol for future Brazilian administration, since the aristocratic public servants looked at their jobs as sinecures.

CARIOCA.   Inhabitant of the city of Rio de Janeiro, portrayed popularly as easy-going, fun-loving, lacking business sense but clever and self-sufficient.   Cariocas lay on the beach, the stereotype holds, while Paulistas and Mineiros make money.   See also BAHIANO; MINEIRO; GAÚCHO; PAULISTA.

CARIOCA, JOSÉ.   Stereotyped Brazilian of Walt Disney's Saludos Amigos (q. v.).

CARLOS, ROBERTO (1943-   ).   Major popular music singer during the years 1965-75.   Carlos, like most Brazilian pop artists, writes his own lyrics and music.

CARMÓ, IGREJA DO.   Rio de Janeiro church which, after the arrival of the Portuguese Crown in 1808, was made the Royal Chapel.

CARNAVAL.   Three days of quintessentially Brazilian celebration preceding Ash Wednesday in the Lenten season. Lower class blacks have, since the nineteenth century, organized into samba clubs, groups which prepare during the entire year for the Carnaval processions, composing theme-oriented ballads, designing lavish costumes, and constructing elaborate allegorical floats, usually depicting

scenes from Brazilian history. Carnaval explodes with
non-stop music, dancing in the streets, and frequent
violence. In more recent years the samba processions
have become touristic (bleacher seats sold by travel
agencies at high tariffs) and many upper class citizens
have taken to leaving their city residences for mountain
and seashore resorts; others attend high priced ($100
a ticket and up) masquerade balls at private clubs.
Waiters and other servants employed during Carnaval
traditionally hold their own Carnaval celebrations days
before the main celebrations.

CARNE DE SOL. Dried beef of the Northeast, made from
    charque.

CARNE DO CEARÁ. Northeastern colloquialism for charque,
    or dried, jerked beef. In Pernambuco, the term used
    is "carne de sol," or sun's meat.

CARNE DO SUL. "Southern meat," a local term for charque.
    See also CARNE DE SOL.

"CARNE SEM OSSO" PROTEST. Literally, "meat without
    bones." An 1858 insurrection among the Northeastern
    peasantry; virtually unexamined by scholars.

CARNEIRO DA CUNHA, JOSÉ MARIANO (1850-1912). An
    outspoken abolitionist from Pernambuco despite the fact
    that he and his family held slaves until relatively late
    in the century, he used his oratorical skills and his pop-
    ularity among urban lower middle class groups, to ha-
    rangue in behalf of the cause. He became a leader of
    the state political opposition after the monarchy
    fell, and, caught up in the political plotting of the 1890's,
    was arrested, driven from the state, and exiled in Rio
    de Janeiro, where he died, still a popular hero.

CARNEIRO LEÃO, HONÓRIO HERMETO (1801-1856). Im-
    perial Foreign Minister in the early 1840's, who, like
    his predecessor, Souza e Oliveira Coutinho, argued for
    nonintervention in hemispheric affairs. The principle
    survived until 1852, when Brazil joined with anti-Rosas
    forces to overthrow the Argentine dictator.

CARREGADEIRA. A poor variety of manioc which yields
    after six months and can be planted in poor soil, but
    which can only be harvested in July or August in the
    Northeast and which keeps for three years rather than six.
    See also MANIPEBA.

CARTA DE ALFORRIA.   A letter of certificate attesting to
the free status of a former slave.   Mulattos generally
were more easily able to purchase such a document than
blacks.

CARTA DE DOAÇÃO.   Land grant, part of the charter issued
in the creation of a captaincy.   See CAPTAINCY SYSTEM;
FORAL.

CARTAS DE USANÇA.   Letters of appointment, given by the
ouvidor (crown judge) to persons, judges or procurators
or other local officials, elected by the indirect system
of voting.

CARUMBÉ.   Miner's bucket, used in panning for gold by
the garimpeiros.

CARURÚ.   An Afro-Brazilian dish made with okra, often
served after the completion of a candomblé (q. v.) or
macumba ceremony.

CARVALHO, MENELÍCK DE (1897-1949).   Mineiro politician
and police official who rose to power as a protégé of
Governor Antônio Carlos.   Carvalho became one of the
first career politicians to study public administration.

CARVALHO E MELO, SEBASTIÃO JOSÉ see POMBAL.

CASA DE ESTUDANTE.   Government-supported student housing facility agency, the parent organization which in 1940
gave birth to UNE, the national student association until
its demise in 1964.

CASA DE FUNDIÇÃO.   Smelting house of the eighteenth century, where all gold extracted from the ground had to
be, by law, brought for smelting.   After the quinto
(fifth) had been subtracted, it was melted into bars and
returned to its owner, properly certified.

CASA GRANDE.   The plantation house or manor, established
in the Northeast during the colonial period as the central
residential unit of the engenho; the center of family life
and, later, the symbol of the patriarchal relationship between owner and slave.   See MASTERS AND THE SLAVES.

CASAS AVIADORAS.   Central trading enterprises in the
Amazon region, buying and shipping crude rubber and

organizing the employment of seringueiros as well as
their housing and, as much as it existed, health care.

CASCALHO. Gravel subsoil mixed with quartz and gold particles which were separated by the washing process of
the garimpeiros.

CASSADOS. Persons stripped of their political rights under
the Atos Institucionais of the post-1964 military regime,
in order to neutralize any potentially disruptive (or popular) influence they might develop. Among the cassados
in the mid-1960's were three former presidents: Quadros, Goulart, and Kubitschek.

CASTELISTA. A supporter of the late military president
Castelo Branco, during the mid- and late-1970's.

CASTELO BRANCO, FRANCISCO CALDEIRA. Chief of an
expedition in 1615 which, in three convoys of river canoes
with a total of 150 men, left São Luís de Maranhão to
explore the Amazon. His explorations set the stage for
the later expedition, in the 1630's, of the Amazon River
up to Quito by Pedro Teixeira.

CASTELO BRANCO, HUMBERTO DE ALENCAR (1900-1967).
Military officer and first president of the revolutionary
government which overthrew the Goulart administration
in 1964. Born in Ceará, Castelo Branco, a member of
the "Sorbonne" wing of the armed forces command--the
group considered moderate intellectuals--was the liaison
officer to the Allied Command in Italy in 1944 from the
Brazilian Expeditionary Force (FEB). Stepping down from
the presidency in 1967, he died shortly afterward in a
crash of his small military aircraft in his home state.

CASTILHOS, JÚLIO DE (1860-1903). Gaúcho leader and
politician, and state boss from 1893 to 1898 when he
passed control of the state's Republican party to Borges
de Medeiros. A positivist and republican, he was responsible for the constitution of Rio Grande do Sul, which
bears his personal stamp.

CASTRO, JOSUE DE (1908-   ). Physician, author and professor, de Castro served in various administrative posts
in Recife and Rio de Janeiro in the area of nutrition and
public health before being exiled under the Estado Novo.
An outspoken social critic, his books Death in the North-

east and Geography of Hunger have focused world attention on the terrible conditions of life in the northeastern
region.   De Castro served as president of the United
Nations Food and Agriculture Agency (FAO).

CATARENSE.   Resident of the state of Santa Catarina.

CATETE.   The official residence of the President of the
Republic, in Rio de Janeiro, during the Old Republic, and
the place where Getúlio Vargas committed suicide in
1954.

CATHOLIC ORGANIZATION.   Brazil is divided into 190
ecclesiastical units (archdioceses and dioceses) under
approximately 241 archbishops and bishops, and subdivided
into 4,947 parishes.   There were 2,000 secondary schools
and 12 universities under Catholic Church auspices in
1975.

CATIMBÔ.   Derived from the word "cachimbo," or tobacco
pipe, referring to an illegal form of spiritism practiced
among Afro-Brazilians in the Northeast.   The leader,
or catimbozeiro, receives spirits on behalf of the faithful, who enter trance-like states through the use of tobacco, marijuana, or jurema, another drug.

CAVALEIROS DA LUZ.   First Brazilian Masonic Lodge,
established in Salvador on July 14, 1797, and coinciding
with the so-called Tailor's conspiracy in Bahia.

CAVALHEIRO DA ESPERANÇA.   The "Knight of Hope," the
romantic name given to Luís Carlos Prestes by his sympathizers and by the left-wing press.

CAXIAS, DUKE OF (1803-1880).   Luis Alves de Lima e
Silva, first Baron of Caxias for his siege of the rebel-
held city of that name in Maranhão (see BALAIADA RE-
VOLT), later for his role in the Farroupilha Revolt
(q.v.) in Rio Grande do Sul, his reputation grew even
further.   After the Paraguayan War he held the army
in check as supreme commander, during a period of
unrest when peacetime officers began to meddle in
politics.   His death in 1880 led to greater political
intrigue among the officer corps and helped undermine
support for the monarchy.

CEARÁ.   Northeastern state dominated by rural poverty and
subject to the consequences of periodic droughts.   Its

capital is Fortaleza; it is bordered by Paraíba, Pernambuco, Rio Grande do Norte, and Piauí.

CEARÁ ABOLITION LAW. A blanket abolition of slavery in
the province, passed in 1884 and thereby preceding national abolition by four years. To some degree, the
question was academic, since slavery played a very
minor role in the regional economy by the mid-1880's.
But the law did serve a symbolic function, and cheered
abolitionists to press their efforts. Abolition laws were
also promulgated in Amazonas and Rio Grande do Norte
prior to national abolition in 1888.

CELSO, AFONSO (1860-1938). Blatantly nationalistic author
of Porque Me Ufano do Meu País (Why I Am Enamored
of My Country, 1901). The book, still read widely in
Brazilian public schools according to Burns, proclaimed
the superiority of Brazilian racial intermixture and lav-
ishly praised the strength and heroism of the Amerindian,
African, and European ancestors of modern Brazilians.
See also RETRATO DO BRASIL.

CENSUSES. National censuses were taken in 1872, 1890,
1900, 1920, 1940, and in each succeeding decade. The
1930 census was never compiled although data was col-
lected--the legacy of the administrative confusion following the 1930 Revolution. The 1920 census is the first
one to ask large-scale questions, but it is known to have
been grossly inflated for political reasons.

CENTRAL WEST. Region encompassing the states of Mato
Grosso and Goiás, and the site of the new (post-1960)
federal district of Brasília.

CENTRO DE INFORMAÇÕES DO EXERCITO (CIE). The
Army's Intelligence Service, under attack during the late
1970's and, in 1977, seemingly destined to be surbor-
dinated to the Serviço Nacional de Informações--Brazil's
CIA--or eliminated altogether.

CENTRO DE PESQUISA E DOCUMENTAÇÃO DE HISTÓRIA
CONTEMPORÂNEA DO BRASIL (CPDOC). Rio-based
research center, created in 1973 at the Fundação Getúlio
Vargas, to house documentation dealing with the history
of Brazil since 1930. It includes the Vargas papers as
well as clipping files, films, and a wide range of bibliographic material.

CENTRO DOM VITAL. Lay Catholic intellectual Center established in 1922 by Jackson de Figueiredo and led, after his death, by lay leader Alceu Amoroso Lima (Tristão de Ataíde). The Centro served as the Catholic hierarchy's vehicle to mobilize opinion among educated Brazilians, and achieved some prestige during the late 1920's and early 1930's; branches were opened in São Paulo, Salvador, and Recife. The Center emphasized liturgical piety, theological thought, and personal austerity and conservatism.

CENTRO INDUSTRIAL DO BRAZIL. A São Paulo-based national association of manufacturers, organized in 1904.

CENTROS POPULARES DE CULTURA. "Popular Culture Centers," sponsored by UNE and other student organizations to bring artists to the people and to shed the "elitist" stance of cultural expression. The Centros were closed down abruptly in 1964.

CHÁCARA. A rural small holding, often outside of town, with fruit trees, chickens, and garden-type agriculture.

CHAGAS, CARLOS (1879-1934). Discoverer of the cause of American sleeping sickness (Trypanosomiasis americana) and successor to Oswaldo Cruz as Institute Director as well as national health director in 1919. See also OSWALDO CRUZ INSTITUTE.

CHAGAS, CARLOS. Head (1977) of the Estado de São Paulo's Brasília office, and prosecuted under national security legislation for publishing an article claiming that yellow fever mosquitos had escaped from a laboratory at the University of Brasília during a police raid on the campus.

CHALEIRA. A slave who collaborated with owners by telling on other slaves who may have stolen goods, run away, or otherwise defied authority. Chaleiras are known to have been ostracized by fellow slaves, and even beaten when the overseer was absent.

CHALMERS, GEORGE (1856-1928). A Cornish mining engineer who spent forty-three years as superintendent of the Morro Velho gold mine in Minas Gerais, and who became a leading landowner and country gentleman. At his death, he was called "a constant and dedicated friend of our country" by the local press.

CHAPADAS. Mountainous areas of the Northeast, generally free from the periodic droughts which afflict lower-lying land, and therefore functioning as oases in the <u>sertão</u>.

CHAPLIN CLUB. A tongue-in-cheek organization of intellectuals in Rio de Janeiro in 1929, made up of young men opposed to the introduction of sound film. Members included Otávio de Faria, Claúdio de Melo and Josué de Castro.

CHARQUE. Dried, or jerked, beef, the principal form of meat in the Brazilian diet, and the chief export of the southern states, especially Rio Grande do Sul. See also BACALHÃO.

CHARQUEADAS. Beef drying stations, the first of which sprang up near São Pedro do Rio Grande, Rio Grande do Sul's port, and along the São Gonçalo River. The town of Pelotas was established about 1800 in the center of this region.

CHERMONT, ABEL. One of five members of the national Congress arrested and imprisoned in violation of parliamentary immunity, for having supported the popular front Aliança Nacional Libertadora, in 1935. The others were deputies Domingos Velasco, João Mangabeira, Otavio Silveira and Abguar Bastos.

CHIMANGO. Literally, a long-legged bird native to southern Brazil that lives off ticks it picks off the bellies of cattle. The Chimangos were a political faction headed by Borges de Medeiros, the state political boss, and were opposed by various groups which finally joined in the Aliança Libertadora in 1922.

CHIMARRÃO. The drink of the gaúcho.

CHIQUEIRO. A small ranch. Literally, the term means "pigsty" or "hovel."

CHORÕES. Instrumental bands popular in Rio de Janeiro and elsewhere at the turn of the century, playing at parties, celebrations, and at Carnaval. Many of the vibrant themes of the chorões were adapted later by Villa-Lobos, himself a member of a <u>chôro</u> group directed by Quincas Laranjeira, especially in a lengthy series of classical pieces based on the chorões written between 1922 and 1930.

CHUCHÚ see XUXU

CÍCERO, ROMÃO BATISTA (PADRE CÍCERO) (1844-1934).
Excommunicated priest and regional folk hero, Padre
Cícero transformed the Cearense sertão village of Joaseiro into a messianistic capital of 30,000 souls by 1914,
with thousands of pilgrims flocking to the site yearly to
sit at the feet of the frail cleric. His romeiros, or
followers, helped him exercise powerful political influence
at the state level and to resist Church efforts to strip
him of his post.

"CIDADE TUBERCULOSA. " Parody of the Carnaval song
"Cidade Maravilhosa," popular in Belo Horizonte in the
early decades of the century:

"Cidade tuberculosa	"City of tuberculosis
Cheia de microbios mil	Microbes fill the air
Cidade tuberculosa	City of tuberculosis
O sanatório do Brasil!"	Sanatorium of Brazil!"

CINEMA NÔVA. Movement during the 1960's to achieve a
national form of cinematographic expression, typified by
the films of Glauber Rocha, which use French Nouvelle
Vague methods to illustrate themes of social protest.
Hit hard by censorship, the Cinema Nôva faded by the
late 1960's.

CISPLATINE WAR. A border war, from 1825 to 1828, between Brazil and Argentina over Uruguay which, under
British protection, emerged as an independent buffer
state.

CLARIM DO ALVARADO. A short-lived newspaper established
in the city of São Paulo by middle class mulattos in the
1930's.

CLASSE OPERÁRIA, A. Communist Party newspaper of the
1920's and 1930's which reached a weekly circulation of
30,000 copies, although it never achieved any measure
of influence among working class groups.

CLAVER, PEDRO. Seventeenth-century Venezuelan "Apostle
of the Negroes," whose canonization by Pope Leo XIII
in the late 1880's served to apply additional pressure
upon the Cotegipe ministry to bring about abolition.

CLIMATE. Ninety-three percent of Brazil lies within the

equatorial zone, although the effects of latitude are tempered by altitude and by differences in the relative humidity of the air. The Amazon region is hot and humid; the northeast dry in the interior and damp on the coast; frost occurs in the three southernmost states, where winters are cold and damp and summers temperate. Brazil's seasons are the reverse of those in the Northern hemisphere.

CLOSING OF THE ASSEMBLY, 1823 see PAMPLONA, DAVID

CLUBE DE ENGENHARIA. An association (1880-) for the dissemination of technological ideas, especially in the area of transportation. In 1882 it sponsored the first railroad congress; in São Paulo, it encouraged the foundation, in 1894, of a state politechnic school.

CLUBE TRÊS DE OUTUBRO see THIRD OF OCTOBER CLUB

CLUBES DE LAVOURA. "Agricultural Clubs," vigilante groups organized through Pernambuco's zona da mata by slaveholders in the late nineteenth century, to counter abolitionists' attempts to sow discontent among plantation slaves.

COBERTURA. Protection or "coverage" by virtue of connections through relatives or friends. See also PANELINHA.

CODI see OPERAÇÃO BANDEIRANTES

COELHO, DUARTE (1554- ?). Donatary of the captaincy of Pernambuco, the most important territory in Brazil, a man whose father had led an expedition of exploration to Brazil in 1503 and who, himself, had acquired major administrative experience in Portuguese India before coming to the New World. Arriving in 1535, he brought with him his entire family, and dedicated himself to the venture of developing sugar cane agriculture. His first settlement, called Marim, was renamed Olinda in 1537. Igaraçú was the colony's first urban center.

COELHO, NICOLAU (? -1504). The first member of Cabral's fleet actually to set foot on Brazilian land, on April 23, 1500, with a boatload of sailors. The main landing was made the next day at a point to the north of the original site of contact between Coelho and the several dozen aborigines who came to greet him.

COFFEA ARABICA. The coffee plant, native to Ethiopia, flourishing in humid tropical climates tempered by higher altitudes than sea level. In Brazil, coffee has done best in São Paulo and Paraná, although historically the earliest coffee plantations were established in Bahia, the Paraíba Valley of Rio de Janeiro, and in parts of the northeastern coast.

COFFEE. First introduced illegally from French Guyana into Pará, later to Rio de Janeiro, and finally, in the 1830's, to São Paulo, where it flourished in the red earth. Coffee prosperity in the Paraíba Valley and in São Paulo led to the decline of slavery--since it could utilize paid free labor, to subsidized immigration, and, by the end of the nineteenth century, to the creation of a manufacturing sector in the Center-South. By 1900 Brazil had become the world's leading producer, and coffee cultivation had spread beyond São Paulo into Paraná and parts of Mato Grosso.

COHAB-GB. State Housing Agency created in Guanabara in 1963 under the Goulart regime to carry out projects to urbanize or remove favela shanties. By the time of the 1964 coup COHAB had removed about 6,000 families to new homes in developments outside the city built in part with United States AID funds, such as Vila Kennedy. See FAVELAS.

COIMBRA, UNIVERSITY OF. Venerable Portuguese university founded in the thirteenth century, and the institution to which sons of Brazilian settlers of the upper class were sent for their education until the advent of Independence. Of the 1824-26 classes at Coimbra, 120 students were Brazilian-born; seventy percent of them, according to the Barmans, gained entrance into the Brazilian Imperial elite upon their return from Europe.

COIVARA. Amerindian methods of clearing land for planting by burning heaped brushwood, branches, and other debris after the land has been levelled except for the tallest trees, which were girdled. Simply setting fire to the woods, practiced by the Portuguese, was called queimada (q. v.).

COLÉGIO. A school corresponding to the Junior High School in the United States. Curricula are generally academic in nature, to prepare students for the higher-level ginásio.

Most Brazilian colégios are privately owned and charge
tuition and fees.

COLÉGIO CARAÇÁ. Secondary school established in 1820,
in Rio de Janeiro, by Lazarist fathers, remembered for
its rigorous discipline and its high educational standards.

COLÉGIO DE DOM PEDRO II. Secondary school established
in Rio de Janeiro in 1837 in honor of the future Emperor,
and during the nineteenth century one of the nation's
most prestigious preparatory schools for sons of the elite.
The school still functioned in the 1970's.

COLONO. A small agricultural property owner of European
origin, usually German or Italian, in the southern states.

COMANDO REVOLUCIONÁRIO DE 1964. A triumvirate of
the three military cabinet ministers--War, Navy, and
Air Force--which took power immediately after the ouster
of João Goulart on March 31, 1964.

COMARCA. A judicial district. In the colonial period and
early Empire, these were often sizable. The Comarca
de São Francisco represented more than half of the territory of Pernambuco before it was ceded to Bahia.

COMARCA DO SÃO FRANCISCO. Expanse of land following
the São Francisco River and giving access to the interior
of Minas Gerais, stripped from Pernambucan territory
in retribution for the 1817 republican uprising in Recife.

COMBES, LOUIS. A French priest who, arriving at Bahia
on the ship L'orientale in 1840, produced the first daguer-
reotype in South America, one of the earliest photographic
reproductions anywhere. Dom Pedro II requested a personal demonstration of the process; the fifteen-year-old
Emperor took steps to acquire his own equipment, and
became one of the first serious amateur photographers
in the world. Father Combes produced various photo-
graphic views of city life in Rio de Janeiro, Petropolis,
and traveled into the hinterland of the state of Rio.

COMISSÁRIO. A coffee broker, usually a Brazilian, who
handled the planters' coffee from its unloading point in
Santos and dealt with the exporter, usually English; the
comissários frequently arranged for loans to planters,
or loaned money himself at very high interest, and often
ended up as fazendeiro himself.

COMPADRESCO. Ritually extended kinship whose relative strength--throughout Latin America--is often used to measure urbanization.

COMPANHIA ESTANÍFERA DO BRASIL. The major private tin producing and processing firm in Brazil (CESBRA), which, in 1961, established a geological center in Porto Velho, Rondônia, to study ways of increasing that territory's tin production. Within a few years a boom had resulted, producing high profits but also exacerbating relations between independent garimpeiros and CESBRA over conflicting claims.

COMPANHIA ESTRADA DE FERRO LEOPOLDINA. Founded by Brazilian interests in 1872, the line, originating in Rio de Janeiro, became insolvent in 1897 after acquiring a collection of other lines, most of which used different track gauges. British creditors took it over in 1897, investing new capital, and the line recovered to some extent. By 1912 it controlled 2,660 kilometers of track and had become the country's largest privately-owned railroad network.

COMPANHIA GRÃO PARÁ E MARANHÃO. Mercantilist trading group given a commercial monopoly for the provinces of Maranhão and Pará by Pombal, as part of his effort to weaken the economic power of the Jesuits. See also POMBAL.

COMPANHIA SIDERÚRGICA NACIONAL. The national steel enterprise, established in 1941, and the administrator of the steel works at Volta Redonda, on the banks of the Paraíba river in Rio de Janeiro state, installed (with United States financing in part, in return for Brazil's support during the war) in 1946.

COMPANHIA VALE DO RIO DOCE. Established by Vargas in 1942 to exploit the iron resources of Itabira, as a government-owned enterprise. Helped along by United States and British loans, the agency broadened its scope to the point where it became, by the 1950's, a regional development agency. In 1976 it employed 10,000 workers.

COMPENSATION MARKS. Special blocked German currency for payment of imports introduced by Berlin trade officials in the mid-1930's to boost sales in South America. The currency, usually known as aski marks, could be used for German products only, thereby encouraging trade.

CONDOR. The German airline serving Brazil until it was
nationalized during the Second World War, remerging as
Cruzeiro do Sul Airlines.

CONFEDERAÇÃO DO EQUADOR. Republican and abolitionist
uprising in Pernambuco, seven years after the 1817 revolt, and considered more serious. Both revolts were
put down without much difficulty; Soares Brandão and
others have suggested that one reason for the lack of
regional support for the 1824 uprising was landowner
opposition to the call for slave emancipation.

CONFEDERAÇÃO DO TIRO BRASILEIRO. The first national
association of Tiro groups (see LINHAS DO TIRO), established in 1906 by a Gaúcho pharmacist, Antônio Carlos
Lopes, with the approval of the military command.

CONFEDERAÇÃO NACIONAL DE INDUSTRIA (CNI). The
principal industrial lobby in the mid-1930's, headed by
Euvaldo Lodi, its president. As Wirth notes, however,
such formal interest groups as CNI became less influential after 1945, as the political system became more
complex and less responsive to direct lobbying.

CONFERÊNCIA NACIONAL DOS BISPOS DO BRASIL (CNBB).
Founded by Dom Hêlder Câmara in 1952 and approved by
the Vatican Secretariat of State (under Msgr. Giovanni
Montini), the organization was designed to forge links
among the Brazilian bishops and facilitate Church efforts
to encourage progressive social change. Most of the
bishops who did join the Conference were from the Northeast; during the 1950's it proved eminently successful,
although Câmara's charismatic leadership and seeming
leftist orientation galvanized Church conservatives to
attack it. After 1964 the group entered into eclipse--
Câmara was made a "non-person" under the new rules
of censorship--and was reintegrated into the Church,
thereby depriving it of its autonomy.

CONGONHAS DO CAMPO. Eighteenth-century town in the
gold region of Minas Gerais, whose Church of Bom Jesus
de Matosinho is the site of the major works of Aleijadinho,
the crippled sculptor who worked with his tools strapped
to the stumps of his arms.

CONGOS. Also known as congadas, dramatic dances akin to
the bumba-meu-boi; the congos originated as a coronation

ceremony honoring the King of the Congo. In Brazil, a
"king" was chosen from among the slaves of a plantation
to act out the part.

CONGREGAÇÃO. Members of a university faculty with pro-
fessorial rank. See also CORPO DOCENTE.

CONGREGAÇÃO CRISTÃ. The second largest Pentecostal
sect in Brazil.

CÔNGRUAS. Stipends for the clergy, paid from the tithe of
10 percent levied on all produce during the colonial period.

CONSCIENTIZAÇÃO see FREIRE, PAULO

CONSELHEIRO, ANTÔNIO (1828-1897). Sertanejo, from
Quixeramobim, Ceará, whose messianic vocation created
a holy city at Canudos, Bahia, and who led the resistance
of his caboclo faithful to military attack from the hated
central government in the Canudos campaign of 1897.
Conselheiro died during the attacks--out of which only
three men survived; his head was severed and carried
to the coast, where it was put on public display. See
also DA CUNHA, EUCLIDES.

CONSELHO NACIONAL DE GEOGRAFIA. The National Geography Council, established in 1937 as part of the Instituto
Brasileiro de Geografia e Estatística (IBGE). Mandell
considers this the high point of prestige for geographers,
who were invited to participate fully in decisions on urban
and rural development and planning.

CONSELHO NACIONAL DE MULHERES. The National Wom-
en's Council, established in 1947 to work for equality
for women in the Brazilian Civil Code, a collection of
laws which made wives, in every legal sense, second
class citizens without such civil rights as the freedom
to have independent bank accounts or to travel abroad
without a husband's written permission. Some changes
were finally achieved in 1962.

CONSPIRACY OF THE TAILORS. An attempted republican
movement in Salvador, betrayed in 1798, and leading to
the trial of thirty-six men, the large majority artisans
and working class persons, ten being tailors. Twenty-
four were mulattos, one black, and only eleven white.

The four principal activists were hanged in 1799, as a
lesson to the Brazilian elite, although as in Minas only
conspirators from the lower classes were punished.
Fear of social revolution, in the wake of the French
Revolution nine years earlier, prevented influential Ba-
hians from supporting the "tailors" cause.

CONSTANT, BENJAMIN (1833-1891). Career military officer,
    mathematics professor, and one of the founders of the
    Republic. With the fall of the Empire Constant (family
    name: Botelho de Magalhães) was made a brigadier
    general and given the Ministry of Education, from which
    post he introduced many reforms based on the doctrine
    of positivism.

CONSTITUENT ASSEMBLY (1822). One of the most important
    steps in the formation of a national political consensus,
    and the precursor of the Imperial Assembly.   Represen-
    tatives from fourteen provinces attended the session to
    draft a Constitution (Piauí, Maranhão, Grão-Pará, and
    the Cisplatine province, later Uruguay, still had not
    formally recognized Brazilian Independence).   The Minas
    Gerais bancada was the largest and most influential, led
    by Antônio Carlos Ribeiro de Andrada e Silva, José
    Bonifácio's brother.   The Assembly acclaimed Pedro I
    Emperor and Perpetual Defender of Brazil; as emperor
    he called the Assembly into session in May 1823, only
    to dissolve it on November 12th.

CONSTITUENT ASSEMBLY (1823-1824). Having dissolved
    the first Assembly in November 1823, over various issues
    rooted in the deputies' almost pathological distrust of
    Portugal and their insistence upon asserting legislative
    authority over the Emperor, Pedro called a second body,
    comprised of ten Brazilians, who wrote a draft constitu-
    tion in early December.   Submitting it to the municipal
    councils across the country, Pedro declared it approved,
    and promulgated the constitution on March 25, 1824.

CONSTITUTION OF 1824. Influenced by French Revolutionary
    thought and the writings of the Swiss-Frenchman Benjamin
    Constant, the document was accepted by Emperor Pedro
    I as Brazil's first constitution.   Its 179 articles gave
    political power to the central government; heads of the
    provinces were to be named by the Emperor; the monarch
    would enjoy virtual veto power over all state affairs
    through the "Moderating Power" granted by Article 98;

the Senate was appointed entirely by the Emperor, and the Chamber of Deputies elected by provincial representatives.   Income and literacy restrictions limited voting; Catholicism was the state religion, and only apostolic Catholics could hold elective office.

CONSTITUTION OF 1891.   Brazil's second constitution, influenced by positivist doctrine and the principles of extreme federalism, under which states (the former provinces) gained the right to tax their own exports, establish their own militias, and otherwise enjoy their own autonomy.   Under this document the country's name was changed to the "Republic of the United States of Brazil."

CONSTITUTION OF 1934.   The country's third constitution, the product of a lengthy constitutional convention called by Getúlio Vargas after the São Paulo constitutionalist insurrection of 1932, and a hybrid document which never held the confidence of the chief executive and which was replaced by the Estado Novo constitution of 1937.   A peculiar mixture of liberal constitutionalism, authoritarianism, and corporatism, the constitution restored some of the privileges of the Catholic Church in the area of education, and sent representatives to congress not only on the basis of geographical constituencies but from interest groups--employers, employees, professionals, and public servants.   Brazil's first labor legislation was incorporated into the constitution in Article 120.

CONSTITUTION OF 1937.   Written by Francisco Campos, the new Minister of Justice and the Interior, the document created executive supremacy and gave the President the right to dissolve Congress, cancel civil rights, and imposed centralized control over state affairs.   Frankly corporatist and hostile to traditional juridical liberalism, the constitution headed Vargas's Estado Novo, or New State, itself patterned after fascist regimes in southern Europe.

CONSTITUTION OF 1946.   A return to political liberalism and federalist principles, and re-establishing the traditional balance of powers among the three branches of government--Legislative, Judicial, and Executive.   Held over from the 1930's was the labor legislation promulgated by the Vargas regime; the constitution also guaranteed individual rights and freedom of religious expression.

CONSTITUTION OF 1967.   Approved by Congress although

written by authorities of the military regime--including
Francisco Campos, who had composed the near-fascist
Constitution of 1937--Brazil's fifth constitution maintained
the principles of the 1946 document but incorporated the
stronger position of the executive branch taken by the
military after the 1964 coup. This was reinforced in
1968 by the promulgation of the Institutional Act No. 5
suspending constitutional guarantees and giving the president exceptional powers.

CONSTITUTIONALIST REVOLT. Uprising of the state of São
Paulo in 1932 (May 25th) over the failure of the Liberal
Alliance administration to convene a constituent assembly
to return the country to constitutional rule. With the
support of a military contingent from Mato Grosso led
by Gen. Bertoldo Klinger, Paulista troops led by Gen.
Isidoro Dias Lopes and Col. Euclides de Oliveira Figueiredo; they were opposed by federal forces under Gen.
Góis Monteiro. With the port of Santos blockaded, the
would-be civil war failed, and was met by Vargas without bitterness: he called the constituent assembly, and
assumed the war debts of the rebellious state.

CONTESTADO CAMPAIGN. A rebellion in the states of Santa
Catarina and Paraná during the period 1912-1916, finally
subdued by the federal army.

CONVENT OF SANTA CLARA DO DESTÊRRO. Brazil's oldest,
founded in 1677. Soeiro notes that before this date Salvador's leading citizens opposed such seclusion of women
on the grounds that it would threaten the colony's population growth. Once established, the Destêrro Convent became both a religious retreat and a functional part of the
city's economic life, since the nunnery played the role of
banker, slaveholder, landlord as well as the repository
for female members of the elite who could not arrange
suitable marriages.

COPACABANA. Elegant and densely populated beach-front
district on Rio de Janeiro's Zona Sul, or South Zone,
linked to downtown Rio by a tunnel at Leme in the early
1920's, which spurred a building boom which made Copacabana one of the most desirable and high-priced neighborhoods in the city.

COPACABANA FORT UPRISING. An outbreak of insurrection
among young tenente officers and their commanders on

July 5, 1922 at the Fort, which stands at the pinnacle
between Rio de Janeiro's Capacabana and Ipanema beaches.
Popular folklore holds that eighteen cadets made their
stand against the counter-attack from the Vila Militar--
based on an anonymous poem which appeared in the
Correio da Manhã--whereas 28 rebels actually started
out, with their ranks depleted by desertions and injuries
to 9 by the end of the conflict.

COPERSUCAR GROUP. One of the largest agricultural product corporations in Brazil. Copersucar purchased, in
1976, the United States firm Hills Brothers Coffee, which
will allow it a direct export line for ground and soluable
coffee products. This is the first arrangement of this
sort in the coffee market.

CORINTHIANS. Most popular soccer team in São Paulo. It
has been noted that when Corinthians win, production in
the city rises 12.3 percent. When it loses, work acci-
dents increase by 15.3 percent. Sociological fantasy or
no, few Brazilians would dispute the psychological impact
of victory and defeat.

CORONEL-COITEIRO. Literally, the "boss-protector," the
rural (or small-town) figure exercising near-absolute
power in political and economic terms.

CORPO DOCENTE. Faculty (teachers). See CONGREGAÇÃO.

CORPOS FECHADOS. Bodies impervious to bullets, attributes
given by folklore to some of the more ferocious cangaceiros and backlands bandits. These jagunços added to
their reputations--deliberately or not--by using no lights
at night, by sleeping in squatting positions, and by wreak-
ing terrible vengeance on their enemies through the use
of torture and other brutalities.

CORREÇÃO MONETÁRIA. Adjustment of mortgage rates and
other fiscal obligations according to the official rate of
interest. This practice, instituted in Brazil in the mid-
1960's to combat monetary and real estate speculation,
has won the acclaim of some economists as innovative,
and has been proposed in the form of "variable mortgage
rates" in New York State and elsewhere.

CORREIA, RAIMUNDO (1860-1911). Maranhense poet of the
Parnassian school, he was a dour, sentimental, and

anguished man whose personality translated itself into his poetic works, the best of which were compiled in the anthology Poesias, published in Lisbon in 1898.

CORREIA, RIVADÁVIA DA CUNHA (1866-1920). Gaúcho positivist and Minister of Justice during the administration of Hermes da Fonseca. Responsible for education as well--the Education Ministry was created two decades later--he was responsible for the enactment in 1911 of the National Education Act, also known as the Reforma Rividávia, a mixture of far-sighted and ill-conceived legislation. Among other things it set the conditions for the creation of the national entrance examination system (vestibular); the livre docente, or full-time faculty; and final examinations in each course instead of at the completion of study. As Nachman observes, many of the individual reforms were flawed, and led to abuses. Correia's successor in 1915 issued a revised set of laws, but preserved the positivist flavor of federal educational policy, also paving the way for the establishment of new faculties of law, medicine, engineering, dentistry, and pharmacy.

CORREIA DE OLIVEIRA, JOÃO ALFREDO (1835-1919). Pernambucan-born Imperial politician named by Princess Isabel, acting as Regent, to head the Ministry which oversaw the final abolition of slavery in 1888. An unreconstructed monarchist, João Alfredo retired from political life when the Empire fell, although he served as President of the Banco do Brasil toward the end of his life.

CORREIO BRASILIENSE. The first "Brazilian" newspaper, published in London by the exiled liberal journalist, Hipólito da Costa Pereira Furtado de Mendonça. The newspaper appeared more or less regularly until 1822, staunchly advocating Brazilian independence.

CORREIO PAULISTANA. The oldest newspaper in São Paulo, dating from 1854.

CORTES. The Portuguese parliamentary body whose influence was greatest during the fourteenth-century reign of João of Aviz; with overseas expansion, its role steadily declined. See FIDALGOS.

CORTESÃO, JAIME (1884-1960). Portuguese historian who lived in exile after 1927, and who took up residence in

Rio de Janeiro in 1940. He wrote to rehabilitate the
Paulistas from what he considered to be the "Black Legend" surrounding bandeirante exploits.

COSTA, DUARTE DA. Second governor-general of Brazil,
from 1553 to 1557, following Thomé de Sousa.

COSTA, JURANDYR. Psychiatrist and medical historian,
leader of the small Brazilian school of mental health
professionals influenced by R. D. Laing and opposed to
behavior modification and other standard forms of mental
health treatment.

COSTA, LÚCIO (1902-). Architect and urbanist; the major
planner of Brasília. Costa studied in England and Switzerland, returning to Brazil seeking to study and interpret
colonial architecture and to develop a modern style compatible with it. By 1930 he was recognized as the country's leading architect, and was invited to reorganize the
Brazilian Architectural Society (SBA).

COSTA, MIGUEL (1872-194?). Argentine-born and Paulista-
bred, Costa became a leading tenente figure and one of
the heads of the Prestes Column even though, at the age
of 50 in 1922, he was more than twice the age of most
of the rebellious cadets and young officers.

COSTA E SILVA, ARTUR DA (1902-1969). Career military
officer and second military president after the 1964 coup,
following Castelo Branco. Born in Taquari, Rio Grande
do Sul, Costa e Silva was "elected" by the National Congress after being named by the high military command
and took office on March 15, 1967. Under Costa e Silva
Brazil was placed under a virtual state of national emergency with the promulgation of the Institutional Act No.
5 in December 1967, which gave the president additional
power to guarantee law and order. After suffering a
stroke in August 1969 Costa e Silva was replaced by a
military junta until his successor, Garrastazú Médici,
was named.

COSTA SEIXAS, PADRE FRANCISCO DE. One of the poty-
guar (Rio Grande do Norte) conspirators in the Confederation of the Equator, who, with José Joaquim de Morais
Navarro and José Joaquim Fernandes Barros, delivered
the support of the Câmaras (councils) of the interior of
their province.

COTEGIPE, BARÃO DE (1815-1889).   João Maurício Wander-
     ley, a nineteenth-century Bahian planter often cited as
     the prototype of the landowner-nobleman who used his
     political influence as head of the Conservative Party to
     fight for the status quo and to resist progressive mea-
     sures of economic modernization.   Pang, however, sug-
     gests that this characterization is unfair, that the po-
     litical structure of the Empire hindered agricultural
     modernization.   Cotegipe, for example, lauded efforts
     at modernization elsewhere, and urged his fellow planters
     to look at the (slave-owning) sugar engenhos of Louisiana
     and Cuba for ways of improving production.   He mecha-
     nized his own engenho at Jacarancangá and became the
     chief advocate of labor division, suggesting that slave
     labor be used in the canefields but that engenhos centrais
     (central factories) be established with government sub-
     sidies.

COUTINHO, AZEREDO (BISPO) (1742-1821).   Bishop of Olinda
     and founder of the Seminary in that city in 1800.   Its
     curriculum included history, geography, geometry, de-
     sign, physics and natural history (science), representing
     the first Brazilian reaction to the curriculum reform at
     the University of Coimbra in 1772 and to French philo-
     sophical currents.   Graduates of the Olinda Seminary
     took part in the Pernambucano insurrections of 1817 and
     1824.   In 1832 it became the Colégio Preparatório das
     Artes, to prepare youths for entrance to the Law School.

COUTO, MIGUEL (1865-1934).   A physician and deputy in
     the mid-1930's who led the (ultimately successful) legis-
     lative campaign for exclusion of Asiatic immigration.

COXIPÓ-MIRIM MINES.   Gold mines in the Cuiabá region
     whose discovery in the 1720's spurred the monsões (q. v.)
     --the riverine expeditions to interior Brazil.

CRAB CYCLE.   A commentary by Josué de Castro about
     hunger and misery in the Northeast, quoted by Tad Szulc
     in the New York Times in the late 1950's, and graphically
     revealing of the terrible conditions of life in the region.

CREENTE.   A Protestant believer.   Often the term is used
     in a pejorative manner by others.

CRIMINAL CODE OF 1832.   A Liberal Party measure, emas-
     culated in 1841 by the Conservative ministry, which elim-

inated locally elected judges and replaced them with appointed officials chosen from Rio de Janeiro. Provincial and county officials also lost their autonomous powers, further weakening the Code.

CRISTIANIZAR. "To Christianize," a term in political slang for nominating one candidate but supporting and voting for the opposition.

CRISTÕES NOVOS see NEW CHRISTIANS

CRUZ, OSWALDO GONÇALVES (1872-1917). Brazilian scientist and medical researcher. Under his impetus, the Serum Therapy Institute of Rio was turned into a major research and investigative institution for the purpose of studying and eradicating epidemic disease. The Institute was named after Cruz in 1907. Born in São Paulo to a wealthy family, Cruz was educated as a physican in Rio and then sent to the Pasteur Institute in Paris. He pioneered in the new tradition of medical research and in public health and sanitation, and helped banish yellow fever from the Brazilian coast. See also OSWALDO CRUZ INSTITUTE.

CRUZADO. Colonial-era monetary unit worth 400 réis.

CRUZEIRO. Brazilian currency unit, replacing the milréis. In 1957, 1,000 were worth $15; in 1964, $1; 1 new cruzeiro (CR$N) was worth 17 cents in 1973, and about 5 cents in 1978.

CUBAS, BRÁS (1505-1592). Governor and Capitão-mor of the colony of São Vicente, a member of Martin Afonso de Sousa's original fleet, and the founder of a hospital to which he gave the name Santos.

CUÍAS. Small split gourds, used by slaves as utensils for eating, along with their hands, and, rarely, spoons. Since the slave workers were only given a few minutes in which to consume their soft, boiled food with primitive instruments (as Stein notes), they earned among whites the reputation for crude manners, "bolting" their food rather than eating it.

CUNHA, ANTÔNIO ÁLVARES DA. The first Conde de Cunha, and the first viceroy to govern Brazil from its new capital in Rio de Janeiro, from 1763 to 1767. His greatest

efforts were in the area of urban development. Although
unpopular in office, he asked to be relieved from his
post after only four years.

CUNHA, EUCLIDES DA   see DA CUNHA, EUCLIDES

CUNNINGHAME GRAHAM, ROBERT BONTINE. English writer
and translator who, in 1920, published a translated and
edited version of Da Cunha's Os Sertões, titling it A
Brazilian Mystic, but failing to indicate clearly that Da
Cunha, and not Cunninghame Graham, was the author.

CURANDISMO. Healing by spiritists or other non-licensed
persons. The practice was tolerated until 1890--in
fact, most Brazilian medicine before the twentieth century was non-allopathic--but outlawed by the 1890 Criminal Code as part of the general trend to outlawing practices in society deemed backward or tending to threaten
the progressive order.

CURSO MÉDICO-CIRÚRGICO. A medical-surgical course,
established at Salvador in 1808 and in Rio de Janeiro a
year later, forerunners of the medical schools in those
cities (1832).

CURUMINS. Name given by Jesuit teachers to Amerindian
children, their pupils in catechism, reading, writing,
and liturgy.

CUSTÓDIA, LUDOVINA. An actress and one of the mistresses
of Pedro I. His attraction to her was public and offen-
sive--he once had sexual relations with her between acts
in a benefit performance in the monarch's honor--and
led to public sympathy for Princess Leopoldina and to the
growing animosity with the Emperor.

-D-

DA COSTA, HIPÓLITO (1774-1823). One of the few Brazilians
to have visited the new United States before Brazilian
independence, and the editor of the Correio Braziliense
(1808).

DA CUNHA, EUCLIDES (1866-1909). Author of Os Sertões
(Rebellion in the Backlands), first published in 1902, and
probably the most significant book ever published on the

subject of Brazilian culture and national identity.   A failed army officer and journalist, da Cunha accompanied the military expeditions sent to Bahia to wipe out the tenacious Canudos uprising in 1897; his book, which shocked coastal Brazilians with the concept of "two Brazils"--a Europeanized coast and a primitive, caboclo interior, became a sensation.   Da Cunha's own views on the meaning of Canudos were ambivalent: he greatly admired the courage of the backlands rebels but, in the spirit of the racism of the day, considered them doomed by miscegenation to racial inferiority.

DANILO   see   ALVIM, DANILO

DANTAS, NATANIEL.   Afro-Brazilian novelist from Rio de Janeiro, whose 1969 work, Ifigênia está no Fundo do Corredor gained little recognition but stands, nonetheless, as a major statement of the alienation and loneliness felt by Afro-Brazilians in white Brazilian society.

DANTAS, SANTIAGO (1911-1964).   Jurist and political office-holder as well as a professor of law, Dantas was a leading intellectual figure and foreign policy expert up until his death.

DASP see   DEPARTAMENTO ADMINISTRATIVO DO SERVIÇO PÚBLICO

DASPINHOS.   State administrative organizations formed under the Estado Nôvo and modeled after the federal DASP, hence their nicknames.

DATAS DE TERRA.   Small grants of land distributed in the eighteenth century to settlers in Brazil, at first to colonists from the Azores, with the purpose of introducing diversified agriculture based upon family labor.   The typical data de terra ranged between 250 and 300 hectares.

DEBRET, JEAN-BAPTISTE (1768-1848).   French artist who arrived in Brazil with the artistic mission of 1816, whose drawings and paintings in and around the capital offer the best glimpse of daily life--including the presence of slavery--available.   Debret became the principal painter for the Portuguese Court, and helped establish the first formal instruction in fine arts.   His drawings were used as the theme for the decorations at the 400th anniversary of Rio de Janeiro celebration during Carnaval.

DEFENSE SPENDING. Brazil's military budget of two-and-a-half billion dollars (1975) ranks it nineteenth in the world. Its armed forces are the largest in Latin America, but military expenditures are relatively low in proportion to GNP: 2. 2 percent in the early 1970's.

DEFESA NACIONAL, A. The leading military journal of the late 1930's, a staunch advocate of nationalistic policies in general and rearmament of the armed forces in particular. "The world," its editor warned in 1938, is divided between "colonizing peoples and colonies. Unhappily there is no room for intermediate categories. "

DEFEZA NACIONAL, A. Newspaper produced in 1913 within the army by tenentes and captains trained by the Prussian Army, to which they had been detached for two years. It called for the armed forces to play a modernizing role within Brazilian society, and seeking a strengthened army under the control of the federal government at the expense of state autonomy.

DELEGADO. A police chief, usually with additional, quasi-judicial functions.

DELFIM NETTO, ANTÔNIO (1928-). Finance Minister during the "economic miracle" of the late 1960's, in office from 1967 to 1974 and constantly rumored to be poised for a return to power after his loss of influence with the accession to the presidency of Ernesto Geisel. Trained in economics at the University of São Paulo, he immediately joined the faculty after graduation; at the same time he rose to the directorship of the powerful São Paulo Chamber of Commerce, then to state secretary of finance, then as an aide to Roberto Campos, the military regime's first finance minister. Chosen from relative national obscurity to replace Campos, he quickly earned an international reputation at the age of 38 for his articulateness and economic daring. Some critics found him cold and apolitical, uninterested in the problems of the poor and in the growing gap between the haves and the have nots under the post-1964 regime. But Delfim replied that he is interested in the longer view, a position which has made him greatly admired by the Brazilian business community and by some military officials, but has also earned him the reputation as a cold-blooded technocrat among his detractors.

DELGADO DE CASTILHO, FRANCISCO. The former governor

of two captaincies who committed suicide upon being recalled to Portugal, since he had taken as his lover a
woman of the lower class, and he would have been socially unable to marry her and take her back to Europe.

DEPARTAMENTO ADMINISTRATIVO DO SERVIÇO PÚBLICO
(DASP). The Administrative Department of Public Service, created by Getúlio Vargas in 1936, Brazil's first
modern civil service apparatus.

DEPARTAMENTO DE IMPRENSA E PROPAGANDA (DIP).
The Estado Novo's Press and Propaganda Agency, headed
by Lourival Fontes and modelled, to some degree, after
Goebbel's Nazi Ministry of Propaganda. Of the difference
between the DIP's clumsy efforts to build Vargas's image
and encourage Brazilian nationalism, Major Adaúto Bar-
reiros, the director of the ARP in 1977, notes: "We
(in the President's Public Relations Department) never
promote personal images; the president's name, for example, is never mentioned in our campaigns. And we
do not stretch the facts. 500 is 500, not 600 or 700."
In the 1930's, however, the DIP satisfied those Brazilians
who were attracted to fascism, and its methods were
not questioned by them.

DEPARTAMENTO NACIONAL DE ENSINO. Federal agency
dating from 1925 under the Ministry of Justice, the
antecedent of the Vargas-era Ministry of Education and
Public Health in 1930.

DESARTICULAÇÃO. "Disarticulation," a term used by intellectuals in Brazil to characterize the inability of groups
to communicate with one another, and the silent gap between reality and "official" reality.

DESCIMENTOS. Expeditions to kidnap Indians from their
native habitats and bring them to the coast. These were
banned under the Reform Laws promulgated by the Marquis of Pombal in the mid-eighteenth century. After
1798, however, a royal decree putting aborigines on
equal footing with all other subjects had the effect of
legalizing the descimentos and other forms of Indian
raids, especially since officials were now allowed to
"allocate" Indians for required work.

DESCOLONIZAÇÃO PORTUGUÊSA. The period of colonial
decline, 1789-1808. Some authors extend the period to
1830, the year of Pedro I's abdication.

DESCRENTE. "Disbeliever," a term used to describe peasants as stubborn, suspicious, and non-cooperative, mainly by those who either have been frustrated in trying to improve their conditions, or those who believe that his case is hopeless. Government agencies such as SOR (Service for Rural Orientation) call the existence of descrente behavior as the major obstacle to organizing rural syndicates.

DESEMBARGADOR. An appeal court judge, a major figure in Imperial and Republican Brazil as intermediary between local coronéis (and other private interests) and the system of governance. Promotion to desembargador frequently served as a stepping stone, moreover, to higher offices in the judicial system, and often was the point of transfer from the judiciary to positions in the executive or legislative branches.

DESGERMINASIÇÃO. Vargas administration policy imposed in 1938 to "deGermanize" the population of the southern states by prohibiting German-language newspapers and journals and requiring Portuguese as the language of instruction in the schools. About 900,000 persons of German "blood" were estimated to live in the three states of Rio Grande do Sul, Santa Catarina, and Paraná; since they were openly courted by Nazi organizers, their presence in concentrated numbers was deemed a threat to national security in spite of the proclivity in the armed forces to support the Axis cause, hence the "degermanisição" program.

DESOBRIGA. The paschal duty paid by communicants during Lent, supplementing regular Church income (paid through côngruas, or stipends).

DESPACHANTE. A professional middle man between the bureaucracy and the citizen, who charges a fee for cutting through red tape, getting favors done, or, at times, skirting official regulations. The despachante, however unsavory as a figure, is absolutely indispensable given the Brazilian way of administration.

DESTACAMENTO DE OPERAÇÕES INTEGRADAS (DOI). Formerly OBAN, the notorious police center in São Paulo where journalist Vladimir Herzog was killed in October 1975 and where scores of prisoners have reported brutality and torture.

DESTÊRRO, NOSSA SENHORA DO. Original Portuguese name for Santa Catarina, whose principal nucleus and administrative capital sits on Santa Catarina island. It was so densely populated--25 inhabitants per square kilometer in 1810--that Saint Hilaire considered it too crowded to support urban life, thus explaining its poverty.

D'EU, COMTE DE. Husband of Princess Isabel and son-in-law to Dom Pedro II. See ISABEL, PRINCESS.

DEUSES E OS MORTOS, OS. A film (1971) by Ruy Guerra, a Mozambique-born, Paris-educated Cinema Nôvo director, which deals, through surrealist images, with the themes of violence, greed, and economic dependence set on a Bahian cocoa plantation.

DEUTSCHE SCHULVEREINE. Association of German-language schools, numbering at least 2,500 in the mid-1930's, mostly in São Paulo, Paraná, Santa Catarina, and Rio Grande do Sul. The organization disappeared when Vargas banned foreign-language schools in 1938.

DEVASSAS. Judicial inquiries, held regularly during the seventeenth century, the first of which was carried out in 1603 in Pernambuco.

DIA DE SÃO JOSÉ. St. Joseph's Day, March 19th, given by northeastern folklore as the time by which rain must come or drought will afflict the region.

DIA DOS BOBOS. April Fool's Day (April 1).

DIÁLOGOS DAS GRANDEZAS DO BRASIL see BRANDÃO, AMBRÓSIO FERNANDES

DIAMANTINA see TIJUCO

DIÁRIO DE AMAZONAS. One of the two leading newspapers during the rubber boom years in Manaos, the other being the Jornal do Commércio.

DIÁRIO DE PERNAMBUCO. The oldest continually publishing newspaper in South America, inaugurated in Recife in 1825.

DIAS, CÍCERO (1907-). Pernambuco-born painter who first studied architecture in Rio, then dedicated himself to imaginative and pathetic scenes from his native north-east, and finally taking up permanent residence in Paris in 1938, where he adopted a purely abstract style.

DIAS, HENRIQUE (early 17th century-1662). An Afro-Bra-zilian, born to freed slave parents, Dias volunteered in the campaign against the Dutch and distinguished himself for acts of bravery in battle. At Comendaituba he lost his left hand, but continued to fight. After victory, he was awarded various decorations from the Crown, in-cluding that of the title of "Governor of all Brazilian criollos, negros and mulattos."

DIAS GOMES, ALFREDO. Author of the screenplay of Pagador de Promessas, the winner of the Gold Palm for the best film at the Cannes Festival of 1962, and an advocate of plays in simple, direct language aimed at social commentary without advocating overt rebellion.

DI CAVALCANTI, EMILIANO (1897-1976). Born in Rio de Janeiro but residing most of his life in São Paulo, "Di" was one of Brazil's greatest modern painters, concen-trating on earthy, lyrical portraits of mulatto women, caboclo men, and scenes of small town and countryside life. By the early 1970's Di Cavalcanti's larger canvases were selling at auction for $50,000 and more. Di Caval-canti is credited with having conceived the idea for São Paulo's Semana de Arte Moderna, and he played a major role in it.

DISPUTED TERRITORY BETWEEN STATES. There are two major disputed areas, still unresolved: one on the border between Amazonas and Pará (2,680 square kilometers) and the other between Piauí and Ceará (2,614 square kilometers).

DISTRITO DIAMENTINO. The "diamond district," the only site of legal diamond extraction, centered around pre-sent-day Diamantinha, in Minas Gerais, and after 1771 exclusively reserved as a Crown monopoly. See also REGIMENTO.

DIVORCE. Illegal in Brazil until December 1977, when a bill introduced by MDB Senator Nelson Carneiro (Rio de Janeiro) and ARENA Senator Accioly Filho (Paraná) was passed, making civil dissolution of marriage legal three years after a court approved separation or five years after de facto separation.   Under the law, Brazilians will be limited to one divorce and remarriage.

DIZIMEIROS.   Tithe collectors, entirely unpopular in the colony not only for the fact they collected 10 percent of all profits and transactions, but for the way in which collections were made: in cash always rather than in kind, forcing producers to raise money (at high interest rates) on their produce not yet sold, with all attendant risks. The dizimeiros, then, exerted a far greater burden than merely 10 percent, and many colonists were driven into bankruptcy or ruin.   Dizimeiros are held responsible for the scattering of rural populations, as taxpayers literally fled from payment.

DJANIRA, DA MATTA E SILVA (1914-).   A major painter of Brazilian themes, especially brightly colored still lifes, decorative graphics, and scenes of nature.

DOCE RIVER VALLEY.   Site of open warfare between Botocudo Indians and white settlers in the early years of this century.

DOCENTE LIVRE.   A title awarded to a faculty member who competes for a full professorship (CATEDRÁTICO) but fails to win it although he performs well in his examinations.

"DR. DOI."   Harry Shibata, the physician accused of the criminal falsification of the autopsy report which claimed that Vladimir Herzog had committed suicide while being held at Destacamento de Operações Integradas (DOI) in São Paulo in October 1975.   Shibata has served as the director of the Legal Medicine Institute.

DOMINGOS DA GUIA (1912-).   Soccer hero of the 1930's born in the slum district of Bangú, Rio de Janeiro; da Guia initiated his career playing for Uruguayan and Argentinian clubs before joining the Brazilian national team in 1931; the low salaries afforded to Brazilian athletes during that decade forced him to return to Argentina, where he played out his career except for a final season-- in 1947--which saw him finish his career for the low-status team, Bangú, representing the district of his youth.

DONATÁRIOS.   Donatories, or proprietary landlords under

the system of captaincies established in the 1530's.   See
also CAPTAINCY SYSTEM; CARTA DE DOAÇAO.

DONDINHO   see   NASCIMENTO, JOÃO RAMOS DE

DOUTOR.   One who holds the doctor's degree or degree in
law.   Over time, the term has been more casually applied, often to anyone who holds a university degree or
who otherwise plays the role of being erudite.

DROUGHT.   Droughts in the Northeast are recorded as early
as 1710-11, and have occurred periodically with ever
more severe effects, since the population of the backlands has swelled over time.   Devastating droughts were
registered, in modern times, in 1877-79; 1888-89; 1898;
1900; 1915; 1931-32; 1942-43; 1951; 1958; 1969; 1972;
and 1977.   See also POLÍGONO DAS SÊCAS.

DUTCH BRAZIL, EXTENT OF.   Five years after the fall of
Olinda, under troops led by Antônio Dias Papa-Robalos,
the Dutch holdings in Brazil included the settlements of
Maranhão, Ceará, Rio Grande do Norte, Paraíba, Pernambuco, Itamaracá, Alagoas, and Sergipe.

DUTRA, DJALMA (1899-1930).   One of the four detachment
leaders of the Prestes Column, killed accidentally in
1930 when a sentry mistook him for an intruder.

DUTRA, EURICO GASPAR (1885-1977).   Professional military
officer born in Cuiabá, Mato Grosso, and educated at
the Escola Militar.   In 1935, as army general, he commanded the counter-attack on the rebellious Third Army
headquarters in Rio de Janeiro, the uprising linked to
the call to national insurrection by the National Liberation Alliance, and organized the Brazilian Expeditionary
Force (FEB) that fought in Italy with the Allies in 1944.
He was elected President at the head of the new PSD in
1946, defeating Brigadier Eduardo Gomes of the UDN.
His presidential term ran from 1946 to 1950.

-E-

"É MELHOR QUE SE VÃO OS ANEIS MAS FIQUEM OS DEDOS. "
Folk saying meaning, "It's better to lose one's rings than
one's fingers. "   Applied by Florestan Fernandes to suggest that while planters were forced to grant freedom to

their slaves with abolition, they managed to retain their power over social, political, and economic relations in the countryside.

EAGLE OF THE HAGUE. Name given by the press to Rui Barbosa (q. v.), Brazilian delegate to the Second Hague Peace Conference in 1907.

"ECONOMIC MIRACLE. " The tremendous spurt in national economic growth accomplished in the atmosphere of re- stored confidence in Brazilian stability after the 1964 military revolution. Especially under Finance Ministers Roberto Campos and Delfim Netto, Brazil's course toward uncontrollable inflation was slowed, and GNP dramatically increased.

   The "Miracle" has created a debate of major propor- tions concerning its solidity and its social costs. Fish- low and others have suggested that income has increased disproportionately for the wealthy, with the burden of the miracle's weight being borne by the poor. For the other view, see DELFIM NETTO, ANTONIO.

EDENIC VISION. The belief, inherited from the Middle Ages by Spaniards and Portuguese, that terrestrial paradise could be discovered in an uncharted corner of the world. This, as Morse suggests, gave impetus to the conquest of America, and fueled hopes for the discovery of such places as the Valley of the Impious (in the mountains be- tween Brazil and Peru, where the wicked earned punish- ment), the Fountain of Youth, and the land of the Amazons.

EDUCANDAS. Secular entrants into colonial-era convents, giving nuns a maternal role in the absence of secular family life. When Ursula of the Virgins petitioned to become an educanda at the age of six, she already had been living under the care of two aunts who were nuns since infancy.

EDUCATIONAL REFORM. By the mid-1920's, educators be- gan to complain about Brazil's inadequate facilities for education and its traditional methods of instruction. Out of a population of 35,000,000 in 1927, there only were two million primary school openings serving less than half the school-age population. At the state level, edu- cators and educational administrators began to press for reform, notably in Ceará (under Lourenço Filho, 1922- 1923); in Rio Grande do Norte, (under José Augusto

Bezerra, 1925-28); the Federal District (Carneiro Leão, 1922-26); Pernambuco (José Escobar, 1928); Paraná (Lisimaco da Costa, 1927-28); Minas Gerais (Francisco Campos, 1927-28); Bahia (Anísio Teixeira, 1928) and others. Many of these reforms, however, were over- turned in the anti-liberal backlash of the 1930's. See also PRIMARY SCHOOL ENROLLMENT.

ELECTRIC GENERATOR, FIRST. Introduced in Minas Gerais in June 1883, a 52-kilowatt unit.

ELECTRIC STREET LIGHTS, FIRST. Installed at Manaos, a full decade before Rio de Janeiro as a consequence of the Amazonian rubber boom, in 1896.

ELEIÇÃO DE BARRETE see PELOURO ELECTION

ELLIS, ALFREDO (1850-1925). A physician, trained at the University of Pennsylvania who returned to his São Paulo birthplace and gave up the practice of medicine; instead, he dedicated himself to clearing forest land and pioneer- ing coffee agriculture in the western region of the state, in Mogi-Guaçú and later Rio Claro and São Carlos. Chosen a member of the Constituent Assembly in 1890 he remained in politics and served as deputy from São Paulo from 1890 to 1902 and senator from 1902 to 1925. He supported Rui Barbosa's civilista campaign in 1910.

EMANCIPADOS. Emancipated slaves, usually freed through manumission. Conrad notes that more than 10,000 of Brazil's free blacks enjoyed this status legally, but in fact were indentured to persons for periods sometimes stretching to fifty years. Some slaves became emanci- pated when the ships carrying them from Africa were seized by the British navy in the years before 1845 when the English set themselves up as watchdogs over illegal entry of slaves. They were badly treated, often housed in jails; they were subject to re-enslavement, and even if they did secure their freedom on a permanent basis their movements were limited and they could perform virtually no work except that of the same kind done by slaves.

EMBOABAS. A pejorative term probably meaning "bird with feathered legs" (for their use of leg coverings against the Brazilian bird) used to designate the foreigners who flocked to the Brazilian gold region in search of fortune. See also WAR OF THE EMBOABAS.

EMPLEITA. A piecework task performed by moradores, or
sharecroppers, for their landowners for which they receive cash payment. This form of extra remuneration,
which is very popular among the rural poor, is rarely
asked for. Usually the landowners finds a way to have
the work done within the formal or informal arrangements
made with the morador, and without payment.

EMPREGUISMO. The practice of making excessive patronage
appointments, enhancing the incumbent's hold on power
but also providing the opposition with a powerful slogan
for attack. Empreguismo was a live issue during the
period between 1950 and 1964.

ENCILHAMENTO. Name given to period of financial speculation and confusion between 1890 and 1892, yielding inflation, bankruptcies, and general economic crisis well into
the Prudente de Morais administration.

ENCUBANIZAR. A word coined by Brazilians to explain the
potential threat posed by Cuba in the Western Hemisphere
--the "Cubanization" of society--as a justification for
Brazil's hard-line stand against subversion and propaganda
for social change.

ENGENHO. A small sugar mill, usually water powered or
utilizing slave labor (through the late nineteenth century)
or oxen to grind the sugar cane. By the 1890's, engenhos
came to be challenged by larger, industrialized sugar
refineries (usinas), financed by government subsidies and
foreign loans, and usually owned by powerful family clans
or newly-formed corporations. Although usina sugar
quickly surpassed cruder engenho sugar as a cash crop,
engenho owners (senhores de engenho) stubbornly hung
on, although some of them stilled their mills and became
simply suppliers of cane to the refineries. In the 1930's
the federal government agreed to subsidize engenho owners to forestall economic disaster.

ENGENHOCAS. Smaller than the conventional sugar plantation, often producing distilled alcohol rather than what
Caio Prado calls "aristocratic sugar." These small
engenhos were also called molinetes.

ENGENHOS CENTRAIS. Central refineries, the predecessors
of the turn-of-the-century usinas, sought by planters
from the 1860's on as an answer to the costly and inef-

ficient process of sugar processing, which was carried
out by animal-powered engenho mills on small scale.
The engenhos centrais required large outlays of investment capital; those that were constructed were usually
built by Europeans, with Imperial or provincial government backing, and few succeeded.

ENGENHOS D'AGUA.   Water-driven sugar mills, with nearly
    double the output of oxen-driven mills, but rarely used
    in Brazil, a fact noted with curiosity by foreign travelers,
    who noted the backwardness of local sugar technology.

ENTRADA.   Term ("entry") used by Paulistas to designate
    their incursionary expeditions to the interior.   See
    BANDEIRA.

ENTREGISTA.   One who hands something over.   In the 1950's,
    the term was applied to Brazilians who collaborated with
    foreign governments or enterprises, as one selling one's
    country out.

EQUILIBRIUM POLICY.   Paraguayan Lopez's insistence--
    even obsession--that power in the Platine region between
    Argentina and Brazil had to be balanced, one that he
    pursued since 1855.   Taking this view into account helps
    to understand Lopez's anger over Venâncio Flores's in-
    vasion of Uruguay in 1863 with Argentinian tacit support,
    and may be used to explain Paraguay's feelings about the
    reasons for the War of the Triple Alliance, which is
    often dealt with as caused by Lopez's personal megalo-
    mania.   With Brazil threatening to intervene in Uruguay
    in 1864, Paraguay (this interpretation holds) felt obliged
    to fight for its own survival.

"ERETZOPOLIS. "   Half-humorous, half-pejorative name given
    to the mountain resort town of Teresopolis, outside of
    Rio de Janeiro, by virtue of the fact that many families
    from Rio's Jewish community have maintained summer
    residences there.   "Eretz" refers to the Hebrew term
    for the Holy Land.

ESCOBAR, ILDEFONSO.   Nationalistic publicist of the 1950's,
    whose essay, "A Marcha para o Oeste," comparing
    Getúlio Vargas to Couto de Magalhães, hailed the chief
    of state as the heir of the bandeirantes and the realiza-
    tion of the dreams of the pioneers who had fought to
    open the Brazilian hinterland.

ESCOLA ANATÔMICA. Brazil's first anatomy course, established in 1808 at the Military Hospital in Rio de Janeiro under the authority of João VI.

ESCOLA LIVRE DE SOCIOLOGIA E POLITICA. One of two
institutions of higher education established in São Paulo
between July 1933 and January 1934 (the other being the
Faculdade de Filosofia, Ciências e Letras), representing
an innovative endeavor of the elites to adapt to changing
conditions, in contrast to the Faculdade, an effort of
young intellectuals to transform Brazil into a modern
society. Roberto Simonsen was one of the school's
founders; the institution was devoted entirely to the social
sciences, which would train new generations of technocrats to, in the words of Charles O'Neil, "justify the
capitalistic transformation of Brazil."

ESCOLA MILITAR UPRISING. An outbreak of insurrection
in the military academy in 1904, accompanied by echoes
of monarchist restoration, which served to increase feeling among the urban middle class in favor of stronger
military prowess and universal conscription. See also
MILITARY SERVICE.

ESCOLA MINEIRA. The literary school of Minas Gerais,
which flourished during the second half of the eighteenth
century. The Escola centered in Vila Rica, the leading
city in the mining region; its poets, Arcadian in influence,
included José Basílio da Gama; Cláudio Manoel da Costa;
and, the most well known, Tomás Antônio Gonzaga,
famous primarily for his love poems.

ESCOLA NORMAL. A middle-level school for the training
of elementary school teachers. When they were first
established, in the late nineteenth century, they enrolled
mostly young men but by the 1920's they had become
virtually all young women in enrollment. This pattern
has survived into the 1970's although some few exceptions
may be noted from school to school.

ESCOLA SUPERIOR DE AGRICULTURA E VETERINARIA.
The first school for agriculture and veterinary medicine,
established by the federal government in Rio de Janeiro
in 1910. During the ensuing decade, other new technical-
vocational schools were opened, in various state capitals,
as well as the Escola de Belas Artes (Fine Arts School)
in 1919, established by the government of the federal
district but shortly afterward transferred to the Union.

ESCOLAS DE SAMBA.   Samba Schools, first formally orga-
    nized to perform at annual Carnaval processions in 1928
    but informally in existence since 1917, when the marchin-
    ho groups began to experiment with samba rhythms.

ESCOLAS MENORES.   Lay public schools of the late colonial
    period, forty-two of which were counted in 1777.   After
    completion of the curriculum, a student could go on to
    secondary-level courses, known as aulas régias, to study
    Latin, Greek, or rhetoric.   See also PRIMARY SCHOOL
    ENROLLMENT.

ESCRAVOS DE SERVIÇO.   Hired slaves, contracted out by
    owners who made a business of the practice.   Some
    slaves were even trained in specific trades in order to
    be "rented. "

ESQUADRÃO DE MORTE.   The "Death Squad," police vigi-
    lantes of the 1960's and 1970's who tracked down, tor-
    tured and killed criminals, drug-traffickers, and other
    social undesirables in an effort to impose "law and order"
    and to protest legal restraint on police power.   The
    mutilated bodies of the victims were frequently left in
    public places as a lesson to future miscreants.

ESQUERDA FESTIVA.   The "festive left," a mildly humorous
    (and cynical) term for playboy radicals: intellectuals
    who espouse politically radical beliefs yet live a life
    style rooted in bourgeois hedonism.

"ESTADÃO, O. "   Slang term for the newspaper O Estado de
    São Paulo.   See also MESQUITA, JÚLIO DE.

ESTRADA DE FERRO DOM PEDRO SEGUNDO.   Established
    with Brazilian government capital in 1855 after the finan-
    cial crisis caused by the Crimean War forced the English
    to withdraw their support, the company built Brazil's
    first major railroad, a line connecting Rio de Janeiro
    with the coffee producing regions of the middle Paraíba
    valley.   In time, the British re-entered the picture by
    providing large loans for further development.   In 1889
    the railroad was renamed the Estrada de Ferro Central
    do Brasil.

ESTRELISMO.   The "star" system in professional soccer in
    which heroes receive astronomical salaries (e. g. , Pelé's
    $341,000 per year in 1970) but average players--the

great majority--receive very meager wages, and are
usually not permitted to hold an outside job besides.

EURO-PLUTOCRATS. Term coined by Ghanaian political
scientist and sociologist, Anani Dzidzienyo, for the Brazilian social elite, the principal beneficiaries of an egal-
itarian, exploitative racial structure. As part of their
status quo behavior they perpetrate the myth of racial
democracy, as it bolsters their own self-image and sense
of security.

EXALTADOS. Radical, federalist-minded members of the
Imperial Liberal Party during the First Empire. See
also MODERADOS.

EXCEDENTES. Students who pass the vestibular examination
(q. v.) but who, owing to a shortage of places, are denied
access to universities. In the late 1960's, three times
as many candidates for vagas took the vestibular examinations, and about two-thirds earned passing grades.
The situation improved somewhat subsequently but the
intense pressure generation by shortages led, in the mid-
1970's, to sporadic scandals and allegations of corruption
involving examinations and admissions.

EXEMPLO, O. Newspaper published in Porto Alegre by
mulattos, between 1892 and 1895, with the specific goal
of awakening Brazilians to the realities of racial prejudice and to forge a united front with blacks against white
racism. The newspaper, copies of which have only recently come to scholarly light, died without having made
much ostensible headway.

EXTRA-CHAPA. "Off the ticket," a term for those few who
managed to win election without having been chosen for
the "official" slate during the Old Republic.

-F-

FÁBRICA CENTRAL see ENGENHOS CENTRAIS

FACULDADE DE FILOSOFIA, CIENCIAS E LETRAS. The
cornerstone of the new University of São Paulo (USP),
established in 1934, the result of reformist demands for
a free university which would serve a democratic society.
Anísio Teixeira, Fernando de Azevedo and others, with

the tacit approval of Getúlio Vargas, initiated the plans
for the new program. The Faculdade's students tended
to be from the rising middle class of São Paulo, unable
to enter the more prestigious law or medical schools;
but socially mobile and prestige-conscious, many were
the sons and daughters of immigrants. See also MANI-
FESTO DOS PIONEIROS.

FAISCADORES. Itinerant gold prospectors, who often barely
earned enough to buy provisions, in such declining mining centers as Paracatú and Goiás. Functionally, they
corresponded to the minifundistas, the independent small-
holders in agriculture barely able to raise enough crops
to provide for his family. Of 5,749 registered faiscadores
in Minas Gerais in 1814, for example, 1,871 were slaves.

FALAS DO TRONO. "Speeches from the Throne," delivered
by Dom Pedro II, especially during the 1870's and 1880's,
when abolition became a major public issue. His tone
was generally moderate, favorable to "free labor" and
"gradual emancipation." Toplin notes that Pedro's speeches never departed from accepted public opinion, and that
they always acknowledged the interests of slaveholders.

FARIA, JOSÉ CAETANO DE (1855-1920). Veteran of the
Paraguayan War and former army chief of staff appointed
by President Wenceslau Bras in 1914 to supervise the
establishment of a conscription mechanism which would
allow the armed forces to weed out individuals unfit for
service for lack of moral character, or other weaknesses,
including "impoverishment." Faria prohibited re-enlist-
ment, in order to preserve the concept of a professional
army; soldiers returning to civilian life automatically
became reservists, and the officer corps maintained its
control.

FAROFA. Manioc meal mixed with melted butter or lard,
chopped eggs, and bananas. An upper class adaptation
is farinha, unadorned manioc powder eaten as a staple
by the rural poor.

FARQUHAR, PERCIVAL see ITABIRA IRON ORE COMPANY

FARROUPILHA REVOLT. A ten-year civil war in Rio Grande
do Sul, between 1835 and 1845. The insurrectionists,
finally suppressed by the Baron of Caxias, Luís Alves de
Lima (who went on to become Brazil's greatest military

hero), were called farrapos, or ragamuffins, by the
legalists. The cease-fire was accompanied by a general
amnesty; Caxias was elected a Senator from the Gaúcho
province. The failure of the revolt helped assure the
future political unity of Brazil.

FAUSTO. Born Fausto dos Santos in poverty in 1905, the
youth became Brazil's first non-white soccer hero--known
as the "black marvel," and cited by a naive press for
his "primitive nobility." He played for Vasco da Gama,
one of the major clubs of Rio de Janeiro; later, attracted
by a salary offer unavailable in the Brazil of the 1930's,
he signed with Barcelona, and finally for a Swiss professional team. These ties kept him out of the 1934 World
Cup, although he finally returned to play for Rio's Flamengo during the closing years of the decade.

FAVELAS. Shacks of wood and tin located in the slums of
major cities in the Center-South, usually concentrated in
settlements of several hundred or thousand as shantytowns.
In recent years, officials have torn down favelas and re-
located their inhabitants, many of whom face greater hardship because their new residences are far from sources
of informal (or formal) employment. Prior to 1964 there
was some pressure to "urbanize" favelas--that is, to
clean them up and make them habitable. Major hotels
and large condominiums have risen on the land formerly
occupied by some of the favela communities. In the
North, the equivalent of the favela is the mucambo; favelas correspond to colonias proletários (Mexico), barriadas
brujas (Panamá), ranchos (Venezuela), pueblos jovenes
(Peru), and contregiles (Uruguay). Favela life was
brought to the attention of the public in 1960 with the
publication of Carolina Maria de Jesus's Child of the
Dark. See also CANINDÉ; COHAB-GB.

FAYGA OSTROWER, AQUARELA DE (1920-). Modern
Brazilian artist; winner of the 1958 Grand Prize of the
Venice Biennial, known for a melancholy and pessimistic
style and dramatic tension.

FAZENDA. A large ranch, estate, or plantation; in southern
Brazil, the term estância is used.

FAZENDA MINEIRA. Unlike the sugar plantation of the northeastern coast, the fazenda mineira is agriculturally diversified, raising coffee, food crops, feed, and livestock.

Tenants generally live as sharecroppers or for wages,
and do not live as moradores as do their northeastern
counterparts in plantation villages.   See also SENZALA.

FAZENDEIRO.   Planter, owner or renter of a FAZENDA;
prior to abolition, a slaveholder.

FEBIANOS.   Members of the FEB, the Força Expedicionária
Brasileira, the Brazilian Expeditionary Force which
fought in Italy in the closing years of World War II.
The troops, badly outfitted and trained owing to official
neglect, were treated well neither in the field nor on their
return, despite a somewhat hypocritical public welcome
led by government officials.   After the war, the febianos
sat marginalized and depoliticized, frustrated and resent-
ful of the civilians who pushed them aside.   But
in 1964 they reappeared, at least symbolically: the new
military president, Castelo Branco, was a febiano, as
was his successor, Costa e Silva, as well as Colonel
Vernon Walters, the United States military attaché and
liaison officer to the FEB twenty years earlier and a
close friend of Castelo Branco.   See FORÇA EXPEDI-
CIONARIA BRASILEIRA.

FEDERAÇÃO FEMINISTA BRASILEIRA   see   LUTZ, BERTHA

FEIJÓ, DIOGO ANTÔNIO (1784-1843).   A liberal priest whose
severe measures as Minister of Justice under the regency
of the 1830's led to the "Additional Act" (Ato Adicional)
of 1834, which appeased federalists by granting more
powers to elected provincial legislatures and which
strengthened the central administration by terminating
the three-man regency.   Feijó himself became regent in
1835, a post which he held for two years.   His harsh
measures against southern successionists, however, and
his authoritarian mien alienated supporters, leading to
his forced resignation in 1837.

FEIJOADA.   Brazil's "national" dish, a stew of dried meats,
sausage, tongue, black beans (feijão), farofa, and orange
sections, served with rice.

FEITICEIRA.   A witch, subject to being burned at the stake
if caught by the Holy Office.   In 1499 Dom Manoel ordered
witches' cheeks to be burned with the letter "F"; the
death penalty came later, after 1516.

FELIZ LUSITÂNIA.   The first name of the area beyond the

mouth of the Guamá River, later to be known as Grão-Pará (Great Pará) and finally as Pará.

FERNANDEZ, MILLÔR (1923-). Carioca cartoonist, play-right, and humorist, writing for the weekly magazine Veja as well as Opinião, and with a sense for the jugular. Frequent censorship of his work on political grounds has never squelched his ability to turn out fresh assaults on social and political behavior each week.

FERREIRA DE ALBUQUERQUE, FÉLIX ANTÔNIO. Leader of the insurrectionary forces from Paraíba in the 1824 Confederation of the Equator conspiracy, from Vila Real do Brejo de Areia. After the affair was put down by force, he managed to escape.

FERREZ, MARC. Brazilian-born despite his French name who, after 1860, came to head the second generation of photographers. His career, which extended to the turn of the new century, produced far more extensive photo-graphic coverage of Brazilian life than the daguerrotypists of the earlier period. Ferrez's work includes photographs of slaves at their labors, and well-known views of Pedro II and of the Thanksgiving Mass for the abolition of slav-ery.

FIALHO, ANFRISO. Republican writer. Economic failure and the obstacles to advancement despite education under the Empire are the reasons given for Fialho's conversion to virulent republicanism; in an 1885 pamphlet he attacked the Emperor as lax in fostering Brazil's progress and for abusing the executive prerogative. Fialho also was a staunch abolitionist.

"FICO" ("I shall remain"). The legendary pronouncement allegedly made by Dom Pedro at Ypiranga, São Paulo, on January 9, 1822, defying the order of the Cortês for his return to Lisbon.

FIDALGOS. Nobles, the highest social group in pre-modern Portugal, who met together in assembly, the Côrtes, to advise and confer with the king.

FIFOS. The lamp of the poor, made of small cast-off glass bottles with a wick passed through the top.

FIGA. Afro-Brazilian amulet in the form of a closed fist

with the thumb inserted between the middle and index
finger; used to ward off evil spells in candomblé (q. v.).

FIGUEIREDO, JACKSON DE (1891-1928). Layman and former
    atheist whose reconversion to Catholicism caused him to
    dedicate his life to Church affairs as a layman. Born
    in Sergipe, he took his career as an educator to Rio de
    Janeiro, where he founded the Centro Dom Vital (q. v.),
    a major center of orthodox Catholic thought. He drowned
    in 1928.

FIGUEIREDO, JOÃO BAPTISTA (1918-   ). Chief of Brazilian
    Intelligence (SNI) during the Geisel administration, and
    chosen to succeed Geisel as President for the term to
    run until 1982. The General is the son of Gen. Euclides
    Figueiredo, the military leader of the constitutionalist
    revolt of the State of São Paulo in 1932. Figueiredo's
    selection ended a period of unrest within the military,
    some of whose high officials supported the candidacy of
    the Army Minister, Gen. Silvio Frota, dismissed by
    Geisel in October as too rightist. Born in Rio Grande
    do Sul, he entered a military academy at the age of ten,
    graduated from the elite military school at Realengo in
    1937, and became an officer of cavalry before taking on
    diplomatic and intelligence duties.

FIGUEIREDO REPORT. Released in 1968 under Attorney
    General Jader Figueiredo, the report charged officials
    of the Indian Protective Service with corruption, sadism,
    slavery, and other crimes against Amerindians. The
    Report ran 20 volumes, and led military officials to dis-
    band the Service and create a new agency, the National
    Indian Foundation (FUNAI). See also RONDON, GENERAL;
    VILAS BOAS BROTHERS.

FILAR. To cheat at an examination. See VESTIBULAR.

FILHOTISMO. Nepotism. Young men who gain positions
    because of their family connections are often called, be-
    hind their backs, "filho do papai," or "son of daddy."

FILIPE. A term applied to a man who is partially supported
    by the earnings of his wife (e. g. the husband of a school-
    teacher). In rural areas this has pejorative connotations,
    suggesting loss of manliness.

FIRMINO, JOÃO. Employee of the Engenho Galileia, in

Pernambuco's Zona da Mata, who founded the first Peasant League in the Northeast in 1955.   See also JULIÃO, FRANCISCO; PEASANT LEAGUES.

FIRST COMMERCIAL, INDUSTRIAL, AND AGRICULTURAL CONGRESS OF THE AMAZON.   Held in Manaos in February 1910, an example of the enthusiasm over the development of the regional economy and a reflection of the new national and regional congress phenomenon which helped to accelerate the pace of national integration and increase contact among elite groups and political leaders.

FIRST EMPIRE.   Term used to designate the period from 1808 to 1840, when Pedro II came to his maturity.

FIRST NATIONAL PLAN OF ECONOMIC AND SOCIAL DEVELOPMENT.   An economic master plan issued in September 1971 by the Medici government, pledging to elevate Brazil to the category of a "fully developed" nation within a decade; to double the 1969 income per capita by 1980; and to maintain an annual GNP growth rate of from 8 to 10 percent.

FIRST REPUBLIC   see   OLD REPUBLIC

FÍSICO-MÔR.   Chief physician, a traditional Portuguese institution introduced to Brazil after the arrival of the Crown in 1808 but abolished in 1927 because of the office's ineffectiveness.   In its place was named a committee on public hygiene; in addition, the Society of Medicine in Rio de Janeiro began to play a role in the creation of public hygiene policies which were put into law in 1830.

FIUZA, IÊDO.   Candidate in 1945 for president on the newly-legalized Communist Party ticket, drawing more than a half-million votes out of five-and-a-half million cast. Fiuza, the subject of a nasty book by Carlos Lacerda, O Rato Fiuza (Fiuza the Rat), merely fronted for Luís Carlos Prestes, the real leader of the Party.

FLAGELADOS.   Literally, the "flagellated," the name given to the victims of the northeastern droughts driven from their homes.   See also RETIRANTES.

FLEMING, ALMEIDA.   Mineiro inventor and cinematographer who, in 1920, developed a series of experiments in sound photography which paralleled the Vitaphone experiments in the United States.   The first full-length sound film was produced in 1929, Bentiví, by Lulu de Barros.

FLÔRES DA CUNHA, JOSÉ ANTÔNIO (1880-1956).   Interventor in Rio Grande do Sul after the 1930 Revolution and desposed by Vargas after conspiring with other state governors to resist the regime's movement in the direction of enhanced executive powers and removal of states' rights.   With the installation of the Estado Novo Flôres took refuge in Argentina.   He served as Federal Deputy from his home state from 1946 until the time of his death.

FLORIANO.   Brazil's only ship of battleship class during the 1930's, and over thirty years old, a source of frustration within naval circles, especially since both Chile and Argentina possessed twice the Brazilian navy's total tonnage.

FLORIANÓPOLIS.   Capital of the state of Santa Catarina, renamed after President Floriano Peixoto.   Founded in the late seventeenth century, it became provincial capital in 1823 under its original name, Destêrro.

FLUMINENSE.   1) Inhabitant of the state of Rio de Janeiro (1889-1976); in the latter years, the state of Rio was merged with the state of Guanabara, the old city of Rio de Janeiro.
2) The soccer team of the Carioca middle class, and the arch rival of Flamengo, a lower-class team.   "Flu" was the last professional club in Rio de Janeiro to hire black athletes.

FOGO MORTO.   An inactive engenho mill, with "stilled hearth."   José Lins do Rêgo used the term as the title of a novel, written in 1911.

FOLIÃO.   A participant in Carnaval (q. v.) revelry.

FOME DOS NOVE, A.   Name given to the "Hunger of 99," the legacy of the 1888-89 drought in the backlands.

FONSECA, DEODORO DA (1823-1892).   Career military officer, hero in the Paraguayan War, and first President of the Republic.   Deodoro graduated from the Escola Militar in 1843, helped subdue the Praieira insurrection in Pernambuco in 1848, and, after the war with Paraguay, was made a brigadier in 1874 and a marshal in 1884.   As

one of Brazil's major military figures he logically was
tapped for a leading role in the civilian-military movement which toppled the monarchy. Once elected by Congress to a four-year term, however, opposition to his
somewhat authoritarian manner increased; after some
disagreements with the legislature he dissolved it, as
an affront to his personal honor, in November 1891.
After a naval revolt later in that month he renounced
the presidency, permitting the vice-president, Marshal
Floriano Peixoto, to assume the office and to reopen
Congress. Deodoro died a few months later.

FONSECA, HERMES DA (1855-1923). Student of Benjamin
Constant at the Escola Militar and Minister of War in
the Afonso Pena administration. In 1909 Hermes, as a
Marshal of the armed forces and nephew of Deodoro da
Fonseca, the Republic's first president, was named by
the Republican Party convention as its presidential candidate. Two states--Bahia and São Paulo--refused to support the nomination, backing instead the civilian candidacy
of Rui Barbosa. Hermes's election was followed by two
severe naval revolts, over the issue of capital punish-
ment--and the Contestado rebellion in the south and political conflict in Ceará over Padre Cícero. As a result, and influenced strongly by gaúcho politician Pinheiro
Machado of the Partido Republicano Conservador, the
Hermes administration implanted the so-called salvacionista campaign, to replace civilian state oligarchies in the
North and Northeast with military interventors. In 1920,
as President of the Military Club, he was placed under
arrest by orders of President Epitácio Pessôa for indis-
cipline; he was released six months later by writ of habeas corpus from the Supreme Court. A sick man, he
retired to Pentropolis, where he died in 1923.

FORAL. A feudal contract which, with the carta de doação
(q. v.), made up the charter granted by the Crown to the
donataries under the captaincy system of the 1530's.
See also CAPTAINCY SYSTEM.

FORASTEIROS. Pejorative term ("outsiders") given to immigrants from Portuguese lands after the discovery of
gold in Minas Gerais.

FORÇA EXPEDICIONÁRIA BRASILEIRA (FEB). Brazil's
military contingent of 25,334 soldiers under the command
of General João Batista Mascarenhas de Morais, sent to

Italy in 1944 as part of the Allied effort. The FEB was integrated into the American Fifth Army, under General Mark Clark. At first topheavy with officers and poorly equipped--the Brazilian soldiers were not outfitted in winter uniforms until after arrival--the FEB performed well under fire and helped take the strategic town of Monte Castelo. During 1944 and 1945, 443 members of the FEB died in action.

FORÇA PÚBLICA. A state police force, in the manner of a militia, which, during the Old Republic, left the stronger states of São Paulo, Minas Gerais, and Rio Grande do Sul virtually autonomous in the sense that they could resist armed intervention from the federal government. São Paulo's Força Pública maintained its own military academy and even had its own air force; munitions and weapons were regularly purchased by state agents from European suppliers.

FORDLÂNDIA. Am Amazonian agricultural village and colony, situated on a plot of land one million hectares in breadth conceded to Henry Ford at his request by the government of Pará in 1928. Fifteen hours by boat up the Tapajós river on fertile soil, the colony was developed with sanitary facilities for workers, schools, housing, churches, and planted with 1,600,000 rubber trees. The first crop was wiped out by a fungus (Dothidela Ulei) and Ford officials were granted new land near Santarém, the present site of Fordlândia. Two and a half million trees of a fungus-resistant variety were planted, although disease was never fully controlled, and Ford's expection of mass, cheap production was never fully realized. In 1946 the lands were returned to the Brazilian government for a token payment.

FOREIGN DEBT. Estimated at 27 billion dollars in 1977, leading one Wall Street wag to comment that "any country with a debt of 27 billion dollars must be a world power. "

FOREIRO. A term for a peasant farmer, akin to morador, referring to one who rented marginal land from senhores de engenho to grow marginal crops, in exchange for corvée labor during planting and harvest seasons. This arrangement predominated in regions dominated by cotton agriculture.

FORRO. A manumitted slave, also known as a liberto.

FRANCEZIA. Bahian revolt of 1798, in which republican adherents, attempting to follow in the footsteps of the French Revolution, were captured and summarily executed.

FREE BIRTH LAW OF 1881 see RIO BRANCO LAW

FREGUESIA. A district, part of a têrmo, the colonial era equivalent of a county.

FREIRE, DOMINGOS. Bacteriologist and faculty member at the Rio de Janeiro Medical School who was sent to Europe in 1877 to study medical education in order to suggest reforms, which were called for by Rui Barbosa and others.

FREIRE, PAULO. Educator and social engineer, a professor of the history and philosophy of education at the University of Recife until 1964, when he was arrested, imprisoned for seventy days, and then allowed to leave Brazil. His work has attained world-wide attention, especially on the subjects of literacy training and on the role of the school in society. Freire holds that an educational system with built-in prejudices about the social inferiority of its pupils cannot possibly succeed; his alternative, conscientização, seeks to develop the quality of self-dignity self-awareness, and dialogue.

FREITAS-VALLE, CYRO DE. A diplomat, chargé d'affaires in Washington in the mid-1930's, and a close relative of Foreign Minister Oswaldo Aranha.

FRENCH ARTISTIC MISSION (1816). The first of a significant stream of foreign artisans, artists, and technicians invited to Brazil during the nineteenth century, under the initial sponsorship of D. João VI. Debret, Taunay, Grandjean de Montigny and others arrived as part of the mission and its successors.

FRENTE NEGRA BRASILEIRA. São Paulo-based "Negro Front," organized in the early 1930's with branches in most Brazilian capitals and as many as 200,000 adherents. It was designed to raise the consciousness of Afro-Brazilians and to encourage them to cross the comportment line set by social mores. The Frente was banned in 1937 along with all other groups and parties with mass followings as part of the Estado Novo crackdown on po-

tentially threatening popular movements.   See also ASSO-
CIAÇAO CULTURAL DO NEGRO.

FRENTE PARLAMENTAR NACIONALISTA (FPN).   The National Parliamentary Front, a group of radical nationalist
congressmen organized in the Kubitschek years (1957) and
active until 1964.   The FPN worked to identify needed
legislation in the areas of foreign investment, land use,
and social policy.

FRÊVO.   A Carnaval dance indigenous to the Northeast; like
the samba, it is danced alone, never with partners.   The
dancers prepare throughout the year in Carnaval clubs,
or escolas (literally "schools"); the frêvo dancers wear
lavish costumes, a small part of the cost borne by the
local prefeitura (city government), since it is part of the
touristic attraction of the region.   Frevo music is sung,
with percussion accompaniment; some of the frêvo-can-
sões are traditional; others written for the annual competition.   The elements derive partly from the polka, the
march, and the quadrille, but the result is unique, and
more spontaneous and compulsive than any of them.
There is no set step or steps for the frêvo, but any
which fit the rhythm.

FREYRE, GILBERTO DE MELO (1900-   ).   Brazil's fore-
most ethnologist and interpreter of its historical evolution.   Born at Apipucos (Recife), Freyre studied under
private tutors and at the American Baptist School in the
city; unlike most other sons of the plantocracy, he attend-
ed college outside of Brazil--at Baylor University, Waco,
Texas.   Following the receipt of his B. A. in 1921, he
took an M. A. degree in Latin American history at Columbia, where he took courses taught by J. H. Hays,
Franz Boas, and Edwin R. A. Seligman.   He then traveled
in Europe, visiting anthropological museums in Britain,
France, Germany, and Portugal.
      On his return to Recife, Freyre became something of
an enfant terrible of Brazilian letters.   In 1926 he organized the nation's first conference on regionalism, em-
phasizing northeastern culture, especially its indigenous
and African roots, and in the early 1930's he helped establish modern sociology departments at the new University of Rio de Janeiro and in São Paulo.   A gadfly and
iconoclast, he alienated traditionalists.   His 1933 classic
Casa-Grande e Senzala electrified intellectual circles (see
MASTERS AND THE SLAVES); in 1934 Freyre's First

Afro-Brazilian Congress, held in Recife, scandalized conservatives for its attention to cultism and its timid suggestions that Afro-Brazilian poverty derived in part from environmental causes. Although politically conservative--he had served as secretary to his cousin, Pernambuco's governor Estácio Coimbra, until the First Republic was deposed in 1930--opponents reviled him as a communist and pornographer. In response, Freyre traveled abroad widely and devoted himself to his writing.

In 1946, with the redemocraticization of the country, Freyre was elected to the national constituent assembly, and served in the Chamber of Deputies from 1946 to 1950. In 1949 he represented Brazil, with the rank of Ambassador, at the United Nations.

Freyre welcomed the right-wing military government which took power in 1964 and became somewhat of an apologist for it. As more specific research began to appear within the broad areas first staked out by Freyre as a scholar--history, anthropology, ethnology, sociology, criticism--Freyre's ideas began to be challenged, especially his thesis that slavery under the Portuguese was more benign than elsewhere. Freyre's magnificent contribution to Brazilian thought, however, will always stand. Virtually singlehandedly he produced the scholarly climate out of which came renewed national pride and faith in Brazil's capacity for development. In his later life Freyre became embittered, never having been invited (by acclamation, which he demanded) to join the Brazilian Academy of Letters, and, at least up through 1978, never receiving a Nobel Prize, for which he had been nominated repeatedly.

FRIEDENREICH, ARTUR (1882-?). Brazil's first major soccer idol, born in São Paulo, team leader of the South American Championship team which tied, 0-0, with Argentina in the 1916 final at Buenos Aires.

FRONTÍN, PAULO DE (1860-1933). Engineer and politician, responsible for a good part of the urban reconstruction of Rio de Janeiro in the 1890's and after; Senator; Mayor of Rio de Janeiro, and the recipient of the title of papal Count.

FROTA, SÍLVIO. General deposed in late 1977 by President Ernesto Geisel for allowing his presidential ambitions to interfere with his military obligation to stay silent politically, using dissident members of the official party, Aliança Renovadora Nacional, as his mouthpiece.

FUBÁ. Corn meal, used primarily in the South, much in
the same way as northerners used manioc meal. See
CANJICA.

FUNCIONÁRIOS PÚBLICOS. Public employees, in a sense
holding administrative tenure under the DASP regulations.
Less secure were the extra-numerários, or supplementary
employees, not protected by DASP statutes.

FUNDING LOAN. Debt-consolidation loan negotiated with
various European banking concerns by the Campos Sales
administration in 1898 and its Treasury Minister, Joaquim
Duarte Murtinho.

FURTADO, AURORA. A member of Carlos Marighela's
Aliança Libertadora Nacional, tortured to death by the
OBAN--the Operação Bandeirante division of the federal
police in São Paulo, and, in the late 1970's, somewhat
of a revolutionary heroine among followers of her cause.

FURTADO, CELSO (1920-). Economist, founder of SUDENE,
the development agency for the Northeast, and, as a cabinet minister during the Goulart administration, ousted in
1964 and exiled. Since 1964 Furtado has lived and taught
in France and in the United States.

-G-

GABRIELA. Mulata heroine of Jorge Amado's novel (1958)
of the same name, she was a ravishing, kind, young woman who could retain her charms only in a free, undomes-
ticated state. Afforded the opportunity to become an
accepted member of "society," with its formal requirements for behavior, she had no choice other than to flee.
As a fictional character, Gabriela may be compared with
that of Twain's Huckleberry Finn. In 1977 a daily television novela (soap opera) was made of the Amado book,
as widely popular in Portugal as in Brazil.

GAIOLAS. Motorized river boats of the Middle Amazon,
called "cages" for the appearance of their one or two-
deck superstructures. (Gaiolas are not unlike car-carry-
ing ferry boats of the type used on the Bridgeport/Port
Jefferson line across Long Island Sound).

GALEÃO. International airport serving Rio de Janeiro, on

the Ilha do Governador. The facility was completely modernized in 1976-77 to accommodate 747 and Concorde aircraft.

GAMA, JOSE BASÍLIO DA (1741-1795). Eighteenth-century poet whose O Uraguai, a blank verse epic, eulogizes the Amerindian population of the mission region for its resistance to European domination, and, as Burns shows, was a precursor of the nineteenth century romantic Indianist movement in Brazilian literature.

GAMA, LUIS (1830-1882). Mulatto abolitionist and republican, born in São Paulo to an African mother and a white father, a member of the Bahian elite. Gama's career varied between dozens of different forms of employment--from militia soldier to clerk to unlicensed attorney to poet; he was the founder of the Paulista Abolitionist Center. Gama died in extreme poverty after a life termed by his biographers of "struggle, suffering, and glory."

GAMELIN, GENERAL. French officer serving as a member of the French military mission to Brazil, and the only instructor at the Military Academy to give Luis Carlos Prestes a low grade--for being "too revolutionary" in his stretegy. See PRESTES.

GÂNDAVO, PERO DE MAGALHÃES DE. Author of the Tratado da Terra do Brasil, an early (sixteenth century) chronicle of Brazilian exploration.

GARIBALDI, ANITA (1819-1849). Santa Catarina-born heroine of the War of the Farrapos. Anita became the intrepid companion of the exiled Italian Giuseppe Garibaldi who had come to southern Brazil to aid in the regionalist insurrection. Fighting by his side, she was wounded; at times she substituted for him in command. She married Garibaldi in Uruguay, in 1843, where they joined the fight against Rosas. In 1848 the couple embarked for Italy where they aided in the defense of Venice against Austrian siege. She died of tuberculosis shortly afterward.

GARIMPEIRO. A prospector for minerals, usually diamonds and emeralds, as well as semi-precious stones. Likened to bandeirantes in spirit, the garimpeiros have a reputation for tenacity and independence: they have been known to murder rivals over land claims, and are reputed to deal with Amerindian residents of their lands with brutality.

GARRASTAZÚ MÉDICI, EMÍLIO (1906-). Military officer
and third president of Brazil after the 1964 coup. Born
in Bagé, Rio Grande do Sul, Médici rose through the
officer ranks after graduating from the Escola Militar at
Realengo. From 1964 to 1966 he served as military
attaché in Washington, and returned to become the head
of Brazilian Intelligence, the SNI. He took office as
president in 1969. A longtime soccer follower, Médici
countered growing unpopularity for his regime by exploiting Brazil's World Cup victory in 1970.

GARRINCHA (1933-). Soccer star of the 1950's and 60's,
he was born Manuel dos Santos to a poor family which
had migrated from Alagoas to Rio de Janeiro. By the
age of 13 the young boy had become the outstanding junior player in the region although his early years as a
professional player were disappointing: he preferred to
play barefoot, and was considered difficult to train. By
the mid-1950's he had overcome his past: he led the
World Cup team to victory in Sweden in 1958, was the
outstanding player on the 1962 champion team, and remained to play through the 1970 event. Unlike his team-
mate Pelé, Garrincha never picked up the social mores
of the elite; instead he cultivated--or was given--a public image of a working-class hero: virile, not terribly
intelligent, earthy. His nickname, "The People's Favorite" (A Alegria do Povo) is best understood in the context of the word "povo," here referring to the underpop-
ulation, the poor. As soon as he left football, he found
himself back in the slums, although he belatedly embarked
on a second career as nightclub performer.

GAÚCHO. A resident of the southernmost state of Rio Grande
do Sul, characterized in popular imagery as dashing and
resourceful. The gaúcho (a Brazilian version of the
Argentine and Uruguayan gaucho) is generally pictured as
a mounted cowboy. See also BAHIANO; PAULISTA;
CARIOCA.

GÁVEA GOLF CLUB. One of several exclusive social clubs
in Rio de Janeiro, originally boasting a British clientele.
Others include the Country Club of Leblón, popular with
high military officials and politicians, and Paissandú, in
Flamengo.

GEADAS BRANCAS. Light frosts which occur in the coffee-
producing regions of São Paulo and Paraná, "burning"

the topmost branches of the coffee trees and reducing yields, especially in low-lying sites.

GEMS.   Brazil produces 90 percent of the world's semi-precious gems, including aquamarine, tourmaline, topaz, and amethyst.

GENERAL ASSEMBLY RESOLUTION 3379.   The United Nation's vote condemning Zionism as "racism," supported by Brazil as a sign of its changing foreign policy towards the nations of the Third World.

GENERAL MINES.   The Minas Gerais gold region, the site of the world's first gold rush, 1690-1740.   Because of the Crown's desire to isolate the region to prevent smuggling and tax evasion, communications were not allowed to develop, and the route to Vitória port on the coast through Espírito Santo was kept closed.

GENOVESI, ANTÔNIO.   Italian philosopher and economist whose books were widely read by Brazilian intellectuals in the early nineteenth century.

GENTE GRAÚDA.   The "good families," in local town usage.

GENTE QUE TEM DESTAQUE.   People of distinction, the term used in rural areas to designate the community's most important figures either in terms of income or power.

GENTLEMAN COMPLEX.   Coined by Gilberto Freyre, the phrase recalls the Brazilian preference--historically--for white collar occupations, with corresponding scorn for manual labor.   The national educational system has always reflected this bias, aiming at cultural refinement in the nineteenth century European sense.   See also BACH-ARELISMO.

GERMAN LEGION.   A regiment of volunteers from among German settlers in Rio Grande do Sul, which fought against Argentina in 1851-52.   Most of the troops had been army regulars in Schleswig-Holstein before coming to Brazil as agricultural colonists.

GESCHICHTE VON BRASILIEN.   A general history of Brazil written in 1859 by Heinrich Handelmann, a lecturer at the University of Keil, and considered by Oliveira Lima

and others to have been the most important history of
Brazil written by a non-Brazilian in the nineteenth century.   Like Southey, Handelmann never traveled to Brazil.

GIRIA   see   SLANG

GMELINA PINE.   Fast-growing Asian tree being planted in
the Amazon by the Daniel K. Ludwig company which has
purchased three million acres, to be processed into kraft
paper at a plant manufactured in Kobe, Japan, and being
shipped 13,000 miles to Brazil.

GOD, COUNTRY, AND FAMILY.   The motto of the Integralists, invented by Plínio Salgado.   See INTEGRALISM.

GÓES E VASCONCELOS, ZACARIAS DE (1815-1877).   Coalition minister from 1866 to 1868 under the new alliance
between moderates and progressives, brought down, however, by Caxias's refusal to become Minister of War.
In the end, the matter weakened the parliamentary system, as Conservatives and Liberals alike viewed Zacarias's ouster as the result of interference by military
officials.

GOIÂNIA.   The new (1933) capital of the state of Goiás, designed and planned by A. Corrêa Lima according to
French theories of urban planning (although all of the
initial blueprints were not actually carried out).   The
city, inaugurated in 1942, is zoned into three distinct
districts; for government building, commerce, and industry.   The latter has never been extensively developed.

GOIÁS.   An interior state, important during the colonial period after the discovery of gold in 1725, but in decline,
like that of the other mining regions, from the third
quarter of the eighteenth century.   Goiás is bounded by
Minas Gerais and Bahia on the east and south; Mato
Grosso to the west; Pará and Maranhão to the north.
The Federal District of Brasília was carved out of southern Goiás in the late 1950's.

GÓIS MONTEIRO, PEDRO AURÉLIO (1889-1956).   Career
military officer and the power behind the Estado Novo
between 1937 and 1945.   Góis, a regular army officer
who had fought against the tenentes in the 1920's, switched to the side of the Liberal Alliance in 1930 and became

one of the military heads of the 1930 coup. In 1932 he
helped subdue the constitutionalist uprising in São Paulo,
and became Vargas's closest military advisor and confidant. In 1945 he played a major role in Vargas's ouster.
He was War Minister twice during his career and Senator
from Alagoas.

GOITERVILLE. "Papudópolis," the name given by jokers to
the rising planned town of Belo Horizonte, Minas's new
capital, because of its high incidence of disease and ill-
health, and because of the presence of diseased caboclos
in the area.

"GOLDEN AGE" OF THE EMPIRE. The years between 1850
and 1870, so-called because of the ostensible establishment of political stability after the discrediting of the
Liberal Party after the Praiaeira revolt and the formation of a Liberal-Conservative governing coalition. Foreign investment helped build Brazil's economic infrastruc-
ture during this period, and Brazilian cities moved to
modernize themselves through public improvements; foreign trade increased tenfold during this period of Pedro
II's reign.

"GOLDEN LAW, THE." The law of May 13, 1888, signed
in the absence of the Emperor by Princess Isabel, granting unconditional freedom to the remaining 700,000 slaves
residing in Brazil.

GOMES, CARLOS (1836-1896). Nineteenth-century Brazilian
composer who produced operas in the prevailing Italian
style. His "Il Guarany" (1870), taken from the romance
by José de Alencar, was performed in Verdi's presence
at La Scala in Milan.

GOMES, EDUARDO (1896-). One of the original tenente
defenders of the Copacabana Fort during the 1922 revolt
which led to the death of 7 young rebels as they walked
into the line of fire. One of the three survivors, he was
entrusted after 1930 with building the Brazilian Air Mail
service and continued his career in the Air Force, heading it in 1954. He unsuccessfully ran for president on
the UDN ticket in 1945 against General Eurico Dutra.
In 1961 he retired from the military with the rank of
Air Marshal.

GOMES PIMENTA, SILVÉRIO (1840-1922). Archbishop of
Mariana (Minas Gerais), one of the first Afro-Brazilians

to achieve such a position, and the administrator of the Vatican's call to re-Catholicize his diocese. Under Dom Silvério Minas regained its prominence as the most Catholic of the Brazilian states.

GONÇALVES DE OLIVEIRA, DOM VITAL MARIA (1844-1878). As a newly appointed bishop of Olinda (Pernambuco) in 1872, Dom Vital, a French-educated Capuchin friar, attempted to enforce the 1864 papal encyclical rejecting freedom of conscience, demanding that the state carry out church policies, and forbidding Catholics to take active roles in masonic organizations. By so doing, he precipitated the so-called "religious question," leading to his decree of interdiction (suspension of sacramental functions in his diocese), conflict with the Emperor, and finally his arrest and sentence to four years imprisonment in 1874. Pedro commuted the sentence to a sort of house arrest, but the damage had been done although the interdictions were lifted after cooler heads came to prevail.

GOULART, JOÃO (1918-1977). Politician, popularly known as "Jângo," president of the Republic from September 1961 until his ouster by a military coup in March 1964. A lawyer and state deputy from Rio Grande do Sul, he became the protégé of Getúlio Vargas and the leader of the PTB, Vargas's Labor Party. Goulart was so close to Vargas when he first entered politics that rumors said that he was Vargas's illegitimate son. Vice-President under Quadros, he became president on Quadros's resignation after Congress bowed to military pressure and stripped the executive office of much of its independent power. A volatile personality and forceful public speaker, he frightened conservatives and moderates by his leftist rhetoric. Personally corrupt, he amassed a large fortune in land during his presidency.

"GOVERNOR OF THE SERTÃO." Name given to cangaceiro Antônio Silvino, who, through exploitation of careful ties with local rural bosses, managed to roam free during a bandit career of two decades.

GRAN FINO. Slang designation for upper class behavior.

GRAO-PARÁ. The name for the territory surrounding the first settlement in the Amazon by Francisco Caldeira Castelo Branco in 1615, first called Feliz Lusitânia, and ultimately known as Pará.

GREAT TRADITION, BRAZILIAN. A term borrowed from
Robert Redfield, the sum of the official and semi-official
institutions and traditions, Portuguese in origin, which
comprise the basic foundation of Brazil's national self-
view. The illiterate and semi-literate portion of the
population stands outside the Great Tradition but, through
the process of socialization, are subject to its influence.
See also CIVISMO.

GREAT WESTERN OF BRAZIL RAILWAY, LTD. Named for
the Great Western in England; it was formed in 1872
and began construction in 1879, in time to complement,
as Graham points out, the optimism raised by the introduction of central refineries in the sugar region. When
the government leased its other lines in the region to
bidders in 1902, the Great Western acquired most of
them, becoming, in the process, the Northeast's largest
railroad company. The target of rising anti-foreign
sentiment over its high rates and labor practices, the
G. W. ultimately sold out, at a substantial loss, to the
Brazilian government.

GRENFELL, JOHN. British naval officer sent by Lord Cochrane with 96 men on the brig Maranhão in 1823 to Belém,
to force the local Junta to recognize Brazilian Independence and swear loyalty to Pedro I. He took the city
through a bluff (he warned that Cochrane was poised outside the city ready to strike).

GRILERO. Jungle-region land speculator and entrepreneur,
the scourge of Amerindians (whose women they commonly
take as concubines) and sometimes-friend, sometimes-
enemy of the agents of the Indian Protective Service and
its successor, FUNAI.

GRITO DE IPIRANGA. Declaration, by the shores of the
Ipiranga River on September 7, 1822, of Brazilian Independence by D. Pedro (I).

GRUPO DE TRABALHO DE FOMENTO ÀS EXPORTACÕES.
A federal commission, the Working Group for the Promotion of Exports, created in 1957 to suggest ways of improving Brazil's balance of payments situation. Although
the problem was dealt with systematically after 1964,
this initial effort produced no visible results.

GRUPOS DE CAÇA. Hand-picked "hunting parties," jagunço

bands deputized into the federal army and sent in pursuit of the Prestes Column by Major Góes Monteiro in 1927. See HORÁCIO DE MATOS; ABÍLIO WOLNEY.

GUAIASES TRAIL see BUENO DA SILVA, BARTOLOMEU

GUAIRÁ. Spanish Jesuit settlements in the west of present-day Paraná, under attack from Paulistas in 1628-29, whose superior, Antônio Ruiz de Montoya, formally protested to the Brazilian authorities and to the Crown of Spain the kidnapping and enslavement of several thousands Amerindians taken from under Jesuit control.

GUANABARA see RIO DE JANEIRO STATE

GUANABARA, ALCINDO (1865-1918). Deputy from the Federal District who presented the bill for obligatory military service through conscription which was signed into law in January 1908.

GUARANÍ, O. The title of a major Indianist novel by José de Alencar; also, the name of a Carlos Gomes opera, Italian in style, but based on the novel and with a Brazilian plot. Its overture was later adapted as the national anthem.

GUARARAPES, BATTLES OF. Clashes between Dutch and Luso-Brazilian troops on the heights of Montes Guarapares, near Recife, in 1648 and 1649. In the final encounter, a victory for the patriots, the Dutch lost one thousand soldiers and their commander.

GUARNEIRI, GIANFRANSCESO. Playwright, the author of "Êles nao usam Black-tie," which opened in 1958. The first Brazilian play dealing with the urban poor, it satirized the lives of victimized favelados, corrupt union leaders, police brutality, and slum landlords. Guarneiro wrote "Eles não usam Black-tie" as a Theater-of-the-People piece, but efforts to bring it to the public failed; street audiences failed to understand its sarcasm and some spectators even threw rocks at the actors.

GUARULHOS. Paulista city, with near 400,000 inhabitants, considered the major locus of Hanson's Disease, or leprosy, in Brazil outside of the Amazon, where there are two reported cases of the malady for every thousand persons. About 7,000 "hanseniásicos" reside in or around São Bento, Guarulhos's treatment center.

GUEDES, LINO. Leading Afro-Brazilian poet and dean of the short-lived school of Paulista Afro-Brazilian creativity in the 1930's, whose work called for the moral elevation of his people, the adoption of puritanical modes of social behavior, and attention to the preservation of the Afro-Brazilian family. See also FRENTE NEGRA BRASILEIRA.

GUIMARÃES, HONÓRIO DE FREITAS (1902-1975). An elite youth whose frustrations in business and landowning led to Communist Party membership in the mid-1930's and undercover life under the code name "M." His prison memoirs, after his arrest in 1936 for subversion, offer valuable insight into the reasons youths of his background felt attracted to the revolutionary left.

GUIMARÃES, ULYSSES. Head of the opposition MDB party in the mid-1970's, and prosecuted in 1977 for contravening Brazil's electoral law by attacking the military government in a nation-wide radio broadcast in June 1977.

GUIMARÃES ROSA, JOSÉ (1908-1967). Novelist whose powerful, sweeping works treating mostly rural life use a remarkable mixture of colloquial Portuguese and words coined by the author to convey new concepts and meanings. His major novel, Grande Sertão: Varedas, is translated into English as The Devil to Pay in the Backlands.

GUINLE, CARLOS (1883-1968). One of three brothers, São Paulo-based, who became millionaires in the 1930's through holdings in hotels, textile firms, metal refining, and banking, and who provided the model for the playboys of the day. The other two brothers were Otávio and Guilhermo.

-H-

HARTT, FREDERICK (1840-1878). American geologist whose The Geology and Physical Geography of Brazil in 1870 was the first general textbook on the subject. He died of yellow fever at the age of 38, in Rio de Janeiro.

HAVAS. The Brazilian national wire service, in part controlled by German capital until the late 1930's; HAVAS and the totally German-owned Trans-ocean Company shared overseas cable facilities.

HENRIQUES, AFONSO. A Christian knight who took Lisbon
from Moslem control in 1147, leading to Portuguese expansion south and, by the middle of the thirteenth century, the reconquest of the southern Algarve (and, as
such, the establishment of the modern boundaries of the
Portuguese nation).

HENRY THE NAVIGATOR. Prince Henrique, the third son
of João I, whose efforts to expand Portuguese influence
to Africa through expanding Portugal's commercial power
has earned him the title in history of "Prince Henry the
Navigator." Master of the Order of Christ, he had access to ample funds; he developed a maritime colony at
Sagres, on the southern coast, and oversaw expeditions
to Madeira, the Azores islands, and to Africa. In the
1440's his ships brought the first African to Europe,
mostly to be used as domestic servants; this marks the
beginnings of the slave trade. At his death in 1460 his
efforts were continued under the authority of fidalgos to
whom trading monopolies were granted by the Crown.
See also FIDALGOS.

HEVEA BRASILIENSES. Brazil's native rubber plant, taken
from its Amazonian habitat in 1876, nurtured in Kew
Gardens, and transported to Ceylon for cultivation. By
1915, the Orient, whose share of rubber production had
hardly existed at the turn of the century, supplied 68
percent of the world market, plunging Amazonian Brazil
into economic depression.

HEYN, PIET. Commander of the Dutch West India fleet
which captured Bahia in 1624 but was forced to relinquish
it a year later.

HIGH SPIRITISM see KARDECISM

HISTORICAL REPUBLICAN. The "históricos" owed their
designations for their advocacy of a Republic before the
fall of the monarchy in 1889. The title was coined to
distinguish "true" Republicans from the many monarchists
who transferred their allegiance either at the "eleventh
hour" or after the Emperor had actually abdicated. Some
of the last-minute Republicans actually went on to major
political careers after 1889 although their allegiance was
known to have been, at the outset, opportunistic.

HOMEMS BONS. "Good men," the leading citizens, usually

planters, of colonial towns who in times of extraordinary
questions were called upon as a type of electorate to de-
cide local issues. Most were seignorial patriarchs who
headed large family clans; they also controlled town government.

HORA DO BRASIL. A national radio program, "The Hour
of Brazil," inaugurated by Getúlio Vargas as a sort of
fireside chat, and maintained through the 1960's although
with little public impact.

HUDSON INSTUTUTE AMAZON PLAN. A scheme designed
by think-tank entrepreneur Herman Kahn to flood the
Amazon basin and create a network of large lakes, to
be used in a global system of hydroponics, which was
seized upon by hardliners in the late 1960's to emphasize
their nationalistic views and to reject foreign attempts
to interfere with Brazilian development. Albuquerque
Lima led the attack on the Kahn blueprint.

HUMAYTÁ (Submarine). Formerly the pride of the navy, by
1932 it had become so run down that it had to be retired
from service lest it sink. See also FLORIANO.

HUMOR see POPULAR HUMOR

-I-

IAIÁ (or YAYÁ). A term used through the late nineteenth
century in addressing girls and young women. From
lingua geral (q. v.).

IBIRAMIRA BUMELIA. A small, tough, spiny shrub native
to the sertão, and eaten in extremis during times of
drought.

IDADE D'OURO. Brazil's second newspaper (1812), and
Salvador's first. See also AURORA FLUMINENSE.

IEMANJÁ. Orixá god, the umbanda (q. v.) equivalent of the
Virgin Mary.

IFIGÊNIA ESTÁ NO FUNDO DO CORREDOR see DANTAS,
NATANIEL

IGAÇABAS. Burial pots of Amerindian tribes lacking cemeteries and skilled in clay ceramics.

IGAPÓ. An area of dense vegetation continually under water, native to the Amazon Basin.

IGARAPÉ. A canoe trail, a river amid the Amazonian forest.

IGREJA MINERAL. The "Mineral Church," so dubbed by the Count of Assumar, Governor of Minas and São Paulo from 1717-1721, noting that priests only would give last rites to slaves if they paid a fee in gold. State officials attempted to reform the situation by introducing permanent, salaried parochial appointments (congrua), but spiritual provisions for blacks and mulattos remained deficient.

IGUAÇÚ FALLS. A series of 275 cataracts which form a four-kilometer wide horseshoe across the Iguaçú River; they form the fifth highest falls in the world. Iguaçú is located at the meeting point of Brazil, Argentina, and Paraguay.

ILHÉUS. City on the Bahian coast in the heart of the cocoa region, immortalized by Jorge Amado's portrayal of its town life in the 1920's, in his novel, Gabriela, Clove and Cinnamon.

"IMMIGRAÇÃO POR FOME" ("Immigration from Starvation"). The term given to the migration of nearly 20,000 northeastern drought refugees to the Amazon in 1877-78. By 1900 another 158,000 flagelados entered Belém to make their way further up river, penetrating westward as far as territory claimed by Bolivia. As many as 300,000 may have entered the Amazonian region by the First World War; Furtado suggests as many as a half-million.

IMMIGRATION. Although Brazil never attracted the large numbers of immigrants who came to Argentina, or to the United States, an estimated 3,300,000 foreigners entered Brazil after Independence, mostly from Portugal, Italy, Spain, and Germany, and mostly to the southern states, especially to the coffee regions of São Paulo and Paraná. Japanese immigrants came to the Amazon and to the São Paulo region through the actions of various colonization enterprises, although in the 1930's anti-Japanese feeling rose and Orientals were excluded from immigration quotas. After World War II most immigration has been from Portugal, the Arab countries, and--illegally--from Bolivia and Paraguay.

IMPERATRIZ. Brazilian frigate attacked by six ships of
the Argentine navy in April 1826, four months after the
declaration of war between Brazil and the United Provinces of La Plata over the Cisplatine Province, later
Uruguay. Luís Barroso Pereira, commander of the Imperatriz, was killed in combat although the attack was
repelled after an hour and fifteen minutes of battle.

IMPOSTO DE RANDA. Income tax. To promote payment of
the tax by persons who formerly diverted their income
outside of the country or into capital investments (real
estate, jewelry, art), the federal government, after 1964,
devised a system whereby stiffer income tax levies were
offset by incentives to invest in domestic industry, offering write-offs of up to 50 percent of earned income for
investment in government-approved programs, many of
which were in the Northeast.

IMPOSTO SINDICAL. Following the Vargas-era creation of
the Ministry of Labor and the establishment of norms
regulating labor organization, the government has relied
on the imposto sindical, or trade-union tax, to provide
much of the revenue for legal trade unions. Equivalent
to one day's pay per year, the tax provides as much as
60 percent of union revenues.

IMPOSTO TERRITORIAL. Land tax. Despite Brazil's agricultural economy, virtually no land taxes were levied
through the Empire and Republic, presumably in deference
to the politically powerful landowning class. In the 1900's,
for example, Pernambuco gained less than one-half of
one percent of its state revenue from land taxes, relying
instead on taxes on consumption and a bevy of nuisance
taxes including levies charged to professionals and businessmen.

INCONFIDENTES. The conspirators in the 1789 movement
led by Tiradentes who sought lower taxes on Mineiro gold,
permission for local manufacture, and the development
of provincial institutions, including a university.

INDIAN PROTECTIVE ASSOCIATION. Established as a federal agency in 1910 under the impetus of General (later
Marshal) Cândido Rondón, with the goal of incorporating
the diminishing aboriginal population of the interior into
Brazilian life and to shield the tribes from economic exploitation. This danger increased significantly with the

Amazon rubber boom of the early twentieth century,
which brought thousands of fortune-seekers and adventurers to the region. The collapse of rubber prices by
1912 exacerbated tensions in the Amazon: preyed upon
by the rubber gatherers (serengueiros), aboriginals caught
up in the steady penetration of "civilizing" influences
soon became the pariahs of the social order. Others
retreated even further into the jungle hinterland. In the
1960's and 1970's, revelations about abuse, even torture
and large-scale murder, began to filter out of Brazil;
allegations of land-grabbing, using indigenous women as
concubines or prostitutes, and other abuses were leveled
at agents of the Protective Association itself. See also
VILAS BOAS BROTHERS; ABORIGINAL POPULATION.

INDIANISM. A literary-cultural movement romanticizing
Amerindian life which flowered between 1840 and 1875,
and which was capped by the career of José de Alencar.
Few of the Indianists ever saw Brazilian aborigines in
their native setting, and would have been shocked had
they observed the squalor of the lives of natives brought
into contact with coastal civilization.

INDUSTRIAIS DA SÊCA. Pejorative term for profiteering
from the droughts afflicting the Northeast, ranging from
thefts of relief shipments to corrupt officials in charge
of public works.

INDUSTRIAL CENTERS. These are led by São Paulo city,
which in 1970 produced almost 30 percent of the nation's
industrial output (in percent of total value); Rio de Janeiro came second (10 percent), followed by three Paulista cities, Santo André, São Bernardo do Campo, and
São Caetano do Sul, with a combined total of 9 percent.

INGENUOS. So-called "free" children born to slave mothers
after the 1871 Rio Branco Law who in reality had to remain in a state of semibondage to their masters until
the age of 21. The Imperial government reported a total
of 439,831 ingenuos as of June 30, 1885, and the number
probably exceeded 500,000 by abolition in 1888. See
also RIO BRANCO LAW.

"INNER SERTÃO." Name given by Capistrano de Abreu to
the hinterland of Bahia and Goiás, within the drought
polygon but nearer to the coast than the "outer sertão"
of Pernambuco and Ceará, and relatively hospitable to
agriculture and grazing.

INQUISITION, PORTUGUESE. Milder than its fierce Spanish counterpart, the Inquisition was brought to Brazil in the early eighteenth century; in all, about 90 colonists were shipped to Portugal, forty of them women, for suspected Judaism, by 1739. No Brazilian was ever put to death for sorcery or other religious deviance, a fact which contrasts sharply with the rest of the world at the time.

INSPETORIA DE OBRAS CONTRA AS SÊCAS (IFOCS). The first federal anti-drought agency (1909), succeeded by the DNOCS ("Departamento Nacional...") in 1945, and ultimately SUDENE in 1959.

INSTITUTO DE PLANEJAMENTO ECONÔMICO E SOCIAL (IP EA). The Institute of Economic and Social Planning, a foundation established by the federal government in 1967, supervising activities in economic research, planning, budgeting, and training.

INSTITUTO HISTÓRICO E GEOGRÁFICO BRASILEIRA. Founded in 1838 under the auspices of the monarchy, the Historical and Geographic Institute was the first major scholarly association of the Empire.

INSTITUTO SUPERIOR DE ESTUDOS BRASILEIROS (ISEB). The Superior Institute of Brazilian Studies, a major center of nationalist activity organized in 1955, established by the federal government as an autonomous agency responsible to the Education Ministry. The ISEB sponsored colloquia, publications, courses, and lectures on a wide range of social science-related topics under a nationalistic orientation.

INTEGRALISM. A fascist movement formally organized as a political party, the Ação Integralista Brasileira (AIB) in 1932, by Plínio Salgado. It considered itself to be the "repercussion of Catholicism on the political plane." The Integralists penetrated the armed forces and enlisted several dozen leading Brazilian intellectuals to its ranks, including Miguel Reale and Padre Helder Câmara, but eventually failed when it was isolated for its extremist tendencies by military officials. Linked semi-formally to the Nazi regime through contacts between its leaders, Integralists were virulently anti-Semitic and mocked what they called effete liberal constitutionalists. The AIB was outlawed in 1938 after a comic-opera attempted putsch.

INTEGRAR PARA NÃO ENTREGAR. "Integrate [the Amazon]

to avoid having to give it up. " A motto publicized by
the ARP to remind Brazilians of the strategic importance
of the opening of the Amazon region by the construction
of the Trans-Amazon highway system.

INTERREGNUM. The period from 1831, the abdication of
Pedro I, to 1840, when the fourteen-year-old Pedro II
was placed on the Imperial throne to forestall a political
crisis, four years before his constitutional majority.

INVASÕES. Literally, "invasions," the term used in the
Northeast for shantytowns, collections of mocambos or
jerry-built shacks.

INVERNADAS. Winter grasslands, found in the south (Sul)
of Minas Gerais and elsewhere, valuable for fattening
cattle.

IPEROÍGUE TREATY. Between the Tamoios and Portuguese
in the area around Rio de Janeiro, in 1563. Jesuit
fathers Nóbrega and Anchieta both aided in the negotiations.

IRMANDADES. Colonial-era voluntary associations linked
to the Church, some of which were purely religious in
function, others of a professional or guild nature. Some
were reserved for blacks. The main hospitals in the
colonial era (and until the twentieth century) were built
and administered by the irmandades--the Santa Casas de
Misericórdia.

ISABEL, PRINCESS (1846-1921). The conservative and ultra-
montane heir to the monarchy, revered by Brazilians as
"the Redemptress" for her aid to the cause of final abolition in 1888, but generally unpopular, in part because
her husband, the Comte d'Eu (a French Prince of the
house of Orleans) was distrusted as a man subservient
to European (and papal) influences. Isabel's reputation
may have, in fact, encouraged the makers of the republican coup.

ITABIRA IRON ORE COMPANY. Company established by
Quaker entrepreneur Percival Farquhar to extract iron
ore from Minas Gerais over a private industrial railroad
to Vitória port, to import high-grade coal, and to con-
struct a 250,000 ton capacity steel mill. The plans were
finally rejected in the 1930's under Vargas's more nationalistic economic policies, and the mill was never built.

"ITALIANI." São Paulo's Italian-born population, addressed
by special radio broadcast in July 1924 by the Italian
Ambassador, General Pietro Badoglio, in an effort to
rally support for "legality" in opposition to the tenente
uprising.

ITAPÚ DAM. The goal of a bi-national project between Paraguay and Brazil to utilize the hydroelectric potential
of the Sete Quedas Falls on the Paraná River. By 1980
it will provide up to one-third of all of Brazil's domestic
production of energy.

ITUZAINGO DEFEAT. Brazilian loss in 1827, leading to
independence for Uruguay and growing unpopularity for
Pedro I, whose foreign policy reverses contributed ultimately to his renunciation of the Crown in 1831.

-J-

JACARANDÁ. Also known as jacarandá-paulista, a hardwood
tree of the Leguminosae family which provides a deep
red-brown wood used widely to carve furniture, bowls,
etc. By the 1970's Brazil's supply was so depleted that
officials began to consider prohibiting the sale of jacarandá wood.

JACQUES, CRISTÓVÃO. Commander of the first military
expedition sent by the Portuguese Crown to challenge
French brasilwood traders, whose activities on the coast
were considered illegal under the Tordesillas Treaty.
Jacques made a number of voyages in the early 1530's.

JAGUARIBE, HÉLIO. A moderate nationalist, and member
of ISEB during the 1950's, whose O Nacionalismo na
Atualidade Brasileira suggested ways to achieve economic
and social development without the socialization of the
economy. Jaguaribe's book angered more militant nationalists for its defense of the use of foreign capital for
development, a stance which earned him the charge of
being an entreguista.

JAGUARIBE BASIN. Watered by the irregularly flowing river
of the same name, in eastern Ceará, and the site of a
population, in 1810, of approximately 60,000 persons,
most of them engaged in cattle raising and cotton production.

JAGUNÇO. Originally, a backlands ruffian. The term is
used as a synonym with capanga and cabra.

JANAK SOCIETY. A para-military association of young Poles,
organized by Polish Catholic clergy in southern Brazil
in the mid-1930's, and linked to the fascist Pilsudski
dictatorship. Some Polish-Brazilian youths were sent
to Warsaw for pilot training; one later-discovered document even revealed a Pilsudski-government plan to join
a future German-Italian invasion of Brazil, and to occupy
the state of Paraná, which would be called Nova Polônia,
or New Poland. The Society was suppressed in 1938.

JANGADA. Balsa-wood raft with a canvas sail, used widely
along the northeastern coast for fishing and coastal transport. The men who sail the craft are jangadeiros (q. v.).

JANGADEIROS. In the early 1880's many of them--for the
most part either caboclo or pardo--helped the cause of
abolition in Ceará--before that province outlawed slavery
in 1884, the jangadeiros refused to carry slaves to ships
in Fortaleza harbor waiting to take them for sale in the
south. Several thousand citizens joined the refusal by
gathering on the beach and offering their vocal support.
Shortly after that event the major southern slave-owning
states legislated against inter-provincial slave traffic,
thereby preventing the legal sale of slaves from the eco-
nomically-destitute northern and northeastern regions.

JAPANESE IN BRAZIL. The first Japanese came as settlers
in 1908 as part of a colonization agreement with the
Japanese Ministry of Agriculture, in a group of 779 immigrants to São Paulo. Most subsequent immigrants
came to the Center-South or to the Amazon. In the
1930's, xenophobia directed specifically at Orientals led
to immigration restrictions; Japanese residents, moreover, were interned during the Second World War. By
1970, an estimated 630,000 Japanese had emigrated to
Brazil, with some Nisei attaining relatively high positions
in public life, including a cabinet minister in the Geisel
administration, S. Ukei. In the Amazon, many Japanese
settlers married local residents, forming a Japanese
variant on the caboclo type.

JARDIM BOTÂNICO. The royal botanical gardens, constructed near Gávea in Rio de Janeiro under the auspices of
D. João VI in 1810, and a leading tourist attraction today

despite the toll pollution has taken on many of the plants and trees.

JEITOSO. Someone who is clever, who knows how to make a deal, who takes advantage of luck and circumstances. To have jeito is a gift that works well, as Aufderheide points out, in a practical situation for which there are specific rules rather than in a world-view guided by generalized ideals. To use jeito suggests manipulating all resources at hand, within the rules or not.

JESUS, CAROLINA MARIA DE. Author of the best-selling Child of the Dark, published in 1960. Carolina enjoyed remarkable fame after the publication of her book, but within a few years had fallen out of the limelight and, since most of her royalties were diverted to others, she was forced back into penury. She died a pauper in 1977. See also CANINDÉ; FAVELAS.

"JEUNESSE DORÉE." A pessimistic, self-conscious school of intellectual thought in the 1930's, so named by sociologist Guererro Ramos, which included the neo-orthodox Catholic traditionalists (Alceu de Amoroso Lima and Jackson de Figueiredo), xenophobic nationalists (Gustavo Barroso and Afonso Arinos de Melo Franco) and writers despondent over national "greed and corruption" (Otávio de Faria).

JEWS IN COLONIAL BRAZIL. The Dutch, who granted religious freedom to Jews in Holland and their colonies, encouraged Jewish settlers to come to the West Indies Company's colony in Brazil after 1630; Sephardic Jews, refugees from Spain and Portugal, could serve as interpreters, and others, under the seven-year governorship of Maurice of Nassau (1637-1644), were encouraged to emigrate. Witznitzer shows that the colony's Jewish population may have reached about 1,450 persons in 1645, a very large Jewish community for the seventeenth century. Once Pernambuco was retaken by the Brazilians, the Jews were forced to leave, some (23) coming to New Amsterdam; others to Martinique and Jamaica (where they were taken prisoner by the Spaniards).

JOANINE ERA. The years from 1808-1821, in which João VI reigned as Emperor (or, in the early years, Prince Regent).

JOÃO III (1521-1557). First Portuguese king to acknowledge

the necessity of developing Brazil lest it fall to foreign
hands, and the initiator of the ill-fated donatory system.
Royal government was only introduced in 1549, at Salvador, a half-century after Cabral's discovery.

JOÃO V (1706-1750).   Portuguese Monarch who, in the early
eighteenth century, permitted the Inquisition to enter Brazil.   See also INQUISITION.

JOÃO, MESTRE.   The first Portuguese explorer to make
scientific observations about Brazilian fauna and flora,
a member of Cabral's expedition to India.

JÔGO DE BICHO.   The ubiquitous "numbers" game which is
played illegally by millions of Brazilians.   The name,
"Animal game," refers to the fact that it was first initiated as an innocent means of attracting people to the
Zoological Gardens in Rio de Janeiro; drawings of animals
were printed on the lottery-style tickets.   In the early
1970's the federal government attempted to capitalize on
the jôgo by establishing a legalized one.   For a number
of years a highly popular lottery based on weekly soccer
matches has captured the attention of the population across
the nation.

JORNAL DO COMMERCIO.   One of Brazil's oldest daily newspapers founded in Rio de Janeiro in 1827.

JUBIABÁ.   Title of a Jorge Amado novel (1961).   Its plot
deals with the life of a prêto, Antônio Balduíno, from
his early shiftless existence to his role in a general
strike, which brings him to the point of political and
social awareness.   Becoming a professional boxer, his
fight with (and victory over) a German champion symbol-
izes, according to literary analysts, Amado's suggestion
of the latent strength of the black masses against white
(and foreign) adversaries.

JUDICIAL REFORM, IMPERIAL   see   JUIZ DE PAZ

JUDICIAL REFORM LAW (1828 and 1832).   Reforms ostensibly
decentralizing authority at lower judicial levels but, at
the same time, professionalizing the magistracy by making advancement dependent upon seniority of service and
keeping control of the higher judiciary in the hands of
the centralized administration.

JUDICIAL REFORM LAW OF 1841.   An act which recentra-
lized judicial power and made it entirely appointive.
This served to professionalize the judiciary but also increased opportunities to incorporate it into the patronage
process, therefore defeating intentions to remove judges
from political factionalism.

JUIZ DE FORA.   City in the Mata zone of Minas Gerais,
known for its early industrial development and called
Brazil's Manchester.   The city's importance, however,
declined after 1920, although it ranked second to Belo
Horizonte by income from 1910 to 1937, with its ratio
slipping from 3:2 to 10:1 by that year.

JUIZ-DE-FORA.   A Crown judge or magistrate appointed
from a region other than the one of his jurisdiction.

JUIZ DE PAZ.   A justice of the peace, an elected, parish-
level judge.   The office was created, along with a jury
system for trying accused criminals, during the so-called
"liberal" years of the early Empire, 1827-1837.   Professional judges reacted by blocking and sabotaging the
new institutions wherever possible.   In 1841, the Conservative majority in the Imperial legislature radically altered the 1832 Criminal Code, under which the justices of
the peace and the jury system had been implemented,
and effectively neutralized them and restored the professional magistrate to his position of colonial-era domination.

JULIÃO, FRANCISCO.   Leader of the Peasant Leagues of
Northeastern Brazil until his exile to Mexico in 1964.
An attorney, he also is an author and teacher.

JULIETA CINEMA.   A French theater in the city of Manaos
during the height of the rubber boom during the first
years of the century, featuring the works of the Compag-
nie des Cinematographes Pathé Frères of Paris.   The
cinema catered to the French tastes of the local elite,
who boasted that their city possessed the "gay spirit of
Parisian life. "

JUNTA DE ADMINISTRAÇÃO GERAL DOS DIAMANTES.   The
Council for the General Administration of Diamonds, a
special administrative body convened to supervise diamond
mining in the name of Crown, headed by the intendant of
the diamond district on Minas Gerais.

JURUPARÍ. Am Amerindian spirit, or deity, identified by Catholic missionaries with the Devil.

-K-

KARDECISM. Spiritist cult named after Alain Kardec, a nineteenth-century mystic and writer whose teachings emphasized the blending of science, philosophy, and spiritist religion. Kardecism is also known as High Spiritism. A Brazilian, Chico Xavier, popularized and adapted Kardec's teachings to the local environment. There were 644,000 registered followers of the cult in 1968.

KÊTU. Ceremonial official historically responsible for circumcision at African rites. The role became symbolic with the transportation of camdomblé (q. v.) to Brazil.

KIBON. Leading ice-cream company in Brazil.

"KING OF THE CANGACEIROS." Name given to Lampião, the scourge of the backlands and the last of the major northeastern bandits.

"KOJAK." Most popular show on Brazilian television in the mid-1970's, an illustration of the phenonemon of imported (second-rate) culture.

KOLONIALISTENTUM. Reich term for the Brazilian German community, 900,000 strong in the mid-1930's, producers of agricultural products and eager purchasers of German manufactured and specialty goods.

KRÉEN-AKARORES. One of the last tribes to be "pacified," inhabiting the Cachimbo forests of northern Mato Grosso, and brought to world attention through the documentary The Tribe That Hides from Man. First contact was made in 1967; they were forced out of their lands in 1972 to make way for the Santarém-Cuiabá Highway, and, failing to retreat further into the forest, shaved their heads and painted their bodies black and presented themselves to Indian agents. By 1974 the survivors were reduced to beggary, and numbered only 135.

-L-

LÁ EM CIMA, LÁ EM BAIXO. Common spatial division, as Epstein notes, in rural Brazilian towns. Literally, "up there," and "down there."

LABOR ORGANIZATION. Trade unionism in Brazil dates from the 1890's, when a handful of anarcho-syndicalists and socialists emigrated to Brazil and spread their message to workers, mostly urban. Those strikes which succeeded usually resulted in the establishment of a union (sindicato). From 1902 to 1907, trade federations were formed, dominated by anarcho-syndicalists, who dominated union activities until the 1920's. The height of union membership was 1913, around 60,000 members; recession until 1916 hurt efforts to organize, but they were revived in 1917. Strikes reached their peak in 1919. By 1920-21 government and employers joined to break the labor movement, and, despite bloodshed, they succeeded. Only in the 1930's under Vargas did labor gain the right to strike, but it did so under the paternalistic and closely manipulated Ministry of Labor, which provided social benefits to trade unionists who would work within the system, and isolated the rest. Labor nominally was represented by Vargas's PTB--Labor Party--after 1945, but it never truly won an independent base. After 1964 militant unions were suppressed, labor returning to a state of docility which was welcomed by the foreign investors who considered Brazil a safe place for industrial development.

LACERDA, CARLOS (1914-1977). The son of a leading opposition politician of the Old Republic, Maurício de Lacerda, Carlos spent his youth in left-oriented student organizations and embarked on a career as a journalist, first writing for the Rio daily Correio da Manhã. A volatile journalist, he started his own paper, Tribuna da Imprensa, and quickly attracted national attention. He promoted a violent campaign against Getúlio Vargas before the latter's suicide and helped support the 1964 military coup as governor of Guanabara. He later fell from grace and had his political rights revoked. Lacerda, a talented translator and critic, died of a heart attack in 1977, out of the spotlight he so ardently pursued.

LADINO (fem. , LADINA). A slave who spoke Portuguese and was otherwise assimilated into Portuguese culture and Christian practices; generally used as field or house workers.

LAET, CARLOS DE (1847-1927). Carioca engineer, secondary school teacher and journalist whose polemic and sarcastic essays won him fame as a writer. His work comprises thousands of newspaper articles and columns, and only one book, Em Minas, an essay collection.

LAGEA FUNDA. One of two cemeteries in Fortaleza, Ceará, in which 56,791 people were buried during the twelve months of the drought year of 1878, out of a total population for the city of 124,000.

LAGOA. The moist land on the edge of a receding reservior or lake, used for planting when available.

LAGUNA. A staging area established in 1694 by bandeirantes in the present-day state of Santa Catarina which changed in time from a farming-fishing community to one rooted in pastoral activities; later, Lagunists themselves migrated south to the plains of Rio Grande do Sul, where a major pastoral industry evolved.

LAMPIÃO (1900-1938). Bandit leader Virgolino Ferreira da Silva whose cangaço bands terrorized the sertão from Bahia to Maranhão until his capture and execution by federal troops in 1938. So widespread was his legend that only the display of his severed head in northeastern towns stilled rumors that he still lived. After his death Lampião became the romanticized subject of regional folk ballads and poetry. See also CANGACEIROS.

LAND AREA OF BRAZIL. Eight-and-a-half million square kilometers, or somewhat more than 6 percent of the land area of the earth. Brazil amounts to about half of the land area of South America and is larger than the United States without Alaska. Brazil shares common frontiers with every South American country and colony (French Guiana) except Chile and Ecuador.

LANGSDORFF, BARON GEORG HEINRICH VON. German diplomat sponsored by the Russian Czar who, in the 1830's, traveled throughout Brazil collecting a herbarium of 60,000 species for shipment to St. Petersburg.

LARGO. Widened section of a street.

LARGO DE PELOURINHO. Picturesque, narrow street in
the city of Salvador which, except for the wooden electric
poles spanning both sides, is almost exactly how the city
was, architecturally, two hundred years ago.

LASTRO. A plot of land set aside exclusively for one crop,
such as beans.

LATITUDE. Brazil extends north-to-south from latitude
north 5° 16'19" to latitude south 33° 45'09", covering about
39 degrees from east to west.

LA TOUCHE, DANIEL. French founder of the city of Saint
Louis (São Luís), Maranhão, in 1612.

LAVOURA BRANCA. Cash crops other than coffee (or other
produce destined for export). These include--in southern
Brazil, where the term is most used--peanuts, cotton,
castor beans, corn, rice, and beans.

LAVOURA DO POBRE. "Poor man's crop," referring to
the cultivation of northeastern cotton during the early
nineteenth century, when cotton exports through the port
of Recife outvalued those of sugar. Most of the cotton
came from small family plots in the agreste; cotton growing of this type in fact, as Barman notes, provided cash
for the creation of a capitalist economy and was the main
economic incentive for the penetration of the backlands
by agriculture.

LAVRADIO, VICEROY. Official (1769-79) who first publicly
argued for the use of the militia as a barrier against
potential lower class unrest; he reflected on the racially
mixed masses and suggested that militia organization be
used to compartmentalize the population and keep it in
check.

LAVRADOR. Small farmer, an independent planter who lived
on his own land, occasionally owned a few slaves, and
sold his cane to the engenho mills.

LAVRADOR, JOÃO FERNANDES. Lavrador's name ultimately
was applied to the coast of Canada. See BARCELOS,
PERO DE.

LAW OF DECEMBER 3, 1841. The Conservative bill which
neutralized the provisions of the Liberal 1832 Criminal

Code and stripped away the independent authority of the
Justice of the Peace and the jury system. As a result,
the return to appointing justices vastly expanded the Empire's patronage system, and opened the system to greater
political manipulation. The intent was to return judicial
power to the letrado, or lettered class, along lines rem-
iniscent of the colonial system.

LAW OF DIRECTIVES AND BASES OF EDUCATION. Introduced in 1961, the Lei de Diretrizes e Bases de Educação
Nacional introduced flexibility and decentralization into
the formerly centralized educational system. The law
was modified in 1967 which dealt specifically with higher
education. The 1961 law extended government control
to private schools as well as public. No student may
gain admission to higher education may do so without a
certified degree or diploma from an approved middle-
level school.

LEAL, ANTÔNIO. Producer of Os Estranguladores ("The
Stranglers"), Brazil's first full-length film (1906), the
story based on an actual series of crimes which occurred
at the turn of the century.

LEGIÃO CEARENSE DO TRABALHO. A curious pre-Integralist fascist party in the state of Ceará, headed by Severino Sombra, a young military officer and follower of
Jackson de Figueiredo imprisoned in 1930 for his refusal
to join the Liberal Alliance, and joined by a young priest,
Helder Câmara, who would move on to prominence as
an Integralist in the 1930's and as a socially progressive
archbishop in the 1950's and 1960's called communistic
by the right. The Legião Cearense was organized in
1931 and claimed 15,000 members; it was linked to
worker associations, and its adepts wore uniforms--
white shirts and tan khaki trousers. It sought to bring
Christianity to the working classes and to protect them
from communism.

LEGIÃO DE MINAS. A semi-fascist movement, briefly lived,
created in Minas Gerais by Francisco Campos and Gustavo Capanema after 1930 to establish tenente-led organizations in place of the old state machines.

LEGIÃO DE OUTUBRO. A sister group to the Legião de
Minas, created by Oswaldo Aranha in São Paulo and Rio
de Janeiro, seeking to institutionalize tenente leadership
on a mass basis.

"LEI AUREA" see GOLDEN LAW

LEI DE DIRETRIZES E BASES DE EDUCAÇÃO NACIONAL
see LAW OF DIRECTIVES AND BASES OF EDUCATION

LEME, SEBASTIÃO (CARDINAL) (1882-1943). Leader of the
Brazilian Church from 1928 until his death, a conservative, and confidant of dictator Getúlio Vargas during the
latter's tenure as head of state. Leme fought successfully for the reintroduction of religious education in the
public schools, and achieved a de facto (if not de jure)
reconciliation of Church and State during the 1930's.
Leme was a political elitist who encouraged the growth
of militant lay groups to win support for Church policies
within the government, and cooperated closely with the
fascist Integralist movement, although he never linked
the Church to it in a formal way. See INTEGRALISM.

LEMOS, GASPAR DE. First commander to explore the Brazilian coast, in 1501, with a small fleet of three ships,
at the specific request of the Crown. The expedition
was financed by King Manoel I, who sought to ascertain
the quantity of pau brasil (brasilwood) available for exploitation.

LEMOS, MIGUEL (1854-1917). Apostle of positivism in its
Brazilian form. Lemos lived in Paris from 1877 to
1881, and helped introduce Comte's cult to Brazil through
his writings.

LERY, JEAN DE. Huguenot chronicler of French Brazil in
the early years of the sixteenth century, when the French
were engaged in the brazilwood trade along the coast
from Cabo Frio to Cabo São Roque.

LIBELLO DO POVO see TORRES HOMEM, SALES

LIBERTADOR, O. "Newspaper" of the Prestes Column, the
first six issues of which were published by Pinheiro Machado while Captain Prestes's forces occupied São Luís,
Rio Grande do Sul in 1924; the seventh issue was printed
on the captured presses of Norte do Goiás in 1925. The
eighth appeared in Tocantins, Maranhão, and so on,
through Piauí, until the last, on July 23, 1926, in the
city of Floriano.

LICENCIATURA. A degree which entitles the holder to teach
in middle-level schools, ginásios and colégios. Gener-

ally, the licenciatura and the bacharelado (q. v.) are considered equal, but Brazilian society has historically treated the bacharel (q. v.) with greater deference. To some
degree the situation parallels the comparison between a
B. A. degree in the United States and a degree from a
college of education.

LICEU PROVINCIAL DA BAHIA. One of the earliest secondary education institutions in Brazil, founded in Salvador
in 1838 under the program of the Regency to increase
the number of pre-law and medical school preparatory
courses.

LIGA ELEITORAL CATÓLICA. The Catholic Electoral League,
formed in 1932 in an effort by the archdiocese, headed
by Cardinal Leme, to exert pressure on political candidates to endorse Church positions on education and social
matters. The Liga did not offer its own candidates, but
screened all persons running for office, offering its en-
dorsement when their views coincided.

LIGA NACIONALISTA. Founded in 1917 by students in São
Paulo under the influence of nationalist poet and writer
Olavo Bilac, the group sought political stability (and assurances against civilian or military coups), the secret
ballot, and lay militancy in defense of national sovereignty.

LIGHT, S. A. Name for the Rio and São Paulo Light and
Traction group, a Canadian-United States-English power
and utility company which has provided all of the electric
power for the two cities since the 1920's and which was
the target of nationalistic opprobrium during the 1950's
and early 1960's.

LIMPEZA DE SANGUE. "Blood purity," a requirement for
those who would hold colonial office during the seventeenth
and eighteenth centuries. See also PESSOA DE SANGUE
INFECTA.

LINGUA GERAL. Because they inhabited the coast, the
Tupís most directly confronted the intruding Portuguese,
French, and Dutch. Their language, Tupí-Guaraní, was
put into written form by the missionaries who came to
Christianize them; ultimately it became the basis of the
"lingua geral," an intertribal jargon invented by the Jesuits to communicate with all Brazilian aborigines. Wagley notes that it became the language of the "mamelucos,"

the offspring of aboriginal mothers and Portuguese fathers, and, in time, the language of the rural common people, even the Negro slaves. "Língua geral" may have been spoken by more Brazilians than Portuguese during most of the colonial period, and in the Amazon it survived into the late nineteenth century. It contributed hundreds and even thousands of terms to Brazilian Portuguese (for example, mandioca (manioc) and tapioca, and many of the concepts expressed through language, e. g. , folk and religious beliefs.)

LINHAS DO TIRO. Shooting clubs, organized at the local level under the growing sentiment of nationalism around the turn of the century, and designed as sort of a civilian reserve militia. The status of the army as a professional force without a mechanism to expand in time of crisis (before the creation in 1908 of the draft apparatus) encouraged the formation of the Tiros, which usually were composed of patriotic young men from elite families who provided their own weapons and equipment.

LINS DE BARROS, JOÃO ALBERTO (1899-1955). Tenente participant in the 1922 and 1930 uprisings, and leader of the Prestes Column. After the victory of the Liberal Alliance João Alberto was named interventor in São Paulo, where he roundly antagonized the Paulistas, and had to be removed from office by Vargas. Sent to Pernambuco, he was elected federal deputy; a year later he was sent to Washington as Minister Plenipotenciary. Under the Estado Novo he held several administrative posts, and headed the Fundação do Brasil Central, an organization concerned with the exploration of Amerindian lands.

LIS, JOSÉ. Portuguese marrano who, in 1644, was arrested in Bahia on his way to Dutch-occupied Pernambuco to find religious freedom; he was sent back to Lisbon and burned at the stake. Lis, who was born Isaac de Castro Tartas after his birthplace in Tartas, France, argued his case eloquently--that he was a Jew, not a New Christian, and thus not subject to the Inquisition's jurisdiction, but the appeal failed. He was twenty-one years old at the time of his execution.

LISBOA, ANTÔNIO FRANCISCO. Aleijadinho, the crippled baroque-era sculptor (1730-1814) whose magnificent statues on religious themes adorn the major urban centers of the mining area of central Minas--Ouro Preto, Sabará,

and Congonhas.   Aleijadinho suffered from leprosy and
used tools strapped to the stumps of his arms after his
fingers no longer could be used.

LISBOA, ARROJADO.   The first director of the national anti-
drought agency, the IFOCS.   He took office in 1909 but
resigned in 1912 when the agency failed to receive the
federal funds he believed to be necessary for effective-
ness.   Lisboa was called out of retirement by Epitácio
Pessoa in 1919, when the government suddenly poured
itself into the anti-drought public works effort.

LISBOA, JOAQUIM MARQUES see ALMIRANTE TAMANDARÉ

LISPECTOR, CLARICE (1926-).   Leading novelist and
writer of short stories in the romantic tradition.   She
was born in Russia but came to Recife as an infant; she
published her first novel in 1944, at 18.   Lispector lives
in Switzerland; two of her books, Family Ties and The
Apple in the Dark have been translated and published in
the United States.

LITERATURA DO CORDEL.   Pamphlet literature, crudely
but charmingly hand printed and sold at rural feiras
throughout the Northeast.   Some of the favorite themes
have been cangaceirismo, religious mysticism (especially
Padre Cícero), and family life, especially aberrant behavior
(youths who go wrong; despoiled maidens, and so forth).

LITORAL.   The low, moist slope along the northeastern and
eastern coast, the site of many if not most of Brazil's
urban centers.

LLOYD BRASILEIRO.   The national merchant fleet, modernized after 1964.

LOBATO, MONTEIRO (1883-1948).   Paulista coffee planter
and novelist, whose writings frequently touched on the
lot of the rural poor, the caboclos.

LOBO, PERO.   Commander of the first expedition from São
Vicente to explore the hinterland.   Sent by donatário
Martim Afonso de Souza in 1531-2, Lobo's force of
eighty people reached the plateau which is the present-
day site of the city of São Paulo.   The exploration party,
forerunners of the bandeirantes, proceeded on to the
Paraná River where they were set upon by Amerindians
and slaughtered.

LOJA MAÇONICA PATRIOTISMO. The first masonic lodge
in Brazil, established in Recife in 1814 by a Portuguese,
Domingos José Martins, sent with the specific mission
of founding lodges in the northeastern provinces. Others
were opened under Martins' direction in Maranhão, Ceará,
and Bahia.

LOPES, ISIDORO DIAS (1863-19??). A retired coronel
sympathetic to the aims of the tenentes who, in 1924,
promoted to "general" by his followers, formally demanded the resignation of President Artur Bernardes and
raised the flag of insurrection in conjuction with the rebel
seizure of the city of São Paulo and outbreaks of revolt
among army garrisons in Mato Grosso, Sergipe, Pará,
and Amazonas. The same "general" played a major role
in the 1932 constitutionalist revolt of São Paulo, having
been restored to grace after the Liberal Alliance victory
in 1930.

LOPES, SEBASTIÃO. Portuguese cartographer whose maps
of Brazil drawn in the 1550's emphasized the territory's
natural riches, especially pau brasil (brazilwood).

LORCH, LUDWIG. Philanthropist and Jewish community
leader in São Paulo who, during the mid- and late-1930's,
headed a strenuous effort to receive those Jewish immigrants who could obtain visas and settle in Brazil after
escaping Nazi Germany.

LOTT, MARSHAL HENRIQUE TEIXEIRA (1894-   ). War
Minister from 1954 to 1960, and the leader of the pre-
ventative military coup which preserved Juscelino Kubitschek's inauguration in 1955. He ran for President in
1960 but lost to reformist Jânio Quadros. He attempted
to run for governor of the state of Guanbara in 1965 but
was removed from the ballot when he spoke out against
the regime. Five years later a persistent rumor swept
the country that he had shot to death the officer responsible for the arrest and torture of his grandson, in Rio
de Janeiro.

LUCCOCK, JOHN (1770-1826). Son of a Yorkshire village
clothier, and, between 1808 and 1818, a commercial
trader in Rio de Janeiro, where his diary has left an
invaluable record of life in the capital city during the
first years of the transmigration.

LUCENA, HENRIQUE DE (1835-1913). Imperial and Repub-

lican political figure who, as a close friend of Deodoro
da Fonseca, was entrusted with a number of important
assignments after the fall of the monarchy.   His intervention in the 1891 elections for governor and state assemblies to punish those historical republicans who had
opposed Deodoro in Congress served to exacerbate tensions and drive a deeper wedge between the administration and the new opposition.   A Pernambucano, Lucena
also failed to pacify political tensions in that state.   In
the closing years of his life he served as a member of
the Brazilian Supreme Court.

LUFTSCHIFFBAU ZEPPELIN.   The German airship company
which maintained regular Zeppelin service between Berlin
and Rio de Janeiro during the 1930's, with stops in Rome,
Dakar, and Recife.

LUNDU.   An Afro-Brazilian dance originating in Angloa,
and using the umbigada, the navel-to-navel bump char-
acterizing the early samba form.   At one point the dance
was prohibited on orders of the King of Portugal, who
saw it performed by slaves brought to Lisbon in the
early 1500's.

LUSARDO, JOÃO BATISTA (1892-   ).   Gaúcho lawyer, physician and revolutionary, partisan in the 1923 civil war
in that state and member of the tenente wing of Vargas's
Liberal Alliance.   After breaking with Vargas in 1932
he went into exile; in 1937 he rejoined the government
and served Vargas for fifteen years as Ambassador to
Uruguay and Perón's Argentina.   Eighty-six years of
age in 1978, he has been an active supporter of the military regime.

THE LUSIADS   see   CAMÕES, LUÍS DE

LUSITANI.   Peoples of western Iberia who resisted Roman
occupation, the ancestors of the present-day Portuguese.
Their leader was a shepherd, Viriatus.

LUSOPHONE AFRICA.   Portuguese-speaking Africa--Cape
Verde, Guinea-Bissau, Angloa, Mozambique--given special status by the Brazilian Foreign Ministry in its post-
1975 effort to woo former African colonies.

LUTHERANS.   One of the oldest Protestant groups in Brazil,
with its first church established in 1823.   Most Lutherans

live in the South; they include military president Ernesto
Geisel (1975-79), the first non-Roman Catholic head of
state.   Lutherans numbered 433,000 in 1970, the date
of the last census.

LUTZ, ADOLFO (1855-1940).   Paulista physician and micro-
biologist who, beginning in the 1890's, began to call attention to the connection between sanitation and epidemic
disease, and whose research touched on plague, malaria,
yellow fever, and leprosy.   He was educated in Europe
and may have met both Lister and Pasteur; he headed
the Bacteriological Institute of São Paulo and later came
to the Instituto Oswaldo Cruz but failed as an administrator owing to his personal aloofness and European mien
(Nancy Stepan).

LUTZ, BERTHA (1894-1976).   Founder of the first campaign
for women's suffrage, immediately following the First
World War.   The movement was formally organized in
1922 with the creation of the Federação Feminista Brasileira, the Brazilian Feminist Federation, which sought
to use public opinion as a weapon to encourage rights
for women.   Despite the worldwide trend in the direction
of such movements, Lutz and other feminists were met
with unusual hostility, as a threat to the Brazilian family.
Vargas finally granted women the vote in 1932, an act
formalized by the 1934 Constitution.   See also PEREIRA
DE QUEIROZ, CARLOTA.

-M-

MACACOS.   Monkeys.   Argentinians, Uruguayans, and Chi-
leans frequently call Brazilians such, if only in private
and in bad taste.   Graham notes that during the War of
the Triple Alliance Paraguayans did the same, as a way
of ridiculing Brazilian slavery.

MACAPÁ.   Established as a fort on the northern bank of the
Amazon in 1687, in order to confirm Portuguese presence
in the area and check French expansion from Cayenne.
The French attacked Macapá but were driven out in 1697;
after diplomatic negotiation, a boundary between French
Guiana and Brazil was set in 1701, ceding to France the
lands between the Amazon and the Oiapoc Rivers.   Portuguese troops occupied French Guiana from 1809 to
1815 in retaliation for the Napoleanic invasion of Portugal,

but the colony was returned to France, with Macapá remaining Brazil's last outpost in the region.

MACHADO, GILKA (1893-197?).   Poet whose work, "Crystal Particles," appeared in 1915 and whose style has been widely imitated. For better or worse, Machado is known in Brazil as the "queen of feminine poetry."

MACIEL, ANTÔNIO VICENTE MENDES see CONSELHEIRO, ANTÔNIO

MACIEL FILHO, JOSÉ SOARES DE (1897?-1975).   Editor and confidant of Getúlio Vargas during the Estado Novo and Vargas's presidential term from 1950 to 1954, and editor of an outspoken Rio de Janeiro, O Imparcial. The owner of a large textile mill, Petropolitana, in Rio de Janeiro state, Maciel Filho served as an unpaid advisor and speech writer for Vargas, and may well have penned Vargas's controversial suicide note in 1954.

MACONHA. Cannabis sativa (marijuana).   Dried herb smoked widely among lower class caboclos (q. v.) over the centuries.   Originally believed to be an aphrodisiac and prescribed by sorcerers in the northeastern region from Alagoas to João Pessôa.

MACUNAÍMA.   Novel by Mário de Andrade (1928) which presented its hero (the title's name) as a cross between Paul Bunyan and Peer Gynt, poking fun at Brazilian racial attitudes and some of the more colorful aspects of Brazilian culture, including cannibalism.   The book was used as the basis for a film made in the early 1970's, starring the black comedian Grande Otelo.

MÃE PRETA.   Literally, "black mother," or "mammy." See BABÁ.

MAGALHÃES, COUTO DE.   Author of O Selvagem (1876), a collection of Tupi legends, a more serious effort (than the romantic Indianist literature) to appreciate the contribution of Amerindian culture to Brazilian life.

MAGALHÃES, DOMINGOS JOSÉ GONÇALVES DE (1811-1882). Romantic poet, writing of the countryside and idyllic indigenous life.

MAGALHÃES, JURACY (1901-   ).   Tenente Interventor (later

governor) of the state of Bahia from 1930 to 1937, ousted
by Vargas for his flirtation with Flôres da Cunha, Armando de Sales de Oliveira, and other liberal constitutionalist figures.   He returned to political life after 1945,
serving several terms as governor through the 1950's
and identifying with the 1964 coup.

MAIA, JOAQUIM JOSÉ DE.   Brazilian student at the University of Montpellier, France, who corresponded with Thomas Jefferson, the United States Ambassador in Paris,
asking for support for Brazilian independence.   Two other
Montpellier students--Domingos Vidal de Barbosa and
José Álvares Maciel--brought back even more activist
notions: they joined the Inconfidência Mineira conspiracy.
Álvares Maciel, in fact, is thought to have coached Tiradentes in French Revolutionary ideology.

MAL CAZADA ("Badly married").   A state frequently referred to in colonial literature, it pertains to wives who
have wearied of their married state because of their husband's inconsiderate behavior.   They were not permitted,
however, to do anything other than languish at home.

MALAGUETA, A.   Newspaper founded in 1821 by Luís Augusto
May (sic), a Portuguese functionary who had arrived in
Brazil in 1815.

MALFATTI, ANITA (1896-1964).   Major Brazilian painter who
studied in Berlin before returning to São Paulo to exhibit
at the 1922 Semana de Arte Moderna; some early critics
called her work "paranoid."   By 1930 she had been acclaimed as one of the country's most important artists.

MALOCAS.   Slum dwellings in the South, similar in construction to the favelas of Rio de Janeiro and São Paulo.

MALUCO.   Described by Freyre as a form of dysentery common to Africans brought over in the days of the slave
trade.   Also known as corrução and mal-de-bicho.

MALUNGO.   Slave children allowed to be playmates of the
white offspring of the senhor de engenho.   Malungo is
an African word for "comrade"; it was used by blacks
to address one another on the slave ships during the voyage from the African coast.   Runaway slave members of
the quilombos (q.v.) also used the term in their inter-
personal relations.

MAMELUCO (fem. , MAMELUCA).   Offspring of Amerindian and Caucasian parents, frequently used as a generic term for all mestizos.

MAMORÉ-MADEIRA RAILWAY.   Built during the 1890's to bypass the river rapids in the rubber region of Acre, it was never extended into Bolivia as originally projected. A new railroad, connecting Corumbá with Santa Cruz, Bolivia, was built in the 1950's by a bi-national commission.

MANAOS.   The capital of the state of Amazonas, in the center of the Amazon, and a bustling river port with about 5,000 inhabitants until about 1890.   Then with the rise in the foreign demand for rubber, its economy boomed: by 1910 it had become the rubber capital of the world, with a population of 50,000, and a breathlessly cosmopolitan life style patterned after that of Paris, and a monumental, ornate Opera House.   With the fall of rubber prices in 1910, the city's fortunes declined.   In the mid-1960's it was made a free port of entry in an effort to stimulate trade and domestic tourism.

MANAOS HARBOR, LIMITED.   British-owned port facility serving Manaos, attacked vehemently during the rubber boom for allegedly inadequate services, over which it held a monopoly.   In 1910, 1,675 ocean-going steamships and river launches visited the port; ships often had to line up in mid-river awaiting a berth for unloading.

MANDÃO.   Rural boss, or coronel (q. v.).

MANGAS.   Farmed-over plots, used principally for pasturage.

MANGUINHOS.   Site of the Oswaldo Cruz Institute, on the outskirts of Rio.   To get there, laboratory workers and other employees had to travel eight miles by train and then continue on horseback.   See also OSWALDO CRUZ INSTITUTE.

"MANIFESTATION TO FRIENDLY GOVERNMENTS AND NATIONS. "   Statement by José Bonifácio, signed by D. Pedro on August 6, 1822, and sent to foreign governments in an effort to establish diplomatic relations as an independent state.   Portugal, refusing to accede to the state of affairs, applied pressure on the other European powers to withhold recognition.   As a result, even Great Britain hesitated, leaving the United States as the first nation to extend formal recognition, in May 1824. Portugal finally ended its intransigence in 1825, after the British-mediated treaty of that year with its former colony.

MANIFESTO DOS PIONEIROS. Manifesto of young educational reformers--Anísio Teixeira, Francisco de Azevedo, M. B. Lourenço Filho and others--published by the Brazilian Educational Association (ABE) in 1932, and resulting in the decision to establish the University of São Paulo (USP).

MANIOC. Brazil's staple food since earliest colonial days. A starchy tuber grown from cuttings which, as Worcester notes, needs virtually no care, and which could be stored indefinitely or left in the ground. The manioc tuber is scraped into a coarse powder and mixed with water, taken dry, or turned into farofa (meal). The word manioc comes from the Tupí mandi (bread) and óca (house). See also MANIPEBA; CARREGADEIRA.

MANIPEBA. The best variety of manioc, which can be harvested any time after 18 months growth, and which can be stored in the ground for up to six years, used as a kind of calorie storage in the drought-ridden parts of the northeast. See also CARREGADEIRA.

MANOEL I (1475-1521). The heir to João I of Portugal, and its king after 1495. One of his first acts was to expel the Jews from Portugal, in part as an effort to ingratiate himself with the Castillians, whose princess, Isabel, was a possible marriage partner. In 1496 Manoel ordered all Jews and Moslems to leave the country within ten months, and he ordered all Jewish children under fourteen years old arrested and prepared for baptism. See also NEW CHRISTIAN.

MARACANÃ. Rio's soccer stadium, the largest in the world with a seating capacity of 200,000. Five other Brazilian stadiums seat more than 100,000.

MARACUJÁ. Passion flower fruit, commonly used as a source of juice and fruit drinks.

MARÁFO. The African word for crude rum, or cachaça, served to slaves during times of unusually hard labor or during festivals.

MARAGATO. A member of the Rio Grande do Sul Federalist Party (Partido Federalista).

MARAJÓ ISLAND. Lying between the two channels of the Amazon River delta, it is the largest fluvial island in the world--100 miles from north to south, and 180 miles from east to west.

MARANHÃO. A poor state lying between Pará and Piauí in the North-Northeast. Originally settled by the French, its capital is São Luís. The state's major economic activity is cotton growing.

MARCGRAF, GEORGE. Dutch astonomer brought to Recife by Maurice of Nassau, to administer the use of his astronomical observatory in the gardens of Vrijburg Palace. A naturalist, he also wrote, with Wilhelm Piso, the first major study of Brazilian flora and fauna, the Historia naturalis brasilae (1648), published in Holland.

MARCHINHA. Dance rhythm related to the samba, first composed for the 1899 Rio Carnaval by Chiquinho Gonzaga, the famous "Abre Alas."

MARIA DA GLÓRIA. Infant daughter of Pedro I, named by him queen of Portugal when his own father, João VI, died in 1826 and he decided to remain in Brazil as Emperor. In consequence, his brother Miguel seized the throne, precipitating the dynastic crisis which led finally to Pedro's abdication in 1831.

MARIA ZÉLIA STOCKADE (ZÉ MARIA). Makeshift São Paulo prison, in an abandoned textile factory complex, holding 400 detainees in the aftermath of the 1935 ANL-PCB uprising, and curiously paradoxical: on one hand prisoners were allowed to publish their own newspaper, hold indoctrination classes (the PCB boasted that Zé Maria was the best "revolutionary school" in Brazil) but on the other conditions were terrible, almost subhuman.

MARIMBA. Stringed instrument once very popular among Brazilian slaves although its use disappeared by the mid-twentieth century among Afro-Brazilian cultists whose use of other traditional instruments continued.

MAROMBAS. Floating rafts or corrals constructed in the Amazon region to protect livestock and even cattle when

the water rises.   The animals, unable to forage, are
fed with canarana grass, cut from canoes by the vaqueiros.

MARRANOS.   Another term for New Christians (q. v.).

MASCARENHAS DE MORAIS, JOÃO BATISTA (1883-1968)
    see   FORÇA EXPEDICIONARIA BRASILEIRA

MASCATES.   Peddlers.   The less-than-complimentary term
    applied by the population of Olinda to the Portuguese of
    Recife, derived from the fact that many members of the
    Olinda-based rural plantocracy by the eighteenth century
    had fallen heavily in debt to the Portuguese merchants
    of the port city.   The planters attempted to trade directly
    with Dutch and English ships, thus bypassing the mascates
    (and Crown duties); in retaliation the King, in 1710,
    elevated Recife to the status of a city, removing it from
    the political control of Olinda.   A two-year-long "war"
    ensued, with the planters seizing the port.   The conflict
    was ended after Portuguese intervention with the proclama-
    tion of a general amnesty, but hard feelings between the
    Brazilian sugar aristocracy and the Portuguese mercan-
    tilist bourgeoisie lingered for generations.

MASCOVADO.   This brown (or engenho) sugar was the prin-
    cipal variety of exported sugar from Bahia through the
    nineteenth century.

MASSAPÊ.   Rich, fertile black alluvial soil which character-
    izes the Northeast's Zona da Mata and which is respon-
    sible, in part, for the region's rich agricultural past.

MASTERS AND THE SLAVES.   English version of Gilberto
    Freyre's pathbreaking work (1933), Casa-Grande e Sen-
    zala.   In his work, Freyre openly praised the legacy of
    miscegenation, claiming that Brazilian slavery had been
    relatively benign and that the Portuguese willingness to
    intermingle with what he termed the "lower races" even-
    tually yielded Brazilian homogeneity and created a "new
    world in the tropics," the amalgam of European, African,
    and Amerindian racial culture.   Controversial and pro-
    vocative, Freyre's writing freed Brazilian intellectuals
    from many of their cultural complexes and feelings of
    national inferiority.   See also RETRATO DO BRASIL.

MATARAZZO ENTERPRISES.   A vast industrial and commer-
    cial empire founded by Francisco Matarazzo, an Italian

immigrant later knighted by the papacy, and the head of
one of the wealthiest family-owned business groups in
Brazil.

MATOS, GREGÓRIO DE. Literary figure of the seventeenth
century. Matos was born on a Bahian fazenda but educated in Portugual, where he later practiced law; he also
wrote poetry but fell out of favor for his penchant for sa-
tire. He returned to Brazil but ultimately was exiled
to Angola. His lyric poems were only published two
centuries after his death, and serve as the basis for
his high reputation today.

MATOS, HORÁCIO DE. "Governor of the Bahian Sertão,"
so named for his defeat of state forces and his virtual
control, as regional coronel during the 1920's, of the
Bahian backlands. In 1926 he was hired by federal officials to pursue the Prestes Column, against which he
held a personal grudge, since a relative had been killed
by Siqueira Campos's detachment. The jagunço troops,
fighting jungle style (and acknowledged by the tenentes as
"revolutionaries on the loyalist side" for their tactics)
never defeated the Column, but they helped push them
away from major population centers and ultimately into
exile.

MATRIFOCAL FAMILY. The twentieth century form of family organization, heretofore believed to have been a product of urbanization and industrialization, but traced by
Donald Ramos to colonial period antecedents.

MATUTO. A rural peasant, or rustic. The term implies
helplessness, and applies to the interior of the Northeast.

MAUÁ, VISCOUNT see SOUZA, IRINEU EVANGELISTA DE

MAZOMBISMO. The upper class tendency, identified by
Viana Moog, to deprecate things Brazilian and to idealize
foreign culture and material goods, especially--at least
during the period before World War II--French. See also
GENTLEMAN COMPLEX.

MAZOMBOS. Brazilian-born sons and daughters of Portuguese
settlers, the counterparts of the criollos of the Spanish
colonies in the New World.

MAZZEI, JÚLIO. Leading soccer trainer who joined the

Santos team in 1965, after post-graduate training in physical conditioning at Michigan State University, and considered a father-figure by the young athletes under his charge. Pelé credits him with keeping him in school until he earned his diploma. He was fired in 1972 after a conflict with management over treatment of players.

MECÂNICOS. Artisans who, as Morse notes, were often indistinguishable from "nobles" and homems bons in colonial days because of the atmosphere of generalized poverty which, at least among the Paulistas, prevailed. See also HOMENS BONS; SÃO VICENTE.

MEDEIROS, MARIA QUITÉRIA DE JESUS. A Cachoeira (Bahia)-born woman who distinguished herself at the Battle of Periquitos during the fight against Portuguese forces loyal to Lisbon after Independence. For her part, she was decorated with the Imperial Order of the Cross by Emperor Pedro I.

MEDICAL SCHOOL OF RIO DE JANEIRO. Established in 1832, along with a sister medical school in Salvador, and one of Brazil's four university-level faculties through the end of the Empire. Standards were high--between 1833 and 1843 out of 2,000 students, only 100 received their medical licenses; as late as the 1880's a large percentage of those who did graduate never practiced medicine, using their degrees instead to enter the bureaucracy as bacharéis, or merely for the social prestige. In general, the school stressed teaching over research, and reflected the generally low levels of scientific information prevalent in medical schools worldwide before 1900.

MEIAÇAO. A sharecropping system used widely in the Paraíba valley and adopted by landowners in Minas and elsewhere after 1900 to attract freed slaves and other rural workers. The sharecroppers were called meeiros.

MEIRA MATTOS, CARLOS. A general and author of Brazil: Geopolitics and Destiny (1975), a nationalistic pronouncement of Brazil's intentions to achieve world power status.

MEIRELLES, VICTOR (1832-1903). Leading nineteenth-century artist, painter of patriotic canvases depicting such Brazilian military victories as Riachuelo and Guararapes.

MELLO, EDNARDO D'AVILA. Commanding general of São

Paulo's military region and a hard-liner, removed by
President Ernesto Geisel in 1976 after public outcry over
the deaths by torture of two political prisoners under his
jurisdiction.

MELLO, THIAGO DE. Poet born in Amazonas, he was a
    close friend of Pablo Neruda, and quiet spokesman for
    the return to introspection and human dignity in Brazilian
    life. De Mello's simple, almost childlike poems call
    softly for resistance to authoritarianism. As such, de
    Mello was exiled in 1969 after harassment and arrest in
    the aftermath of the 1964 coup. Collections of his poems
    include "O silêncio e a palavra," and "Madrugada cam-
    ponêsa. "

MELO, PADRE ANTÔNIO. A priest from the city of Cabo,
    Pernambuco, who during the early 1960's spoke out
    against the Church for its conciliatory role in the pea-
    sant movement and who, in 1963, led a successful strike
    in the zona da mata which resulted in an 80 percent
    salary increase for 200,000 rural workers.

MELO, CUSTÓDIO DE (1840-1902). Rear Admiral and veteran
    of the Paraguayan War whose opposition to Deodoro da
    Fonseca's closing of Congress in November 1891 led him
    to head an insurrection in the navy two weeks later.
    Training his fleet's guns on the official buildings of down-
    town Rio de Janeiro, he attempted to force the govern-
    ment to abdicate. The revolt succeeded, and Floriano
    Peixoto, the vice-president, took office. Custódio de
    Melo served as Navy Minister from the day of the revolt
    to mid-1893 when he resigned over Floriano's refusal to
    set elections for the succession. De Melo also backed
    the Federalist revolt in Rio Grande do Sul and led a
    second, more serious, navy revolt in September 1893,
    this time calling for a restoration of constitutionality.
    The revolt failed and, in March, de Melo took refuge
    in a ship of the Portuguese navy and escaped into exile;
    others who participated in the revolt were shot. He
    returned after an amnesty was proclaimed.

MELO DE MORAES FILHO, ALEXANDRE JOSÉ DE. Author
    of several works on Brazilian custom and folklore, in-
    cluding História e Costumes, at the turn of the twentieth
    century. See also PEREIRA DA COSTA, FRANCISCO
    AUGUSTO.

MELO FRANCO, AFRÂNIO DE (1870-1943). Known princi-

pally for his writings on law and his service in the diplomatic corps. His son, Afonso Arinos de Melo Franco,
published his biography, Um Estadista da Republica.

MEMORANDUM OF UNDERSTANDING. A mutual interest
pact between the United States and Brazil, signed after
two years of discussion, signed in Brasília in 1976 by
Henry Kissinger and Foreign Minister Azeredo de Silveira.
The pact establishes a special relationship between the
two nations shared only by the United States by a few
Western Allies, Japan, and Saudi Arabia.

MESQUITA, JÚLIO DE (1862-1927). Owner of the leading
newspaper O Estado de São Paulo and leading political
figure during the Old Republic.   Mesquita worked his way
up the ranks of the paper until he bought it in 1902; he
also was a member of the 1891 Constituent Assembly
and a state legislator. His son, Júlho de Mesquita Filho,
took over the reins of the paper and held them until the
1970's.

MONTOYA, ANTÔNIO RUIZ DE see GUAIRA

MOQUECA DE PEIXE. One of the most traditional dishes of
the northeastern plantation zone. In the nineteenth-century Casa-Grande it was a ragout of fish and shellfish
cooked in oil and pepper, then wrapped in banana leaves
and roasted in coals. Moqueca today is prepared in a
saucepan on the stove.

MORADORES. Sharecroppers. Persons in this category who
are particularly destitute are known, in the Northeast,
as moradores de sujeição ("residents of subjection").

MORAES, RUBENS BORBA DE. Author, former librarian
of the Biblioteca Nacional (National Library), and the
owner of one of the best private collections of Brasiliana
in the country until he sold most of it in 1963 to José
Mindlin, a Paulista industrialist.

MOREIRA, DELFIM (1868-1920). Mineiro politician elected
Vice President in 1918 on the Rodrigues Álves ticket.
When Álves died, before taking office, Moreira acted as
president of the Republic for seven months before a newly
elected successor--in this case, Epitácio Pessoa--could
take over. But his own health was sufficiently weak so that
his interior minister, Afrânio de Melo Franco, for all practical purposes exercised presidential decision-making power.

MORENO.   Code name for "black" in polite Brazilian usage
in the 1970's.   In the 1960's, the term pardo (q. v.) was
used; before that, preto.   Afro-Brazilians have complained
that they are often called "moreno" in their presence but
"preto" behind their backs.

MORGADO.   Law affecting inheritance, abolished in 1835 and
therefore effectively destroying the rule of primogeniture
and entailment, making both legitimate and natural progeny
of both sexes eligible for inheritance.

MORUBIXADA.   The military chieftains of the Tupi tribes,
selected by the taxauá, the tribal leader.

"MOSCA NA LEITE" ("A fly in the milk").   A term used in
jest to show Brazilian social distaste for marriages between partners of widely divergent colors.

MOVIMENTO.   A cultural journal sponsored by the popular-
front Aliança Nacional Libertadora, edited by Jorge Amado,
José Lins do Rêgo, and others.   Suppressed after the
failed insurrection in late 1935, it was succeeded several
decades later by a political-social newspaper of the same
name, published in São Paulo, just as frequently in trou-
ble with the censors (although with no known connection
to its ancestor).

MOVIMENTO COMUNISTA.   The frequently-suppressed, underground newspaper of the Brazilian Communist Party,
issued monthly from 1922 to 1925, after which time it
was given up in favor of a weekly, A Classe Operária.

MOVIMENTO DE EDUCAÇÃO DE BASE (MEB).   Church-
sponsored organization for social change through literacy
mobilization, centered in the poorest areas of the coun-
try--the North, Northeast, and Centerwest--growing out
of radio schools pioneered by Dom Eugênio Sales in Natal
in 1958.   MEB flourished from 1960 to 1963, seeking to
raise social awareness among the illiterate and to offer
remedial training, and was dismantled after the military
coup in 1964.

MOVIMENTO DEMOCRÁTICO BRASILEIRO (MDB).   The im-
potent "opposition" party, formed in 1964 from centrist
elements in the former Partido Social Democrático and
the União Democrática Nacional (qq. v.), and the token
anti-government party in the docile Congress.   Strong

MDB showings in state-wide elections in every year they have been held since the middle 1960's has led the military government to slow its timetable for return to civilian government.

MOVIMENTO REVOLUCIONÁRIO DEMOCRÁTICO. A secretive group within the Army, presumably castelista in orientation, which in 1977 distributed thousands of tape cassettes speaking to the general political situation couched in "progressive" and nationalist language, while possibly representing an anti-Geisel, hard-line group or faction.

MR-8 (MOVIMENTO REVOLUCIONÁRIO 8). A guerrilla group, mostly made up of students, responsible for the kidnapping of the United States Ambassador, Charles Elbrick, in 1969. The group was loosely allied to a splinter Communist Party organization, the Ação Libertadora Nacional (ALN), which was headed by expelled Party leader Carlos Marighela.

MUCAMA. A favorite slave or black maid who frequently served as a wet-nurse. See also BABÁ.

MUDAS. Seedlings, usually of coffee trees, sold by traveling muleteers from fazenda to fazenda.

"MULATTO ESCAPE HATCH." As explained by Degler, the opportunity afforded within Brazilian society for mulattos to achieve upward social mobility by acting according to the values and rules of "white" society. In this sense Brazil, more than the United States, offers persons of color the opportunity to be accepted, although at the same time it suggests that non-whites who fail to climb the social ladder do so out of inadequacy and not because of societal prejudice or discrimination. See also BRANQUEAMENTO.

MÜLLER, FELINTO (1900-1973). Mato-Grosso-born, Müller emerged as a prominent police official after the 1932 São Paulo insurrection, and soon became a confidant of Getúlio Vargas, who gave him the command of the new Political and Social Police and its undercover branch known as S-2. Müller openly sympathized both with the Integralists of Plínio Salgado and the German Nazis; he maintained correspondence with several high officials of the Reich. Müller reported directly to Vargas, although technically he was subordinate to the Minister of Justice.

Vargas even used him to keep the Catholic Church under surveillance, despite his publicly warm friendship with Cardinal Leme.

MUMBANDA. A favored female slave.

MUNGUZÁ. A porridge prepared from corn and coconut milk (or cow's milk), served in the big houses in the Northeast and like the Paulista canjica, a dessert made from grated green corn, butter, and coconut.

MUNICÍPIO. Literally, municipality. But Brazilian municípios correspond, demographically speaking, to counties in the United States. Município seats are called sédes.

MUNICÍPIOS, LARGEST. According to the 1970 census, the largest municípios were São Paulo (5,924,615); Rio de Janeiro, formerly Guanabara (4,251,903); Belo Horizonte (1,235,030); Recife (1,060,701); Salvador (1,007,195); Porto Alegre (835,545); Fortaleza (857,980); Nova Iguaçú, in Rio de Janeiro State (727,140); Belém (633,374); and Curitiba, in Paraná (609,026).

MUSEU GOELDI. Located in Belém, Pará, and one of the country's most important centers of tropical studies, based on the flora, fauna, and ethnography of the Amazon.

MUSEU IMPERIAL. The former summer palace of Emperor D. Pedro II, now a museum dedicated to the Brazilian Empire.

MUSEUM OF BLACK ART. Founded in Salvador in 1968 by playwright and writer Abdias do Nascimento in an effort to focus attention on Afro-Brazilian life and culture as the first step "toward the restoration of the values of African culture" in Brazil.

MUSIC see POPULAR MUSIC

MUTIRÃO. Community efforts to help an individual or family in the Northeast, usually in construction, of a house, corral, or in the field in the case of hardship.

-N-

NABUCO DE ARAÚJO, JOAQUIM AURÉLIO (1849-1910). Leading abolitionist and the figure most closely identified with the anti-slavery campaign. Nabuco, who spent part of his career in London and Washington as a diplomat, maintained contact with foreign abolitionist groups. An unreconstructed monarchist, he retired from public life after the advent of the Republic, and dedicated himself to writing his memoirs. An eloquent orator, Nabuco's role in history has been compared in Brazil to that of Abraham Lincoln's, although Nabuco never held elected office. Some criticism has been leveled in recent years at the fact that Nabuco showed little concern with the plight of the slaves (and of the freedmen after abolition); his interest was mostly legalistic.

NADEZHDA. The first Russian ship to visit Brazil, in 1803, outbound from Kronstadt on a circumnagivation of the globe. In the early 1800's, some Brazilian products reached Russia through trade: cacao, tapioca, vanilla, cinnamon, rum, tropical wood, and, especially, cotton and sugar. Most of the products were shipped either through Portugal or Manchester. A Russian tariff in 1816, however, hindered the further development of trade, and Portuguese pressure forced Russian-Brazilian relations even further apart. With Independence in 1822 Russia forcefully supported Portugal; only in 1828 did the Czar recognize the new nation.

NAMES. Brazilians have shown a refreshing and at times delightful propensity for choosing names, often modifying family names in keeping with unwritten rules of status (taking the matrilineal name if of a more established family) or inventing them, as was the fashion early in the century (Brasil, or Pernambucano, or names from the Tupi). First names include children named after historical figures ranging from Marconi to Edison to Mussolini to Getúlio Vargas to John and Robert Kennedy to Garrastazú. Verified names include the following: Veneza Americana Derecife; São Sebastião do Rio de Janeiro; Jerônimo Dix-Neuf Rosado; Céu Azul Soares (the last, "Blue Skies" Soares). The most common names in the 1970's are José and Maria, followed by Antônio and João, but invented names widely used include Suely, Jarbas, Moacir, Jacy, and Millôr. Sr. Kuroki B. de Menezes, of Recife, named his eight children: Kilza, Kátia, Keila, Kénia, Kadja, Kilder, Katiane, and Kleber.

NASCIMENTO, EDSON ARANTES DO (1940-   ). The great soccer star Pelé, whose career from the mid-1950's to

1977 spanned three World Cup championships. Playing
mostly for Santos, Pelé, a self-effacing black from a
poor town in Minas Gerais, became the highest-paid team
athlete in history before leaving Brazilian competition.
His post-retirement decision to join the New York Cosmos
is considered the prime reason for the success of soccer
in the United States. Pelé's personal conservatism and
apolitical posture has led the military government to
laud him even further; his example is widely used in
civismo texts for his willingness to avoid militancy, to
play within the system, and to obey the rules of hierarchy.
Pelé's marriage to a white woman, Rosemeri Cholby,
has been widely cited as an example of Brazil's liberal
attitudes toward intermarriage.

NASCIMENTO, JOÃO RAMOS DE. "Dondinho," the soccer
name of the father of Edson Arantes do Nascimento
(or Pelé). A star in his own right although of regional,
not national stature, Dondinho's career was cut short by
a knee ligament injury in 1942 while playing for Atlético
Mineiro, a leading Belo Horizonte club.

NASSAU, COUNT MAURICE OF (1604-1679). Dutch governor
of New Holland, the West India Company's Brazilian territory on the northeast coast including the captaincy of
Pernambuco. As governor-general and military governor
Nassau embarked on an ambitious plan to win cooperation
from local planters, build a port city at Recife, and improve coastal sugar agriculture. He is known for his
accomplishments in urban development and for his sense
of religious toleration. Affected by diminishing financial
support from Holland for his colony, he returned to Europe in 1644, paving the way for the Luso-Brazilian reconquest. As a Protestant, Nassau holds a peculiar position in Brazilian history: efforts in 1937 to celebrate
the anniversary of his arrival in 1637 were defeated by
right-wing groups in Recife for reason of his religion
and his service to a foreign enemy.

NATIONAL ANTHEM, BRAZILIAN see Guaraní, O

NATIONAL EDUCATIONAL ACT OF 1911 see CORREIA,
RIVADÁVIA

NATIONAL LIBERATION ALLIANCE (ANL) see ALIANÇA
NACIONAL LIBERTADORA

NATIONAL SECURITY LAW OF 1935. A law, directed prin-

cipally against the left (decreed in April, it forced the
ANL to close) but representing the first step in Vargas's
move to the right and leading, two years later, to the
Estado Novo.

NATIONAL TELEPHONE COMPANY. A subsidiary of International Telephone and Telegraph (ITT), one of the first
foreign-owned firms to be nationalized by the state of
Rio Grande do Sul, under its Governor, Lionel Brizola,
João Goulart's brother-in-law, in the early 1960's. ITT
was paid $400,000 for assets it valued at $8,000,000.
Loud protests from the United States led to federal action
which resulted in the purchase of ten additional subsid-
iaries for $135 million, a figure attacked as excessive
by nationalists.

"NEGO" ("I refuse"). The terse rejection by Paraíba governor João Pessoa of the Júlio Prestes candidacy in 1929
which led to his own choice as Vargas's vice-presidential
running mate on the Liberal Alliance slate. After Pessoa's assassination in 1930, the phrase "Nego" was incorporated into Paraíba's state flag.

NEGRÃO DE LIMA, FRANCISCO. Former ambassador, PSD
leader, and friend of Castelo Branco who won the governorship of Guanabara in the 1965 elections with 52 percent of the vote. Negrão de Lima represented the MBD,
defeating the ARENA candidate, and symbolizing the first
public rejection of the military government; as a result
army hard-liners, led by General Afonso Albuquerque
Lima, organized a plot to overthrow the government and
install a hard-line dictatorship, but it was thwarted.

NEGREIROS, ANTÔNIO VIDAL DE. One of the leaders of
the Luso-Brazilian resistance against the Dutch, decorated
by D. João IV after taking Recife's Fortaleza das Cinco
Pontas on January 27, 1654.

NEGRO DA TERRA. Literally, "a black person of the land,"
but in colonial days the term was applied to aborigines
as well.

NEGRO DE GANHO. During slavery, a bondsman who worked
at a trade or other gainful occupation and whose wages
were turned over to his master.

NEGROS BOÇAIS. "Raw" blacks, a term designating the

lowest Negroes on the social ladder, deemed fit only for
rough manual labor. Caio Prado holds this attitude--and
that toward the Amerindian as "apathetic"--as a cause
for the sluggishness of the colonial economy.

NEPOMUCENO, ALBERTO (1864-1920). Composer known for
his use of folkloric themes, à la Villa-Lobos.

NERI, ANA JUSTINA FERREIRA (1814-1880). One of Brazil's national heroines for her volunteer work during the
Paraguayan War as a nurse.

NEVES DA PONTURA, JOÃO (1887-1970). Riograndense
bacharel, journalist, legislative officeholder and member
of the Liberal Alliance, Ambassador to Portugal, Foreign
Minister, and elected member of the Academy of Letters,
more for his political weight than his literary merit.

NEW CHRISTIANS ("Cristãos Novos"). Persons forcibly converted to Christianity in Portugal after the edict of 1496
under King Manoel I. Owing to the threat of the Inquisition and the rigorous requirements of demonstrated piety,
many sought to emigrate to parts of the Portuguese Empire where enforcement might be more lax. Many of
the first agricultural settlers of Pernambuco and Bahia
were New Christians; their contacts with family members
in Amsterdam is given as one reason for the commercial
success of these captaincies. Fernando de Noronha,
holder of the first license to trade in brasilwood, may
also have been a Cristão Nôvo. See also MANOEL I.

NICOT, JEAN. French ambassador to Portugal who, according to tradition, introduced the tobacco plant into France
from Portugal, where it had been exported from Brazil,
and set the stage for the creation of European consumer
demand. From him, "nicotine" derived its name.

NIEMEYER, OSCAR (1907-). Leading architect whose
works in Belo Horizonte, Rio de Janeiro and especially
Brasília, have brought him worldwide acclaim. Born
in Laranjeiras (Rio), he studied at the Escola de Belas
Artes and won a position with planner/architect Lúcio
Costa by sheer persistence. He worked on the Le Corbusier plan for the revolutionary building for the Education
& Culture Ministry in Rio (1936). His structures in Brasília include the Planalto (executive office building), Al-
vorada (presidential residence), and the legislative building.

NINA RODRÍGUES, RAIMUNDO (1862-1906). Mulatto physician, born in Maranhão and graduated from the Bahian Medical School who, in 1891, won that institution's chair in legal medicine. In spite of his own origins, Nina Rodrígues was deeply influenced by European racial thinking, and his own courses and writings touching on genetics, ethnology, and social questions reflect an elitist (and somewhat racist) viewpoint.

NOBILITY, IMPERIAL. From Independence to the fall of the monarchy in 1889 the two Emperors granted a total of 1,278 titles to 980 men and women: 930 baronates, 248 viscountages; 50 titles of count; 47 of marquis, and 3 dukes (in ascending order of status). The concession of titles was the personal prerogative of the emperors; in theory, service to the Empire was the sole criterion for an award of nobility but in reality social and political considerations were important.

NÓBREGA, MANOEL DE (1517-15?). Leader of the first six Jesuits who arrived in Brazil in 1549 with Tomé de Sousa, and a critic of the behavior of the colonists, whom he considered insensitive to their new land. See also SOUSA, TOMÉ DE.

NOBREZA DO CAFÉ. The "coffee aristocracy" of the states of the Center South during the Old Republic.

"NOITE DAS GARRAFADOS." The "night of the bottles," March 13, 1831, when pitched street battles were fought in the capital of Minas Gerais over the visiting Emperor and his failure to abide by the constitution. The event widened the gulf between Brazilians and Portuguese and helped set the stage for abdication in April.

NORDESTINADOS see NORDESTINOS

NORDESTINO. Inhabitant of the northeastern region. In a play on words, local writers have coined the term "nordestinados," or "destined-northeasterners," to speak of the population of that region's troubled past and problematic future.

NORMAL SCHOOL see ESCOLA NORMAL

NORONHA E BRITO, MARCOS. The eighth Conde dos Arcos, and the last viceroy of Brazil, from 1806 to 1808. After

the arrival of the Crown, he retired to Bahia, where he
later distinguished himself as an official of the royal
government.

NORTH. Region stretching from the deep Amazon to the
border of the state of Maranhão, encompassing the states
of Amazonas, Pará, and Acre as well as the territories
of Rondônia, Roraíma, and Amapá. The North contains
42 percent of Brazil's land area and only 4 percent of
its population.

NORTHEAST. The region of greatest poverty, encompassing
the states of Bahia, Sergipe, Alagoas, Pernambuco,
Paraíba, Rio Grande do Norte, Ceará, Piauí, and Maranhão. Geographers have differed on the size and composi-
tion of the Northeast; historically, the Northeast has been
dominated by Pernambuco in the middle of the region and
Bahia in the south. See also DROUGHT POLYGON.

NOVA LUZ BRASILEIRA. Newspaper of the Exaltado faction
during the era of the Regency, published in Rio de Janeiro.

NUCLEAR ENERGY PACT. Signed between West Germany
and Brazil in 1977 over strenuous United States opposition, since Brazil has not signed the nuclear proliferation
treaty. West Germany will provide reactors, components
to service the reactors, and training for Brazilian personnel; by 1990 Brazil should produce 10,000 megawatts
of nuclear energy. The value of the pact was estimated
to run as high as 8 billion dollars. The pact will allow
Brazil to become a full-fledged nuclear power by the end
of the century; nuclear weapons as well as a delivery
system may be ready within a decade.

NZAMBI. Congolese Supreme Being, called Zumbi in Brazil.

-O-

OBALUWAIYE see OMOLU

OBRIGADOS. Sharecroppers, or copyholders, living on engenho land.

OBSERVADOR ECONÓMICO E FINANCEIRO. Rio de Janeiro-
based financial newspaper, published by Valentim F.

Bouças during the mid-1930's, and the source of useful information about economic conditions, the cost of living, and policy making under Vargas.

OCA.   Indian dwelling unit, made of bamboo, a horizontal structure with two or three separate entrances for family groups.

OCUPANTES.   Squatters, occupying land owned by absentees or in the public domain.

OFFENSIVA, A.   The Integralist weekly newspaper.   Its title is Portuguese for Der Angriff.

OGUN.   St. George, one of the orixás (the West African gods simultaneously identified with Catholic saints) in Umbando cultism.

OLARÍA.   A fazenda kiln, used to produce clay roofing tiles.

OLD REPUBLIC.   The years from 1889 to 1930, when the Old, or First, Republic was overthrown in the 1930 Revolution.

OLHO DE BOI.   Literally, "bull's eye," the designation for the first series of Brazilian postage stamps, issued in 1843, the second set of regularly-issued adhesive stamps in the world.   In three denominations, 30, 60, and 90 réis, the stamps show an oval design not unlike that of a bull's eye target.

OLIVEIRA, EDUARDO DE.   Paulista poet and writer of prose fiction whose themes, especially after 1960, reflected more and more the frustrations of Afro-Brazilians economically and culturally dependent upon a white society. Typical of this is his short story collection, O Carro do éxito.

OLIVEIRA LIMA, MANUEL DE (1867-1928).   Leading historian and diplomat whose career spanned assignments in Lisbon, Tokyo, Venezuela, Brussels, and Washington.   There, on his retirement, he lectured at various local universities on Brazilian history, and, on his death, donated his library of more than 40,000 volumes to the Catholic University.   Considered to have written the best histories of nineteenth-century Brazil, Oliveira Lima himself lived as an expatriate, rarely returning to Brazil in his later life.

OLIVEIRA VIANNA, F. J. DE (1885-1951). Historian of
conservative bent; popularizer of the view, later challenged,
that the bandeirantes' lives reflected aristocratic culture
and that the Paulistas were relatively wealthy. See also
ALCÁNTARA MACHADO, JOSE DE.

OMNIÓGRAPHO. Brazil's first cinema, on Rio de Janeiro's
Rua do Ouvidor, established in 1896 by the Lumière
brothers.

OMOUL. The goddess of contagious diseases, whose face
in spiritist representations is usually covered by a shawl
to hide smallpox. Other names for the same figure are
Obaluwaiye and Shapana.

ONDULAÇÕES ("Waves"). Joaquim Nabuco's term for Brazilian revolutionary movements of the nineteenth century,
which he saw as weak echoes of events in Europe.

OPERATION BANDEIRANTES. Established in São Paulo in
1969 as a pilot project to coordinate military and police
efforts to combat terrorist activities. Known as OBAN,
the new agency included representatives from the Army,
Air Force, and Navy intelligence sections; local state,
and federal police organizations. During late 1969 and
1970 the OB concept was extended in the form of Centros
do Operações de Defesa Interna (CODI). These "public
safety" programs drew upon United States equipment and
training facilities, and were alleged, in the early 1970's,
to be centers of ill-treatment and torture of political
prisoners. The United States' role was investigated during Senate hearings in 1971 held by the Committee on
Foreign Relations.

OPERATION CENTRAL PARK. Alleged maneuver through
which Brazilian buyers, in order to keep the price of
coffee high in 1976 and 1977, purchased more than 122,000
excess bags of coffee from El Salvador on the New York
Coffee and Sugar Exchange, then shipped it to Brazil for
eventual resale in the United States. In Dec. 1977, the
United States government began to investigate the practices of Interbras, the Brazilian coffee trading agency,
as well as Coscafe, an affiliate of Anderson, Clayton, a
major United States commodity firm and investor in Brazil. "Operation Central Park" got its name because it
was fashioned at a series of meetings in hotels in mid-
town Manhatten, and the Plaza.

OPERATION LYSISTRATA.   Tongue-in-cheek call by Deputy
Márcio Moreira Alves in 1968 for military men to be
boycotted by their wives and lovers until they renounced
the use of violence against citizens, which led to his expulsion from Brazil (and contributed to the confrontation
which resulted in the closing of the Congress).

OQUENDO, ANTÔNIO DE.   Portuguese naval commander
whose victory over the Dutch fleet under Adriaan Pater
in 1631 checked the Dutch drive south from Pernambuco.
See BATTLE OF ABROLHOS.

ORDENANÇAS.   Militia troops of the colonial period drawn
from the general population, men between 18 and 60 years
of age and who could not claim exemptions.   The ordenanças were not given serious military duties and were
limited to occasional parades, although in times of crisis
in theory they would serve as a sort of ready reserve.

OSORIO, GENERAL MANUEL LUIS (1808-1879).   Military
hero of the Paraguayan War, rewarded with a triple
title of nobility: Baron, Viscount, and Marquis of Erval.
At the time of his death he held the post of Minister of
War.

OSWALDO CRUZ INSTITUTE.   Brazil's major medical research institute, named in 1907 after public health pio-
neer Oswaldo Cruz, and the first of its kind in Brazil
to carry out an ambitious program of research.   Under
Cruz's direction, the institute turned out a generation
of Brazilian medical researchers and technicians, all of
whom formerly had been foreign-educated.   See also
CRUZ, OSWALDO; MANGUINHOS.

OTHON PALACE.   Leading São Paulo hotel, and the center
of controversy in the early 1950's when on two occasions
it refused to admit visiting American entertainers Kath-
erine Dunham, a dancer, and Marian Anderson, the
singer.   Two deputies, Gilberto Freyre and Afonso
Arinos, introduced a bill in the legislature prohibiting
discrimination on the basis of race in response to the
incidents.   For its part, the hotel management blamed
the fact that its American guests would not feel comfor-
table with Anderson or Dunham, and pointed to racial
segregation policies in the United States.

OTTONI, CHRISTIANO.   One of the first authors during the

mid-Empire to write of the consequences of slavery on
Brazilian life, warning that if the system were not re-
formed or eliminated it would lead to civil or race war.
He became a leading abolitionist senator; his 1908 auto-
biography details the history of the anti-slavery campaign.

OURO PRETO.   New name given to the town of Vila Rica
during the gold rush, which transformed the Minas region, in the words of Robert Southey, into "the richest
place in the world, if gold alone were riches." At its
height, Ouro Preto may have had a population of 100,000.
After the eighteenth century the population declined; today
its major activity is tourism, with the town turned into a
Baroque museum.   Ouro Preto is now a national monument.

OURO PRETO SCHOOL OF MINES.   Founded in 1876 under
the sponsorship of the Emperor, part of the overall reform of education during the 1870's separating scientific
from military education.   See also POLYTECHNIC SCHOOL.

OUVIDOR.   Crown judge.   See also RUA D'OUVIDOR.

OUVIDOR-GERAL.   Chief Justice of the colonial-era Crown
captaincies.

-P-

PACHECO PEREIRA, DUARTE.   Claimed by some to have
discovered Brazil in 1498 on a voyage financed by the
Portuguese Crown.   There is little evidence if any to
substantiate the assertion.

PADILHA, RAYMUNDO.   Leading Integralist official and
chief of the AIB in Rio de Janeiro state.   In the 1960's
and 1970's Padilha resurfaced as a prominent member
of ARENA, the pro-government political party.

PADRE-CORONEL.   A figure described by Pang and others,
a priest-local boss, some of whom, during the Old Republic, rode careers to the state or federal legislatures,
or to the governorship.   The influence of such men tended
to counter the competing lure of messianistic movements,
since they politicized their followers and kept them within
the established system.

PADROADO.   Spiritual jurisdiction of the Portuguese state
following from colonial-era precedent.

PAGADOR DE PROMESSAS.   A film by Alfredo Dias Gomes
    which won three national awards in 1960 and the Palme
    d'Or in Cannes in 1962, depicting the story of a humble
    Bahian Catholic believer who attempts to repay a "pro-
    messa," or vow.   The film speaks to the impossibility
    of communication between the hero and the aggrandizing
    elements of the city, whose personages--priests, jour-
    nalists, politicians, merchants--are seen as twisted by
    material and bourgeois values.

PAGELANÇA.   A syncretistic cult prevalent among blacks in
    the Amazon, fusing elements of African religion and
    Amerindian spiritism.   The African gods were brought
    to the region by escaped black slaves.   Bastide considers
    the cult to represent coexistence as much as fusion, a
    conscious desire to join the most powerful elements of
    two religious traditions.

PAI-DE-SANTO.   A cult leader; the "father" of a candomblé
    or macumba ritual group.   Women who perform the same
    role are called "maê-de-santo."

"PAI DO POVO, O."   Affectionate name--"the father of the
    poor"--given to Getúlio Vargas by his admirers.   Others,
    of course, considered his paternalistic image to be dema-
    gogic, the product of carefully planned public relations
    efforts.

PAIS LEME, PEDRO TAQUES DE ALMEIDA.   Paulista (1714-
    1777) and descendant of bandeirantes whose Paulista Pe-
    erage helped create the bandeirante legend and who por-
    trayed them as heroic and aristocratized frontiersmen.

PAJÉ.   Tribal medicine man, or healer.

PALACETES.   The palatial homes built by newly affluent
    city dwellers, often planters lured to the coast by the
    surge of cosmopolitanism in the late nineteenth century;
    in São Paulo they lined the aristocratic Avenida Paulista;
    in Rio de Janeiro the districts of Laranjeiras, Cosme
    Velho, and Flamengo.

PALÁCIO BOA VISTA.   Constructed along Recife's Capibaribe
    River by Maurice of Nassau, along with a 318 meter-
    long bridge linking the Island of Antônio Vaz to the main-
    land.   Its Dutch name was Schoonzigt.

PALÁCIO FRIBURGO.   Called Vrijburg by the Dutch, Friburg

Palace was built by Maurice of Nassau on the shores of
the Beberibe River, to be his official residence. The
Boa Vista Palace was his headquarters for private enter-
tainment and relaxation.

PALMAS. Disputed territory in southern Brazil, lying between the Peperi-Guaçu and Chapecó rivers, and claimed
by Argentina. Its urban center, Palmas, is about 400
kilometers west of Blumenau, Santa Catarina.

PALMATÓRIA. Punishment for unruly or disobedient soldiers,
in which the victim was lashed to stakes on the ground
before their tents and beaten brutally on the hands and
feet. The practice caused mutinies, especially during
the early Old Republic, but was defended by officers as
the only way to deal with the dregs of society who comprised the enlisted ranks.

PALUDISMO. Malaria, a major cause of death in the Amazon
region until World War II.

PAMPLONA, DAVID. Merchant, accused by Portuguese officials of being the author of "Um Brasileiro Resoluto"
(A Resolute Brazilian), an anonymous pamphlet circulating
in Rio de Janeiro in late 1823 attacking the military for
pro-Portuguese sentiment. He was severely beaten by
officers of the Army; as a result, his case was taken to
the Assembly, where the representatives protested. When
Pedro sided with the military, Antônio Carlos proposed
that the Assembly meet in permanent session, to establish
its authority. Pedro responded by closing it, sending
troops to enforce his edict. Antônio Carlos, José Bonifácio, and others were arrested and imprisoned.

PAMPULHA. Modern church in the Pampulha district outside of Belo Horizonte, designed by Oscar Niemeyer and
decorated with murals by Portinari. The church is so
striking that for years it was not consecrated by the
Catholic Church; in recent years it has begun to run down.

PANELINHA. "Little pot," an informal horizontal network
of mutual assistance. During the Old Republic, coronéis
often constructed panelinhas by sending one son to law
school, by making another study accounting, or enter the
bureaucracy, and by marrying his offspring into similarly
useful circumstances.

PAPA-FIGO. In folklore, a goblin who eats the livers of
small children.

PAPA-ROBALOS, ANTÔNIO DIAS. A Dutch Jew who visited
Brazil in the early 1500's and who led the invading Dutch
troops in 1630. After three days of siege he took the
capital of Pernambuco, Olinda, on February 16, 1630.

PARÁ. Brazil's second largest state, totaling 1,248,000
square kilometers, with a population in 1970 of two million. Its two major cities are Belém, at the mouth of
the Amazon, and Santarém, 800 kilometers up river in
the direction of Manaos. In colonial times, Pará was
known as Grão-Pará.

"PARA INGLÊS VER." Colloquialism meaning, "for English
eyes." Refers to acts, presumably political or legal,
promulgated with the intention of satisfying critics. An
example would be the Brazilian pledge to terminate the
slave trade as part of the Brazilian-Portuguese negotiations after independence, arbitrated by Lord Canning.

PARAGUAÇU. Indian folk-heroine who is known, rather in-
accurately, as "the Indian woman who conquered the
[Portuguese] conquerors" in Brazilian popular history.
See FREYRE, GILBERTO.

PARAGUAYAN WAR. Also known as the War of the Triple
Alliance, the fray (1865-70) pitted Paraguay against the
combined forces of Argentina, Uruguay, and Brazil. As
Brazil's first major war, it afforded the armed forces
a chance to demonstrate their prowess, leading to military frustration in peacetime after the Paraguayan defeat.
The war made the Brazilian commander, Caxias, a national hero. It cost Brazil a quarter of a billion dollars
and 50,000 dead, many from cholera.

PARAÍBA. Northeastern state located between Rio Grande do
Norte and Pernambuco, and dominated by the latter although its own leading city--Campina Grande, the largest
and most important urban center in the northeastern
agreste--itself dominates commerce in its region. The
capital João Pessoa, was renamed after the assassination
of its governor (and Paraíba's vice-presidential candidate
in 1930); formerly its name was Parahyba do Norte.

PARAÍBA VALLEY. Region lying between Rio de Janeiro
and Minas Gerais, drained by the Paraíba River, and the
center of coffee cultivation in the nineteenth century before
the opening of new lands to the south, in São Paulo. The

clay loam and sandy loam soils of the valley allowed
coffee groves to flourish, but only for a number of years
after which the soil began to lose its fertility due to
leaching its native organic material and the failure of
planters to replenish its nutrients.

PARANÁ. State bordered by São Paulo on the north; Santa
Catarina to the south; Mato Grosso and Paraguay to the
west, enjoying pleasant, temperate climate and an abun-
dance of good soil and fresh water. A comarca (judicial
district) of São Paulo during the colonial period, it was
settled by cattle ranchers; in the mid-nineteenth century,
and after, coffee cultivation began to penetrate from the
São Paulo coffee region. St. Hilaire called Paraná "Brazil's Paradise on Earth." Its capital is Curitiba.

PARANÁ BASIN. Formed by the Paraná River and its tributaries, the basin occupies 891,309 square kilometers,
making it the second in breadth only to the Amazon basin.
Within the Paraná system are found four major water-
falls with hydroelectric potential or utility--Dourada,
Santo André, Sete Quedas, and Urubupungá.

PARANAPUÁ. The present-day Ilha do Governador, in Guanabara Bay. The island was the site of one of the decisive battles between the French and Portuguese in 1567,
which led to the expulsion of the former from the region.

PARDO. Term used for a mulatto. See MORENO.

PARNASSIANISM. School of poetry imported from France in
the 1860's, the counterpart of the Naturalist movement
in literature, and championed by Olavo Bilac (1865-1918)
and Alberto de Oliveira (1857-1937).

PARTIDO COMUNISTA BRASILEIRO (PCB). Organized in
the aftermath of the Russian Revolution, and enjoying
legal status only for the brief period between 1945 and
1947, the PCB was led by former anarchosyndicalists,
later by intellectual Marxists who never succeeded in
constructing a mass base of support. From 1935 on,
its head was Luis Carlos Prestes, the tenente hero who
had been converted in Argentinian exile.

PARTIDO COMUNISTA DO BRASIL (PB do B). Peking-line
Communist faction, a breakaway in 1962 from Prestes's
PCB, and immediately suppressed after the 1964 Revolu-
tion.

PARTIDO DA MOCIDADE. The "Youth Party" of São Paulo,
an inpromptu group which offered Luís Carlos Prestes's
name as candidate for state deputy in 1927, the year of
the Column's exile, since "at the moment Prestes repres-
ents all (of our) national aspirations. "

PARTIDO DEMOCRÁTICO (Pernambuco). Founded as an opposition party to the incumbent machine led by Governor
Estácio Coimbra. Its chieftain, Carlos de Lima Cavalcanti, was an usineiro and the editor-in-chief of two
opposition newspapers, Diario da Manhã and Diario da
Noite. In 1930 the PD backed the Liberal Alliance Revolution; as a result Lima Cavalcanti was named Interventor
by Vargas after his victory.

PARTIDO DEMOCRÁTICO (Rio Grande do Sul) see ALIANÇA
LIBERTADORA

PARTIDO DEMOCRÁTICO (São Paulo). Opposition party
founded in 1926. A year later it joined with the Rio
Grande do Sul Libertadores to form the Partido Democrático Nacional.

PARTIDO DEMOCRÁTICO NACIONAL. Established in 1927
as a coalition of state opposition parties. See PARTIDO
DEMOCRÁTICO (São Paulo and Pernambuco); ALIANÇA
LIBERTADORA.

PARTIDO FEDERALISTA (Rio Grande do Sul). Opposition
party founded by Gaspar Silveira Martins in 1892 as
the successor to the old Liberal Party of the Empire.

PARTIDO NACIONAL SINDICALISTA. A pre-Integralist party
organized by Mineiro journalist Olbiano de Melo, later
an Integralist leader, and dedicated to the establishment
of a fascist state in Brazil along the lines of Mussolini's
Italy. Like Severino Sombra, de Melo rejected the 1930
Revolution as not genuinely revolutionary. Members
were to dress in prescribed uniforms and swear loyalty
to "Family, Country, and God. " The movement was
swallowed up by the national AIB after 1932.

PARTIDO REPUBLICANO CONSERVADOR. The PRC, or
Conservative Republican Party, a loose coalition of state
parties backing President Hermes da Fonseca, led by
Gaúcho party chieftain José Gomes Pinheiro Machado
until his assassination in 1915. The PRC died soon after.

PARTIDO REPUBLICANO FEDERAL (PRF). An alliance of state parties pledged to support Paulista Prudente de Morais for the presidency in 1897, though they destroyed him once he took office. Its organizer was fellow Paulista Francisco Glicério Cerqueira Leite.

PARTIDO REPUBLICANO FEDERAL DO RIO GRANDE DO NORTE. The oligarchic party of the state which, in 1926, voted to give the vote to women, although this was illegal under the federal constitution. Its leader was José Augusto Bezerra de Medeiros.

PARTIDO REPUBLICANO FEMININO. A brief-lived nationalist group of women, founded after the establishment of the Indian Protective Association in 1910, who dressed in Amerindian costume and worked for the adoption of Tupí as the official language of Brazil.

PARTIDO REPUBLICANO MINEIRO (PRM). The establishment state party which dominated Mineiro politics during the Old Republic, normally in alliance with São Paulo's PRP and the Gaúcho PRR.

PARTIDO REPUBLICANO PAULISTA (PRP). The dominant state party in São Paulo during the Old Republic.

PARTIDO REPUBLICANO RIOGRANDENSE (PRR). Of Rio Grande do Sul, it was the establishment party during the Old Republic, and the political home of some of the most powerful figures of the political arena: Júlio de Castilhos, Borges de Medeiros, Pinheiro Machado, and Getúlio Vargas.

PARTIDO SOCIAL DEMOCRÁTICO (PSD). Founded by followers of Vargas in 1945 uncomfortable with the more left-leaning Labor Party, the PTB, the PSD was the party of Juscelino Kubitschek; it drew its electoral strength from the countryside and from small towns.

PATER, ADRIAAN JANSZOON. Dutch naval commander sent to reinforce Dutch holdings there and to threaten the fleet of silver ships from Peru. Arriving at Bahia in July 1631, Pater's ships were engaged by Portuguese naval forces under D. Antônio de Oquendo, and were defeated at the Battle of Abrolhos, on September 12th. After this event, the Dutch restricted their efforts to the Northeast.

PATRÃO.   Patron, or boss.   According to anthropologists,
"a paternalistic figure in an asymmetrical but persona-
listic dyadic relationship, especially in rural areas"
(David Epstein).

PATROCINIO, JOSÉ DO.   Editor and fervent abolitionist,
whose Gazeta da Tarde served as the major journal of
the anti-slavery movement.

PAU-DE-ARARA ("Parrot perch").   1) A truck converted for
passenger transportation, used to ship migrants to the
south from the impoverished rural northeast.
   2) A widely-used form of torture used by Brazilian
police and military officials, in which the victim is sus-
pended from a pole and suffers electric shocks to the
most sensitive parts of his or her body.

PAULISTA.   Resident or inhabitant of the state of São Paulo,
and (historical) descendant of the first settlers of São
Vicente, the caboclo bandeirantes.   The Paulista is considered (by cariocas and others) to be energetic, business-
like, humorless, drab--to the point of working too hard
and being too serious.   For their part, Paulistas consider cariocas frivolous and given to excessive revelry.
See also CARIOCA; GAÚCHO.

PAULISTA PEERAGE   see   PAIS LEME, PEDRO TAQUES
   DE ALMEIDA

PAULO AFONSO.   Major hydro-electric plant in the northern
part of the state of Bahia.

PEASANT LEAGUES.   Established in the mid- and late-1950's
in the rural northeast by lawyer and state deputy Francisco Julião, who took up the cause as defender of the
rights of peasant renters who seized agricultural lands
to protest high rent charged by absentee landlords.   The
Leagues were particularly successful in the agreste,
where farmers were better able to organize than in the
more poverty-striken zona da mata and in the sparsely
inhabited sertão.   In 1964, then the military took power,
the Leagues were dismantled and Julião stripped of his
political rights; he sought exile in Mexico.

PEÇANHA, NILO (1867-1924).   Elected Vice President on
Afonso Pena's ticket in 1906 and elevated to the presidency on Pena's death in 1909.   During the rest of his

career Peçanha held various posts, including the governorship of his state of Rio de Janeiro, and in 1921 ran
for the presidency again at the head of the so-called
Reação Republicana, against Artur Bernardes, but lost.

PÉ-DE-CHUMBO ("Leadfoot").   An expression applied to
Portuguese immigrants, often tradesmen, in the early
eighteenth century.   See also MASCATES.

PÉ-DE-MOLEQUE.   A cake made of fermented manioc meal.
Literally, "black boy's foot."

PEDRO I (1798-1834).   The son of monarchs married as
children (1785), Pedro was brought up in Brazil, but by
Portuguese tutors and advisors.   Once he became monarch,
in 1821, only his support for Brazilian independence
earned him any popularity.   His suspension of civil rights
to crush the 1824 Pernambucan revolution won him the
enmity of liberals, and, as Stein notes, his constant
meddling in Portuguese domestic affairs and his repeated
violations of his own constitution forced many to doubt
his allegiance to constitutional monarchy.   In 1831 he
finally abdicated, and returned to Portugal, leaving his
five-year-old son, Pedro, as a kind of hostage for the
dynasty.

PEDRO II (1825-1891).   From his first days as Emperor in
1840 to his abdication at the monarchy's end in 1889, the
symbol of Imperial Brazil.   Pedro, a bourgeois soul
dedicated to a life of the intellect, nonetheless presided
over a system dominated by slaveholders and governed
by a small privileged elite.   Biographers have treated
Pedro kindly, a product of his times.   Later writings
have attacked the emperor as weak, tradition-bound, and
bureaucratic, a man whose very incapacity made the
republic inevitable.

"PEDRO PEDREIRO" ("Pedro the bricklayer").   A popular
song by Chico Buarque de Holanda in the late 1960's:

> "Pedro Pedreiro awaits the Carnival,
> And for a stroke of luck with a lottery ticket...
> Waiting, waiting, waiting,
> Hoping for the sun,
> Waiting for the train,...
> Hoping for luck,
> And his wife expects a baby who also will be
>   born to wait...."

PEDRO I.   Makeshift prison ship, used to hold captured leaders and soldiers of the 1935 ANL-PCB uprising at Rio's Praia Vermelha.   The ship was anchored in Guanabara Bay.

PÉ-DURO.   Name given to a native breed of Amazonian cattle, meaning "hard-foot." The term refers to the resistance of its hoofs to constant immersion in wet and swampy soil.

PEIXOTO, AFRÂNIO (1876-1947).   Novelist, literary critic, and author of scholarly studies of Camões and Castro Alves, his favorite poets.   As an educator, Peixoto wrote a number of influential works, including Ensinar a ensinar (1923): (Teaching to Teach).

PELÉ see NASCIMENTO, EDSON ARANTES DE

PELEGOS.   Union leaders considered government puppets. The term gained currency during the Vargas presidency. Literally, a pelego is a sheepskin horse blanket, worn to cushion the weight of the rider for the horse.

PELOURO ELECTION.   During colonial days, the names of citizens deemed fit to serve in local offices had their names rolled into small wax balls (pelouros), which were drawn out of a chest by lot, usually during the "first week of Christmas" (December 8th).   The remaining pelouros were kept in the chest and the procedure repeated three years in a row, at which time new names were added.   When a vacancy occurred through death or from any other reason, councilors chose a substitute themselves; this impromptu method was known as eleição de barrete (election by cap).

PENA, AFONSO (1847-1909).   President of Brazil from 1907 to 1909, when he died in office.   A Mineiro, Pena followed a career in state politics; as governor he issued the law which moved the state capital from Ouro Prêto to Curral del Rei, the site of the newly constructed planned city of Belo Horizonte.

PENTEADO, AMADEU AMARAL LEITE (1875-1929).   Leading nineteenth-century journalist; editor-in-chief of the Estado de São Paulo, and a poet of note as well.

PEÕES.   Ranchhands of southern Brazil, the name presumably taken from the Spanish "peónes."

PEREIRA, ASTROJILDO. One of the original founders of the
Brazilian Communist Party, a newspaperman and intellectual. In the 1950's Pereira was expelled from the
party for not following the party line. He was the editor
of the party's clandestine newspaper, A Classe Operária,
from 1925 through the mid-1930's.

PEREIRA, LUÍS BARROSO see IMPERATRIZ

PEREIRA, VITORINO. Vice-president of the Republic from
1894 to 1898, and acting President for several months
after November 1896 when Prudente de Morais fell ill.
Following divergent policies from his predecessor, Pereira
provoked a split in the administration when Prudente
came back to office.

PEREIRA BARETO, LUÍS. Positivist philospher and journalist for the Província de São Paulo who opposed abolition
because he held blacks to be inferior; therefore, he argued, liberating them would risk insurrection and bring
a conservative reaction that would make the condition of
the former slaves even worse.

PEREIRA DA COSTA, FRANCISCO AUGUSTO. Author of
Folclore Pernambucano (1908), a major compendium of
tales, poems, and legends from the northeastern state
of Pernambuco. The work accompanied a generally rising interest in folk customs throughout the country at
that time. See also MELO MORAES FILHO, ALEXANDRE
JOSÉ DE.

PEREIRA DE QUEIROZ, CARLOTA. Feminist leader during
the late 1930's, who, with Bertha Lutz (q. v.), worked
for legislation in favor of women's rights. The two,
however, disagreed substantially over the desirability of
a National Woman's Agency, a social services department,
which Pereira de Queiroz worked for as Congresswoman
from the state of São Paulo.

PERES, LUCÍLIA. The greatest Brazilian actress of the turn
of the century, playing the south and the rubber capital
at Manaos to adulating audiences. Her most famous role
was in The Lady of the Camelias.

PERNAMBUCAN REVOLT OF 1817. A republican and abolitionist revolt rooted in the examples of the American
and French Revolutions, and favoring freedom of the press
and religious toleration.

PERNAMBUCAN REVOLT OF 1824   see   CONFEDERAÇÃO
DO EQUADOR

PERNAMBUCO.   The principal economic and commercial center of the Northeast and the center of a Satellite Bloc of
neighboring states (Paraíba, Rio Grande do Norte, Alagoas, and Ceará) drawn to its economic orbit.   Formerly
the most prosperous agricultural center of the colonial
era owing to its extensive sugar plantations, Pernambuco
declined as its sugar became uncompetitive on the world
market and the focus of Brazilian economic activity moved
south.   It played a major role during the Empire in terms
of providing members to the national elite, but its rebel-
liousness--leading to insurrections in 1817, 1821, 1824
and 1848--and isolated location led to its political decline
after the fall of the monarchy in 1889.   Its capital, Recife, remains a commercial and transportation hub; it
is a living museum as well as way-station for hundreds
of thousands of impoverished rural poor from the interior,
many of whom bypass the state entirely en route to hoped-
for employment in the industrialized south.

PERULEIROS.   Portuguese adventurers who entered Paraguay
on route to Peru and Potosí in search of mineral wealth.

PESSEDISTAS.   Followers of the Partido Social Democratico
(PSD), a national party from 1945 to 1964.

PESSOA, EPITÁCIO DA SILVA (1865-1942).   President of
Brazil from 1919 to 1922.   Pessoa, the only elected head
of state in modern times from the Northeast was from
the town of Umbuzeiro, in Paraíba; as a youth he studied
in Recife, followed the typical career pattern for entrance
into the regional political elite, and then decided to break
the pattern by going to Rio de Janeiro, where he arrived
two days before the proclamation of the Republic.   He
then was named secretary-general of Paraíba's new government and proceeded to hold several high level state
and national posts, including Justice Minister in the Campos Sales administration.   The head of the Brazilian delegation to Versailles, he was chosen by the "big state"
machines to take over the presidency after the death of
Rodrigues Alves, as a compromise which ultimately led
to the presidencies of Artur Bernardes of Minas and
Washington Luis of São Paulo.   As president he allocated
the largest proportion of federal revenue in history for
public works assistance to the drought-ridden northeastern

states, but most of his programs were cancelled after he left office.   His nephew, João Pessoa, became the Liberal Alliance candidate for Vice President in 1930; his assassination in Recife was one of the sparks which set off the 1930 Revolution.

PESSOA, JOÃO (1878-1930).   Nephew of Paraíba state boss (and President of the Republic) Epitácio Pessoa; governor of the state from 1928 to 1930.   Pessoa was chosen the vice-presidential candidate on the Liberal Alliance slate to run with Getúlio Vargas.   Following the election, a defeat for the insurgents, Pessôa was assassinated on the streets of Recife by João Dantas, for a combination of political and personal reasons.   The murder helped set off the military rebellion which culminated in the Liberal Alliance coup and Vargas's presidency.   Paraíba's capital, Paraíba do Norte, was renamed after the fallen governor by the state legislature.

PESSÔA, PANTALEÃO DA SILVA.   Army General, chief of Vargas's Casa Militar from 1934 to 1938, and an open supporter of the fascist Integralist Party and its link to the president.

PESSOA DE SANGUE INFECTA ("A person of infected blood"). A term used during the colonial period to connote Jews converted to Christianity and non-whites.

PETROBRÁS.   The state petroleum monopoly ("petro," for petroleum + "brás," for Brazil) established by President Vargas in 1953, and responsible for all petroleum policy, including contracts to foreign multinationals in the energy area.   Petrobrás, in recent years, has invested in exploration ventures in other countries, including Ecuador and Nigeria.

"PETRÓLEO É NOSSO, O".   Nationalistic slogan--"The Oil Is Ours!"--whose dissemination preceded the creation in 1953 of Petrobrás (q. v.), the state petroleum monopoly, as part of the publicity campaign designed to raise public awareness of the issue.

PETROPOLIS.   The summer residence of the royal family, in the low mountains surrounding Rio de Janeiro, first linked to the capital by telegraph in 1857.

PIAUÍ.   One of Brazil's poorest states, located on the North-

Northeastern coast between Ceará and Maranhão.   Its
capital is Terezinha.

PICANÇO, JOSÉ CORREIA.   Brazilian-born personal physician
  to the Prince Regent (D. João), trained at Coimbra, and
  the most effective arguer after the arrival of the Court
  in 1808 for the establishment of medical and surgical
  courses in Brazil.

PICO DA BANDEIRA.   Brazil's highest peak, more than
  3,000 meters (9,482 feet) in altitude, on the border between Minas Gerais and Espírito Santo.

PIGNATARI, FRANCISCO "BABY" (1917-1977).   Famous Brazilian playboy, crowned by Life magazine in 1959 as the
  "king of the international set," and grandson of Count
  Francisco Matarazzo.   Heir to vast industrial wealth,
  Pignatari pursued a life of hob-nobbing with European
  royalty.   One of his wives was Princess Ira von Fursten-
  berg.

PIN E ALMEIDA, MIGUEL CALMON DE   see   ABRANTES,
  MARQUES DE

PINHEIRO MACHADO, JOSÉ GOMES (1851-1915).   Leading
  gaúcho politician and power broker during the Old Republic.   As a student, he fought as a volunteer in the
  Paraguayan war; later, as a lawyer, he founded the Partido Republicano Rio-Grandense, in 1879.   A protégé
  of Júlio de Castilhos, he fought in the state's federalist
  revolt and gained renown for his victory over troops
  commanded by Gumercindo Saraiva.   After the revolution's defeat he returned to political life, coming to dom-
  inate the federal senate.   From 1900 until his death he
  held as much power as the chief executive, or more.
  In September 1915 he was assassinated by Manso de
  Paiva, called euphemistically in Brazilian texts a "man
  of the people" (homem do povo).

PINTO DE MAGALHÃES, FRANCISCO.   A Goiás trader who,
  in 1810, built a settlement on the right bank of the Tocantins River, which had been opened to navigation by
  the end of the previous century.   The town of Carolina
  evolved from the initial settlement-trading post.

PIRANHA.   River fish of the Caracinidae family, known for
  its razor-sharp teeth and voracious appetite.   Piranhas,

properly stuffed and mounted, are sold to tourists along with butterfly trays and carved figas.

PIRATINI. The governor's palace in Pôrto Allgre, Rio Grande do Sul.

PISO, WILHELM see MARCGRAFF, GEORGE

PIUMES. Minute gnats common to the upper Amazon, whose sting produces blood blisters. The piumes are the scourge of mining camps, leaving the exposed skin of workers covered with blisters and sores; some of them, along with ticks, carry typhus.

PLANTATION ORCHESTRAS. By the mid-nineteenth century, some of these were polished and professional, although composed entirely by slaves. Fletcher and Kidder described one such orchestra in Minas Gerais during the 1850's, an all-black fifteen piece orchestra with violins, flutes, trombones, bugles, an organ, and a choir of young slave boys. They performed an operatic overture, a Latin Mass, and, at the request of the guests, a Sabat Mater. Advertisements for slaves often described their musical abilities, which made them more valuable.

PLATIBANDA. Raising the façade of a house, usually colonial in style, so that the roof tiles become invisible from the street. This, Harris notes, is taken as an admired sign of modernity, a fact which others lament.

PODEROSOS DO SERTÃO. Literally, "lords of the backlands," the name given to the ranchers and landlords of the interior during the colonial period.

POLÍGONO DAS SÊCAS. The drought polygon, designated by law to include those portions of eight northern and northeastern states (Maranhão, Piauí, Ceará, Pernambuco, Rio Grande do Norte, Sergipe, Alagoas, and Bahia; Minas Gerais sometimes has been included as well). The area has received millions of dollars in federal and foreign aid designed to permit residents to cope with local conditions. See also DROUGHT.

POLÍTICA DOS GOVERNADORES. The so-called "politics of the governors" of the Old Republic, instituted as an unwritten alliance between the President of the Republic, his backers, and the leading state political machines.

Love defines the "política dos governadores" more broad-
ly, calling it "the policy of establishment groups at all
levels of government to maintain each other in power indefinitely."

POLITICAL DIVISIONS. In 1978 Brazil comprised 21 states,
4 territories (Rondônia, formerly Guaporé; Roraima,
formerly Rio Branco; Amapá; and the island of Fernando
de Noronha), and the Federal District of Brasília.

POLITICS OF THE GOVERNORS see POLÍTICA DOS GOV-
ERNADORES

POLYTECHNIC SCHOOL. Opened in Rio in 1876 as the first
civilian school of engineering. A second polytechnic institute was begun in São Paulo in 1893, and another briefly operated in Recife although without offering the civil
engineer's degree.

POMBAL, MARQÛES DE (1712-1782). Sebastião José Carvalho e Melo Pombal was Portugal's War and Foreign
Affairs Minister during the reign of José I, and virtual
dictator of Portugal and its colonies from 1750 to 1777.
Pombal was a reformer and modernizer who sought to
streamline administration in order to reap greater profits
for the metropolis and to make Portugal a power to be
reckoned with in Europe. His economic reforms, and
changing economic conditions in Brazil and in the Atlantic
world, brought a favorable balance to Anglo-Portuguese
trade in the 1770's. His decline and removal in 1777
and the removal of his policies led to a renewed mer-
cantilism on the part of Portugal and, in consequence,
to strains between Portugal and the Brazilian elite which
eventually heightened feelings for independence.
    Pombal ordered the Holy Office to end its distinction
between Old and New Christians, and pressed a forceful
campaign against the Jesuits, whom he considered an
obstacle to Portuguese progress; they were finally expelled from Brazil in 1759, a circumstance which had
the effect of destroying Brazil's modest educational system. For contrasting views of Pombal's impact, see
Alden and Maxwell.

POMBEIRO. Owner of several fishing rafts, or jangadas,
who rents them out, receiving in return a portion of the
catch and the first option to purchase the remainder,
usually at a price lower than the current selling price.

Pombeiros are frequently the moneylenders in fishing communities, and loan cash to fishermen who want to buy their own jangades.

POMPEIA, RAUL (1863-1895). Rio de Janeiro state-born literary figure, somewhat tormented in his writing, and a passionate abolitionist. His Ateneu is particularly interesting for its autobiographical dimension.

POPULAR HUMOR. Brazilians display a cynical and often sacrilegious sense of humor about their own society, and especially about national politics. This humor is self-effacing, and helps soften the strident nationalism which is heard at the official level. Baron Rio Branco, for example, wrote that "The only organized things in Brazil are Carnaval and the general disorder." Pithy, uninhibited jokes make the rounds about virtually every political figure, especially the military, who are portrayed as insensitive and stupid, never fooling for one minute the urbane man of the street. Jokes mocking Portuguese immigrants are particularly rife, and amount to Brazilian versions of the classical American "Polish joke."

POPULAR MUSIC. With the emergence of radio as a successful form of mass communication during the 1930's, popular music began to assume a greater importance in daily Brazilian life. Radio stimulated public interest both in music and sports; as a result, both soccer players and musicians were able to professionalize their status during these years. The major singer of the 1930's was Nöel Rosa, whose compositions began, after a while, to treat social themes. Others used allegory and parody to mask social criticism: in 1939 two samba composers wrote a Carnaval tune based on the foxtrot "Yes We Have No Bananas." The Brazilian version, "Yes We Have Bananas," not only made a sexual joke but parodied Brazil's reliance on agricultural exports.
    Along with samba parodies, the 1930's saw the Vargas regime use popular music for propaganda purposes--for example, Luís Gonzaga's "Cotton," a paean to the Chief of State.
    The 1950's saw the birth of the bossa nova, a rejection both of traditional Brazilian folk music and the over-commercialized "Latin" music popularized abroad. Bossa nova was essentially a middle class phenomenon. By the early 1960's, popular music had split into two divergent camps--apolitical, centered around experiments in tech-

nique (Edu Lobo, Sérgio Mendes) or out-and-out rock
and roll (Roberto Carlos); and the more dynamic socially
conscious school, led by Geraldo Vandré, Caetano Veloso,
and, ultimately, Chico Buarque de Holanda, whose first
popular successes were either apolitical or only mildly
critical.   Subject to constant harassment from censors
and other critics, the socially-conscious songwriters--
who nearly always performed their own work--represented
by the late 1970's about the only form of popular protest
against the excesses of the military regime.   See also
TROPICALISM.

POPULATION.   The growth rate was 2.9 percent annually
in 1976.   In the year 2000, the estimated population will
be two hundred and sixteen million.

PORÕES.   Basement housing units in multiple dwellings,
rented to lower class families.

POROROCA.   A tidal phenomenon in the Amazonian Basin
caused by the tremendous discharge of river water into
the sea--140,000 cubic meters per second in the rainy
season--threatening small craft or anything else in its
path.

PORQUE ME UFANO DO MEU PAIS.   Blatantly simplistic
and nationalistic book (1901) by Afonso Celso, eulogizing
Brazil's past and seeking to arouse a sense of unbridled
nationalism in order to counter the spirit of cultural inferiority exhibited by educated citizens.   In spite of its
exaggerations, the book went through fourteen editions
since its first appearance, although its message was
countered by the equally exaggerated pessimism of such
writers as Paulo Prado (q.v.).

PORTINARI, CÂNDIDO (1903-1962).   Brazil's major painter,
a student at Rio's Fine Arts School and later a visitor
to Europe, where he specialized in frescos, he returned
to Brazil to become, in the words of his biographer, as
"indefatigable painter of Brazilian popular life."   One of
his murals hangs in the United Nations building in New
York; another at Washington's Library of Congress;
another at Rio's Ministry of Education and Culture.

PÔRTO FELIZ.   Point of embarcation for some of the river-
borne monsões in the early eighteenth century.

PORTO VELHO.   The administrative capital of Rondônia ter-

ritory, situated on the Madeira River barely ten kilometers
from the border with the state of Amazonas.

POSITIVIST CHURCH. Founded in Brazil by followers of the
    French philosopher August Compte, the so-called Church
    of Reason developed its own ritual practices, which were
    called by critics "Catholicism without God" or "Catholi-
    cism without Christianity. " The Positivist Church sur-
    vived in Brazil down to the 1970's although in near mori-
    bund state.

"POSITIVIZERS. " Name given to followers of Posititivist
    thought in the late nineteenth century who were not them-
    selves members of the Positivist Church. Unlike ortho-
    dox Positivists, they tended to be secularists and liberals.

POSSEIRO. A peasant farmer, often the owner of a small
    plot of land (minifundia).

POST, FRANZ (1612-16??). Dutch painter contracted by
    Maurice of Nassau's court in Recife whose works illustrate
    the pastoral side of life under the Dutch occupation.

POTYGUAR. Inhabitant of the state of Rio Grande do Norte,
    a name from the Amerindian tribe which inhabited the
    region before the conquest.

"POVO ARMADO, O" ("A people in arms"). An 1890 char-
    acterization of the armed forces by officers seeking to
    reform military education and use the military to educate
    the general population.

PRADO, ANTÔNIO (1840-1929). Leading Paulista political
    figure whose career spanned the Empire and the Republic.
    After the 1890-91 constituent assembly he served as mayor
    of São Paulo for ten years.

PRADO, EDUARDO (1860-1901). Wealthy and urbane Paulista
    aristocrat who, after several years in Europe, returned
    to become one of Brazil's most militant monarchist writ-
    ers. Prado defended the Empire for its stability and
    liberal foundations, and attacked the Republic for its mili-
    tary origins. Twice, after Canudos and after the 1893
    Naval revolt, he had to flee the country. A conservative,
    independent thinker, his writings praised the caboclo's role
    in history; he similarly lauded the bandeirantes. His na-
    tionalism has been given as a major source of the Catholic
    conservatism revived by Jackson de Figueiredo in the 1920's.

PRADO, PAULO.   Author of Retrato do Brasil (q. v.).

PRAIEIRA REVOLT.   A major outbreak of regional insurrection, centered in Pernambuco in 1848-49, and, unlike
the 1842 Liberal Revolt, cutting across class lines.
Stein calls it the last attempt before 1889 to push the
1821 independence movement (and its sequel, Pedro I's
abdication in 1831), to its republican and federal conclusion.   With the collapse of the Praieira revolt Brazil
entered a period of complacency and conservatism, dilut-
ing even further whatever radicalism might have survived
within the Liberal Party.

PRAXEDES DE ANDRADE, JOSÉ (ZÉ).   A mulatto shoemaker
and member of the short-lived Natal Revolutionary Junta
of November 1935, who, unlike his less fortunate comrades, escaped after the suppression of the insurrection,
and was never seen publicly again.   Rumors placed him
in Salvador in the late 1960's, but they were never con-
firmed.   Zé Praxedes was one of the few working-class
members of the revolutionary ANL-PCB movement.

PRAZERES, HEITOR DOS (1908-1967).   The most consistent
of Brazilian artists of the primitive genre, painting samba
scenes and other glimpses of everyday life.   Prazeres
was entirely self-taught.

PREBISCH, RAUL.   Argentine-born economic planner who
headed during the 1950's the U. N. Commission for Latin
America and the U. N. Conference on Trade and Development, and who greatly influenced the development plans
of the Kubitschek administration (1956-1961).   Prebisch's
writings gave the impetus for the entire dependency theory
debate.

PRENSÁRIO.   "Squeezer," or extortionist.

PREPARAÇÃO AO NACIONALISMO.   A book by Afonso Arinos
de Melo Franco, published in 1934, reflecting the xenophobia and anti-Semitic feeling prevalent during the mid-
Vargas years.

PRESTES, JÚLIO (1882-1946).   Paulista chosen by Washington
Luis as his success in 1930 and duly elected but prevented
from taking office by the Liberal Alliance Revolution.
After he returned from exile in the mid-1930's he retired
to his family's fazenda at Itapetininga.

PRESTES, LUÍS CARLOS (1898-   ).   One of Brazil's most
charismatic and tragic figures.   A brilliant military cadet
at the Escola Militar, he led a rebellious tenente contingent during the 1924 revolt to meet with other rebel units,
joining them to form the guerrilla band which came to be
known as the Prestes Column.   In 1931, after contacts
with Comintern officials and other Marxist exiles in
Buenos Aires and Montevideo, he journeyed to the Soviet
Union, where he was named titular Comintern representative for the Brazilian Communist Party.   Prestes and
his German wife, Olga Benária, returned secretly to
Brazil in 1935 to lead the organization of the popular
front National Liberation Alliance to revolt, but his movements were known to police and the revolt crushed.
Upon her arrest, Olga, a Jew, was deported to Nazi
Germany, where she was liquidated; Prestes was sentenced to prison, and was held until 1945, when he was
amnestied by Getúlio Vargas, now seeking popular support.   Never a Marxist until his exile in the late 1920's,
he now stepped forward as the head of the newly legalized
Brazilian Communist Party, and ran for president in
1945.   The PCB was outlawed again in 1947 and Prestes
returned to a clandestine existence.   After 1964, he was
placed under virtual house arrest, deprived of his political rights, and kept out of public view.

PRÊTO ("Black").   The lowest category in the broad spectrum
of racial terminology, used to describe a Brazilian of
African descent with black pigmentation and pronouncedly
Negroid features.

PRÊTO RETINTO.   A very dark prêto.

PRIMARY SCHOOL ENROLLMENT.   As recently as 1973,
of 100 school children enrolled in first grade classes,
only 40 were expected to reach the second grade (compared with 74 in Argentina, 50 for the Latin American
average, and 92 in the United States).   By grade five,
only 7 were expected to be still in school (compared
with 49 in Argentina; 14 in Latin America; and 82 in the
United States).

"PRIMEIRA MISSA. "   The title of a mural-like painting by
Vitor Meireles, depicting what actually was the second
mass celebrated on Brazilian soil by Cabral's men.   The
work hangs in the National Museum of Fine Arts in Rio
de Janeiro.

PRIVATE LIBRARIES (Colonial Period). Although no printing press was allowed to operate in the colony, many intellectuals and others accumulated large private libraries, especially during the second half of the eighteenth century. The library of Canon Luís Vieira da Silva, for example, one of the Inconfidência Mineira conspirators, contained nearly 800 volumes (170 titles), representing most of Europe's leading thinkers, especially the French.

PROCURADOR. A government official corresponding to attorney general.

PROFESSOR CATEDRÁTICO. Full-professor rank at the university level, attained after extensive preparation and competetive examinations. In 1969 the title was replaced with that of Professor Titular. Some critics have argued that political influence and cronyism have occasionally entered into catedrático competitions; even in the 1910's and 1920's, however, the catedrático enjoyed the highest prestige and respect, and such accusations were usually dismissed as irrelevant.

PROFESSOR TITULAR see PROFESSOR CATEDRÁTICO

PROTESTANTISM. In the mid-1970's, Protestant groups claimed a total membership of 2,600,000, many of them adherents of such evangelical pentecostal sects as Jehovah's Witnesses and Seventh Day Adventists. Older Protestant groups--Methodists, Baptists, and Presbyterians--date back to the late nineteenth century and the foreign communities, as well to missionary efforts.

PROVEDOR-MÔR. Colonial official who served as chief financial advisor to the governor-general.

PROVISÓRIOS. Provisional troops, frequently maintained by local bosses to wage political battles. Vargas, as national finance minister in the 1920's, commanded São Borja's Seventh Provisional Corps, mostly as an honor, but in the tradition of Gaúcho military-political linkages.

PUÍTA. A friction drum producing a strange, lugubrious grunting sound, used in Afro-Brazilian cult ceremonies.

PURÚS RIVER. Brazil's second longest navigable river, part of the Amazon basin, 1,773 miles long.

PUTNAM, SAMUEL (1892-1950). Literary critic, journalist

and translator whose English language editions of Da
Cunha's Os Sertões (Rebellion in the Back-lands) and
Freyre's Casa-Grande e Senzala (The Masters and the
Slaves) have come to be considered literary masterpieces
in their own right.

-Q-

QUADRAGESIMO ANNO.   Papal Bull of Pius XI, praising
    corporative association of classes as the best means to
    combat the evils of individualism, used by Integralist
    sympathizers in the Brazilian Church to justify their po-
    sition.   See INTEGRALISM.

QUADROS, JÂNIO DA SILVA (1917-).   Governor of São
    Paulo, federal deputy (from Paraná), and President of
    Brazil from 1961 until his renunciation after seven months
    in office.   After the 1964 coup his political rights were
    suspended and he was confined in Corumbá, Mato Grosso.
    Quadros is known for his reformist rhetoric and his frus-
    trations in attempting to govern during a volatile time in
    recent Brazilian history.

QUARESMA, POLICARPO.   Fictional hero (or anti-hero) of
    novelist Lima Barreto's Triste Fim de Policarpo Quares-
    ma (1911), a nationalist and empty-headed patriot, given
    to learning Tupi, citing the achievements of the Father-
    land, and otherwise acting in a silly and lugubrious man-
    ner.

QUARTO DE DESPEJO.   Brazilian title of Carolina Maria de
    Jesus's Child of the Dark (1960).   Its first printing sold
    out its 10,000 copies in three days; another 90,000 copies
    were sold in Brazil within six months.   In all, the book
    has sold more than any Brazilian book in history.   Car-
    olina's own story was less spectacular: within a decade
    of the publication of her diary she had been evicted from
    her brick home and was back in the favela.   See also
    CANINDÉ.

QUEBRA-QUILOS REVOLT.   A violent uprising among north-
    eastern peasants from November 1874 to January 1875,
    where rioters invaded markets (feiras) and smashed the
    weights and measures of the newly introduced metric sys-
    tem.   Although tax records and notarial registers were
    also destroyed, little violence was directed against citi-

zens or officials.   Reaction among the four provincial
governments (Alagoas, Pernambuco, Paraíba, Rio Grande
do Norte) was predictably angry, but the disorder subsided spontaneously before massive repressive measures
could be applied.   Barman notes that little really is
known about the dynamics of the revolt, although he suggests that examination of the affair makes clear that the
peasantry, pictured as docile and lethargic by the traditional literature, actually comprised an independent group
capable of defending their own way of life and challenging
the existing order.   See also CANUDOS.

QUEIMADA.   System of burning over the land for cultivation,
a variation of the Amerindian method of coivara, used
widely since the early colonial period despite the ineffe-
ciencies and waste produced by slash-and-burn techniques.

QUEIROZ, RACHEL DE.   Novelist (1911-   ) and the first
woman to gain entrance to the venerable Brazilian Academy of Letters (see ACADEMIA BRASILEIRA DE LE-
TRAS), in 1977.   Her work deals with the northeastern
region.

"QUEM NÃO ROBA NEM HERDA ACABA COMENDO MERDA. "
Widespread homily illustrating Brazilian attitudes towards
work: "He who neither robs nor inherits ends up eating
shit. "

"QUEREMOS. "   Slogan--"we want"--used by pro-Vargas groups
during 1945 to stir up support for keeping the chief of
state in power.   The movement, probably officially inspired, failed; Vargas was ousted from office in late October.   The pro-Vargas forces were individually and
collectively known as Queremistas.

QUILOMBO DO TRAVESSÃO.   A secret slave society which
existed between 1879 and 1884 in Campos, in the province
of Rio de Janeiro.

QUILOMBOS.   Fugitive-slave settlements, at least ten of
which are known to have been established during the days
of slavery.   Seven of these were destroyed within two
years of their founding; the longest lived, at Palmares
in the interior of Alagoas, reached a population of 20,000
through most of the seventeenth century as a quasi-inde-
pendent pseudo-African state.   Between 1672 and 1694
Palmares held off government attacks on the average of

one every fifteen months. It was finally destroyed by
expeditions of bandeirantes sent by royal authorities.

QUINA-QUINA. Native tree producing quinine, used in treatment of malaria. The drug is taken from the tough,
horny bark, which is stripped and brewed to make an
acid tea. It is indigenous to the Amazon basin.

QUINTA DE BOA VISTA. The Rio de Janeiro residence of
a wealthy Portuguese merchant, Elias Antônio Lopes,
turned over to be the royal palace on the arrival of the
Court in 1808 from Lisbon.

QUINTO. The one-fifth levy applied by the Crown to all mineral wealth. The practice, originating in medieval Portugal, brought tremendous wealth to the metropolis but
also encouraged smuggling; up to 1713 the total amount
of confiscated gold taken by Crown officials virtually
equalled its revenue from the quinto.

QUIXADÁ DAM. Completed in 1906 after some two decades
of construction, the dam, with a capacity of 128 million
cubic meters and located in the heart of Ceará's drought
region, became the symbol for waste and governmental
inefficiency in the area of drought relief.

-R-

RABELO, JOAQUIM DO AMOR DIVINO. Carmelite friar
known as Frei Caneca.

RÁBULA. One who practices law without a formal degree.
See also BACHAREL.

RADIO BANDEIRANTES. São Paulo radio station, one of the
first to broadcast intercity soccer matches, and, ultimately, international contests.

RANGEL, ALBERTO. Fiction writer whose short stories,
Inferno Verde (Green Hell), published in 1907, bemoaned
the fate of the Amerindian, at a time when Brazilians
were beginning to recognize the harmful impact of coastal
civilization on aboriginal life.

RAPADURA. Crude, brown engenho sugar, usually sold in
kilo blocks.

RAPARIGA. Accepted term in colonial days (and to the present in Portugal) for an adolescent girl; in modern Brazil, however, the term has come to connote a prostitute.

RAPAZINHO. "The young lad," referring to D. Pedro II prior to his ascession to the Brazilian Imperial throne.

"RATIO STUDORIUM." Codification (1599) of the educational orientation of the Jesuits in Brazil, indicating a shift from emphasis upon educating aboriginal peoples to training Brazilian youths in the liberal arts.

RAZÃO, A. Newspaper, established in São Paulo in 1931, which became the official organ of the Integralists under Plínio Salgado. Its editorial offices were looted and burned during the Constitutionalist insurrection of 1932, but there is no known connection between this fact and the paper's Integralist orientation. In the mid-1930's the newspaper carried the viciously anti-Semitic columns of Gustavo Barroso despite the AIB's assurances that it did not share the same anti-Semitic line as the European National Socialists.

REAÇÃO REPUBLICANA. The 1922 coalition of state parties from Bahia, Pernambuco, Rio Grande do Sul, and Rio de Janeiro which broke with the establishment candidate, Artur Bernardes of Minas Gerais, and backed instead Nilo Peçanha, of Rio state. The break was occasioned by the PRR's failure to consider a Gaúcho as vice-presidential candidate on the Bernardes ticket; Bahia and Pernambuco were similarly slighted. Peçanha, President of Brazil from 1909-10, was still a popular figure but the campaign, which involved attempts to win the support of the armed forces, was close and bitter, with the Reação emerging as the loser amidst allegations of fraud. The events helped set the stage for the 1922 tenente revolt.

REALE, MIGUEL (1910-). Paulista jurist, educator, and member of the fascist Integralist party in the mid-1930's. Reale reached the post of catedrático in the Philosophy of Law at the University of São Paulo at the age of 30; in his later life he served as the institution's rector.

REBELO, JOSÉ SILVESTRE. First Brazilian minister to the United States, received by President James Monroe in May 1824. The act symbolized the first formal recognition of Independent Brazil by a foreign nation.

REBOUÇAS, ANDRÉ (1838-1892). One of the few abolitionists
of Afro-Brazilian origin. Rebouças studied at the Escola
Militar in Rio de Janeiro and gained a teaching post at
the Polytechnic Institute in that city. A dedicated monarchist, he left Brazil with D. Pedro and lived until his
death in Portuguese Africa. His body was found floating
beneath a high cliff on the island of Madeira; it is unknown whether his death was accidental or a suicide.

RECIFE AND SÃO FRANCISCO RAILWAY COMPANY, LTD.
The first British railroad in the country, running southwest from Recife with the intention (fulfilled only years
later) of linking up with the navigable portion of the São
Francisco River. The line was a financial drain; its
engineers' plans were hastily drawn, and the region it
served was insufficiently prosperous to provide adequate
revenue.

RECIFES. Stone reefs paralleling the northeastern coast
from the Ponta dos Três Irmãos to a point south of Ma-
ceió. The reefs make coastal navigation treacherous,
and give the name to Pernambuco's capital and chief port,
Recife.

RECOLHIDA. A secular recluse taken into a Convent. See
CONVENT OF SANTA CLARA DO DESTÊRRO.

RECONCAVO. The region outside the city of Salvador, bordering the Bahia de Todos os Santos, stretching into the
interior, the former seat of the slave-holding plantocracy.

REDE FERROVIARIA FEDERAL S. A. The government-owned
railway network, the largest single employer in Brazil
with 121,492 employees in 1976.

REDUÇÕES. Settlements of converted Amerindians, usually
in southeastern Brazil near the Paraguayan border, where
Jesuits established agricultural colonies under virtual
self-rule.

REFORMA RIVADÁVIA see RIVADÁVIA CORREIA

RÉGIA PRESS. One of Brazil's first, and publisher in 1811
of Adam Smith's Wealth of Nations.

RÉGIME CAPACITAIRE. Term given to the Brazilian political
system in 1891, when the new constitution gave the vote

to all literate males over twenty-one years of age.   During the Empire, Brazil had been a régime censitaire,
where income and property requirements effectively limited suffrage to the privileged few.

REGIMENTO.   Decree law of August 2, 1771, which established a crown monopoly on all diamond mining, a sharp
change from the condition of free exploitation subject to
the royal fifth (quinto) from 1729 to 1740; exploitation on
a monopoly-contract basis (1740-1771); and finally the
notorious Regimento, which, although it applied only to
the Distrito Diamantino (Diamond District) of Minas Gerais, diamond mining was forbidden elsewhere, and no
one allowed even to enter districts where diamonds were
known to exist, such as the region of the Claro and
Pilões rivers in Goiás and the Jequitinhonha River in
Bahia.

REIS VELLOSO, JOÃO PAULO   see   VELLOSO

RELAÇÃO.   Brazil's first high court, established in Bahia
in 1609; the second was inaugurated in Rio de Janeiro a
century and a half later.   The governor-general acted
as its chief presiding officer.   Colonial justice, as Worcester notes, was a relative term: it was applied dif-
ferently to rich and poor.

RELATIVE DEMOCRACY.   Term used by President Ernesto
Geisel on a speaking tour in November 1977 to define
his regime's approach to governance.   Old fashioned
liberalism, he said, was a dead letter.   According to
critics (in this case, the Estado de São Paulo), the president really intended to "organize democracy by dogmatic
indoctrination and authoritarian implementation, in effect
by suppressing democracy."

RELIGIOUS QUESTION OF 1874   see   CONÇALVES DE OLI-
VEIRA, DOM VITAL

REMÉDIOS DA MATA.   Herbal medicines, used in spiritualist
healing.

REMOÇÃO.   The process of transferring a judicial official,
used during the middle years of the Empire for politically-
inspired manipulation, since the Constitution of 1824 for-
bade outright dismissal of professional magistrates.

RENÓIS.   Portuguese who came to Brazil to become rich and

then return. The renóis constitute the counterpart of
the peninsulares (in Spanish colonies) or gachupines
(Spaniards resident in New Spain).   See also MAZOMBOS.

RENOVAR. To "renovate," a term used often by Getúlio
Vargas to describe the task of his (authoritarian) administration in the mid-1930's and early 1940's. Tenentes
preferred this concept to what they considered the corrupt and cynical promises for evolutionary democracy
and social change under the liberal constitution of the
Old Republic.

REPARTIÇÃO GERAL DAS TERRAS PÚBLICAS. General
Bureau of Public Lands, organized in 1854 for the purpose
of supervising sale of unused public land to would-be
small farmers.

"REPUBLIC OF SILENCE. " Term coined by Chilean writer
Eduardo Galeano to describe Brazil (and other Latin
American countries) in the light of the massive post-1964
restrictions on free public expression.

REPÚBLICA. Literally, a "republic," a boarding-house occupied by secondary or university-level students in the
nineteenth and early twentieth centuries, popularly known
for their bohemian atmosphere.

RESCATES. Officially-sanctioned expeditions of slave hunters
into the interior, who bought or ransomed Indians held
as prisoners by rival tribes.   The practice was prohibited
by the Pombaline Reform Laws.   See also DESCIMENTOS.

RESTINGAS.   Hummocks of land on the Amazonian floodplain,
protruding in roughly parallel contours.

RETIRANTES.   Refugees from the Northeastern drought.
Also called flagelados (q. v.).

RETRATO DO BRASIL.   A book-length essay by Paulo Prado
(1928), typifying the intellectual's self-doubt and pessimism
which characterized the nineteenth and early twentieth
centuries in Brazil.   Prado viewed Brazilian history as
the sad legacy of sensuality and greed.   This morbid
pessimism contrasted violently with the buoyant optimism
of other writers, such as Afonso Celso (q. v.).   These
extreme viewpoints, equally fashionable during Brazil's
Belle Epoque, were too grotesque to be tested by mun-

dane analysis; thus some of their theories were absorbed into popular belief to the detriment of scientific investigation.

REUNIÃO.   The first regular Masonic lodge in the city of Rio de Janeiro, founded in 1801 by a man known as "Chevalier Laurent," whose real identity is unknown. Freemasonry, which was feared and hated by many as a conduit for the transmission of revolutionary ideology, served to integrate Brazil more closely into the international arena, but it touched only a handful of members of the elite, and never threatened to undermine the social order.   Pedro II, as Emperor, was also a Mason of the thirty-second degree.

REVÉRBERO CONSTITUCIONAL FLUMINENSE.   A newspaper of the 1820's, published by Gonçalves Ledo, which helped influence the climate of opinion in favor of a break with Portugal.

REVISTA BRASILIENSE.   A scholarly review which published from 1955 to 1964, representing the position of the "development nationalists," linked to the Instituto Superior de Estudos Brasileiros (ISEB).

REVISTA DO EXÉRCITO BRASILEIRO.   Founded in 1882 by some of the persons associated with the outspoken Tribuna Militar as well as other military intellectuals of the post-Paraguayan War generation.   It advocated reform, reorganization, and measures to increase efficiency and morale.   The view of the newspaper reflected the outlook of the military command, and it was not as critical as its predecessor.   But in 1888 it attacked the parliamentary armed forces reorganization bill as not going far enough, and it ostensibly was suppressed: in any case, it ceased publication without explanation.   One year later, angered military officers helped overthrow the monarchy.

REVOLUTION OF 1842.   The first major revolt against the newly-crowned D. Pedro II, led by Liberals angered at the Conservative ministry's emasculation of the Liberal 1832 criminal code and the Emperor's dismissal of the newly elected Chamber of Deputies.   Stein notes that it is still unclear why the bitterest fighting was centered in the Paraíba valley, the locus of a coffee boom.   The revolt, which developed from a rift in the elite, was

put down by Imperial troops dispatched from Rio to Santos
by steamship.

RIBEIRO, JOÃO (1860-1934).   Like Tobias Barreto and Silvio
Romero, a Sergipiano.   Most of his early literary career
was spent in Europe--Germany, Austria, Switzerland,
and Italy--where he wrote essays, poetry, works of gram-
mar, and taught.   He is considered one of Brazil's major cultural theorists.

RIBEIRO, JÚLIO.   Author of one of Brazilian literature's
few portrayals of the black as evil, A Carne (Flesh),
written in 1888 and paralleling Thomas Dixon's The
Leopard's Spots (1902) and The Clansman (1905).

RICARDO, CASSIANO (1895-197?).   Poet and spokesman,
during the late 1920's, for a vision of an industrialized,
urbanized Brazil.   His most widely known poem is "Martim Cererê" (1928).

RIO BRANCO, BARÃO DO (1845-1912).   Born José Maria da
Silva Paranhos Júnior, Rio Branco was Brazil's greatest
diplomat and is credited with favorable negotiations over
disputed territory with Argentina, French Guiana, Bolivia, Dutch Guiana, and Colombia.   Rio Branco also
was a major historian.

RIO BRANCO LAW OF 1871.   An act by which the Imperial
Parliament seemed to take meaningful legal activity
against slavery but in fact prolonged it, by allowing free-
born children--born after the law to slave mothers--
to remain in a state of semibondage until the age of 21.
See also INGENUOS.

RIO GRANDE DO NORTE.   Northeastern state on the tip of
the Brazilian bulge into the Atlantic.   The state is poor,
and historically has been dominated politically by Pernambuco, to its south.   Its capital is Natal.

RIO GRANDE DO SUL.   Southernmost state, bordering Uru-
aguay and Argentina, and the center of Brazil's cattle
raising industry.   Belligerant and rebellious during the
nineteenth century, the gaúchos finally settled down to
coexistence with Rio de Janeiro; during the Republic the
state played a major political role, with São Paulo and
Minas Gerais forming the "big three" states in terms of
political and economic influence.   Several presidents,

including Getúlio Vargas, Garrastazú Médici, Ernesto Geisel, and João Batista Figueiredo, come from Rio Grande.

RIO GRANDE DO SUL-GHANA ACCORD. A commercial and cultural initiative established in 1976, dedicated to exchanges and mutual trade agreements, on the unusual basis of state-based "foreign policy."

RIO DE JANEIRO (City). Founded on March 1, 1565, in the rolling hills rising from what later became known as Guanabara Bay, Rio de Janeiro may well be the most beautiful city on earth. The city had to be fought for: the Portuguese only subdued the French settlers who had occupied what they called "Antarctic France" (and their Tamoio Indian allies) after two years and at the cost of the life of their leader, Estácio de Sá. Rio became the Brazilian capital in 1763 and the home of the Portuguese Court after the transmigration of the royal family from Lisbon in 1808. It ceased being the national capital with the inauguration of Brasília in 1960 but remained a major commercial and touristic center.

RIO DE JANEIRO (State). From 1889 to 1975, the state lying across from the city of Rio de Janeiro, which was variously the Federal District and, after the early 1960's, the state of Guanabara. In 1975, facilitated by the construction of a bridge between Rio and Niterói across Guanabara Bay, the city and state were merged into the larger state of Rio de Janeiro.

RIOGRANDENSE. Inhabitant of the state of Rio Grande do Sul, synonymous with Gaúcho.

RISCHBIETER, KARLOS. New (1977) President of the Banco do Brasil, and an example of the rising group of technocrats and administrators whose careers have been cultivated under the management-minded military administrations of Garrastazú Medici and Ernesto Geisel.

RITA DURÃO, SANTA. Author of the epic poem Caramarú, published in 1781, a history of Brazil from 1500, culminating in the expulsion of the last non-Portuguese foreign invader.

RITTER, KARL. German Ambassador during the critical years of the mid to late-1930's, a skillful diplomat who sought to use the presence of 800,000 Teuto-Brazilians (and 100,000 German nationals) as leverage to influence Vargas in the direction of alliance with the Reich. After the 1938 Integralist putsch, however, his influence diminished, and he began to receive criticism for his too-obvious support of Integralist activities. In September, 1938, he was declared persona non grata, and recalled.

ROÇA. 1) A clearing in the forest. 2) A cultivated plot of land.

ROCEIROS. Small-scale farmers who may have some share-croppers or hired laborers but who never are freed from labor themselves. The roceiro often lives on another plot of land from his agricultural parcel; many live in villages, and travel to work.

ROCHA, GLAUBER. Leading filmmaker and member of the Cinema Nôva, known for his extreme realism: for example, his Deus e o Diabo na Terra do Sol, a powerful amalgam of themes taken from the cangaceiros, the influence of messianism on the rural Northeast, and the impact of the drought. Rocha spent thirteen years in European exile before returning in late 1977.

ROCHA PITA, SEBASTIÃO DE (1660-1738). Author of História de América Portuguêsa, 1500-1724, one of the first (and most striking) works on nativist sentiment and Brazilian grandeur. Rocha Pita, a charter member of the Bahian Academy of the Forgotten, published his work in 1730, in Lisbon, the first new history of Brazil in nearly a hundred years.

RODGERS, JAMES HEIDE. A United States citizen involved in the conspiracy of the Confederation of the Equator, captured after the fall of Recife to Lord Cochrane, and executed with Frei Caneca and the other secessionists.

ROMEIROS. Followers of Ceará's Padre Cícero.

ROMERO, FRANSISCO. The first administrator of the captaincy of Ilhéus, sent by the donatory, Jorge de Figueiredo Correia. Romero founded the village of São Jorge (after his patron?), distributing land among Portuguese colonists who had agreed to settle there, and negotiating an alliance with the Tupi tribes inhabiting the region. But conflicts between Romero and his Portuguese subjects led to his return to Portugal and to the economic weakening of the colony; on Figueiredo Correia's death it was sold to another noble, Lucas Giraldes.

ROMERO, SILVIO (1851-1914). Sergipe-born critic, a friend of Tobias Barreto and a member of the Escola de Recife out of the Faculdade de Direito in the 1880's.

RONDON, GENERAL CÂNDIDO MARIANO DA SILVA (1865-1958). Mato-Grosso-born, the career army officer and follower of positivist Auguste Comte spent twenty-five years traveling among Amerindian tribes and headed a commission which mapped over 50,000 square kilometers of land and laid over 2,270 kilometers of telegraph wire. He was named the first director of the Indian Protection Service (SPI) in 1910. The territory of Rondônia was later named in his honor.

RONDÔNIA. Federal territory on the border with Bolivia, in an inhospitable corner of the Amazon basin, and until recently inhabited only by Amerindians and scattered rubber gatherers. Since the early 1960's, however, a mining boom (tin, gold, and other metals) has brought thousands of settlers, prospectors, and major private and public investment. Its capital is Porto Velho.

RORAIMA. Federal Territory in the uppermost portion of the Amazon, reached via the Rio Negro from Manaos, and bordering Guiana and Venezuela. Its administrative center, Boa Vista, serves principally as a guard station against smuggling. Its population in 1970 barely reached 46,000 persons.

ROSA, NOËL. The major popular music composer and performer of the 1930's, the decade in which the radio brought such music to the public as a whole. Trained as a physician, he abandoned his medical career to concentrate on music. After some years, his songs began to take on social consciousness. His "With What Clothes?" (1932) speaks of a downtrodden street hustler, seeking to improve his lot through personal struggle, presumably with an unconcerned society. Other Rosa songs addressed the social contradictions inherent in the proximity of a glittering urban elite and the wretched urban slums. Rosa's followers, however, were mostly middle class; he made little inroads into lower class perceptions.

ROSA E SILVA, FRANCISCO DE ASSIS (1857-1929). Political

boss of the state of Pernambuco from 1896 to 1910 and
a leading national political figure; vice-president of the
Republic in the Campos Sales administration. Rosa e
Silva, a vain, elegant man who preferred Europe to Brazil (and Rio de Janeiro to Recife) dominated northeastern
political affairs from afar. His father was a Portuguese
immigrant who had become a successful merchant; his
wife the daughter of the Viscount of Livramento.

ROSADO FAMILY. Centered in the second city of the state
of Rio Grande do Norte, and headed by a powerful merchant and state politician, the Rosados named all their
male children Jerônimo and all of their female children
Isaura, each followed by the number, in French, of their
birth. Jerônimo Dix-sept later served as governor of
the state; Vingt became a federal deputy.

ROSEBAUGH, LARRY. Milwaukee-born Oblate priest, former
draft resister (member of the "Milwaukee 14") arrested
for working with the poor in Recife, in 1977. Father
Rosebaugh, whose meeting with Rosalynn Carter during
her 1977 visit to Brazil embarrassed the Brazilian regime, was deported from the country later in the year,
having told of inhuman conditions in local prisons.

ROSSI, GIOVANNI. Founder of a short-lived anarchist colony
in the state of Paraná in the 1890's.

ROSSIO. An outlying, generally communal piece of land,
eventually absorbed by the core city when it expands.
For example, Caxangá, in Recife.

"ROUBA MAS FAZ." "He steals but he does," the unofficial
electoral slogan of the late ex-Governor of São Paulo
Adhemar de Barros, in the early 1960's.

RUA D'OUVIDOR. Narrow street in downtown Rio de Janeiro,
in recent years restricted to pedestrian traffic owing to
its girth. In the heart of the old commercial center.

RUGENDAS, JOHANN MORITZ. German-born landscape
artist who came to Brazil in 1821, returned to Europe
in 1825, and came again in 1845, where he spent the
rest of his life.

RUSSIAN-BRAZILIAN RELATIONS see NADEZHDA

-S-

SABARÁ. Mineiro town founded in 1694, whose baroque architecture has remained untouched and which, like Ouro Preto, attracts architecture-minded tourists to its mining museum and its Chapel of Nossa Senhora de O, built between 1720 and 1730 by Chinese artisans brought by Portuguese officials from Macão.

SABINADA. A local revolt in the province of Bahia (1837-1838). See CABANADA.

SACASAIAS. Non-poisonous Amazonian ants which travel in large herds, stinging anything or anyone in their path.

SAINT-HILAIRE, AUGUSTE DE. Nineteenth-century French naturalist, whose various accounts of his travels beginning in 1816 through the interior appeared in 1852 under the title Voyages dans l'intérieur du Brésil.

SAINT JOHN DEL REY COMPANY. The largest private gold mine in Brazil down to the 1930's, and the largest single industrial employer in the state of Minas Gerais to that date. A British stock company held majority ownership.

SALES, ALBERTO (1857-1904). Campinas-(São Paulo state) born, engineer (as a student at R. P. I. in Troy, New York, he wrote various articles published in the Província de São Paulo), republican, and positivist.

SALES OLIVEIRA, ARMANDO DE (1887-1945). Paulista businessman, industrialist, and governor (1934-1938) who was named by liberal constitutionalist groups in 1936 to run against the "official" candidate, José Américo de Almeida for the presidency. The elections were ultimately cancelled with the promulgation of the Estado Novo in November 1937.

SALTE. Dutra-era program to promote public health, nutrition, transportation, and general national development in the face of rising inflation in the late 1940's.

SALUDOS AMIGOS. Disney film of the 1940's, focusing on José Carioca and samba, and the basis (or crystalization) of much of the stereotypical North American view of Brazil as an exotic paradise filled with lazy, fun-loving natives.

SALVAÇÕES. A movement of reform-minded army officers
who, after the victory of presidential candidate Hermes
da Fonseca over civilian Rui Barbosa, used the theme
of anti-corruption to uproot the entrenched state oligar-
chical parties in a number of northeastern states. The
reformers, or "salvacionistas" (redeemers") were unable
to accomplish any long-reaching changes; the new state
machines which took power from the ousted parties quickly turned to similar forms of political behavior. By
1914, the salvações had disappeared as a movement.

SALVADOR, VICENTE DE. Franciscan priest and author of
Brazil's first history (1627). Salvador uses a vocabulary
--as Burns notes--infused with words from the "língua
geral" (q. v.).

SAMBA. Brazilian rhythmic dance, frequently performed to
specially-prepared lyrics, evolving from such African
forms as the batuque, which was danced by slaves at
night in colonial days. See also CARNAVAL.

SAMPAIO, CID. Governor of Pernambuco from 1958 to 1962,
generally conceded to have been the first holder of that
office to owe his election to urban votes. Traditionally,
rural districts have held a greater weight in electoral
representations, and local coroneis always exercised
tight control over the votes of their constituencies.

SAMPAIO, TEODORO. Historian and ethnographer (1855-
1937) who wrote on the bandeiras.

SAN ILDEFONSO, TREATY OF. Accord in 1777 between
Portugal and Spain, giving the Misiones province and
Colônia do Sacramento, in the La Plata estuary, to Spain.
The treaty, however, was ignored a quarter century later,
when Portuguese troops penetrated Misiones as far as
the Chuí River; Spain ceded it to Portugal.

SAN PAULO RAILWAY COMPANY, LIMITED. So spelled,
the English company ran the most important railway line
in Brazil, linking the port of Santos to the heart of the
coffee region; only 139 kilometers long at completion, it
still became the wealthiest and most powerful railroad in
the country, as Graham notes, serving as a funnel to
gather, with the help of connecting lines, the agricultural
produce of the interior of the state and pouring them into
British ships at Santos.

SAN TIAGO DANTAS, FRANCISCO CLEMENTINO DE (1911-1964). Author, jurist, intellectual figure, ambassador, and foreign minister under Jânio Quadros. Dantas was a member of the Integralist Party in the mid-1930's.

SANTA CASA DE MISERICÓRDIA. Church-sponsored institutions which served as hospitals, orphanages, and general charitable centers during the colonial period and through modern times although in reduced scale. See IRMANDADES.

SANTOS, FAUSTO DOS see FAUSTO

SANTOS, NÍLTON (1925-). Born in the slums of Rio de Janeiro's Ilha do Governdaor, Santos rose to become the soccer hero of the late 1940's and early 1950's, and one of the "brains" of the sport after his playing days ended.

SANTOS DUMONT, ALBERTO (1873-1932). Minas-born inventor and Paris-trained engineer whose experiments with aircraft brought him the title "father of air-flight." Santos Dumont was European by preference but is considered one of the most notable Brazilians owing to his birth. His father had been a French immigrant to Diamantina and his mother a member of the wealthy Paula Santos family, whose gold mine he managed.

SANTOS VILHENA, LUÍS DOS. Turn-of-the-eighteenth-century historian, and the author of Recopilação de noticias soterpolitanas e brasilicas (1802). Santos Vilhena's views on race border on the paranoid (Schwartz), and he counseled coerced settlement and deportation as means to deal with the "vagrant, insolent, uppity, and ungrateful" mulattos.

SÃO CARLOS, FRANCISCO DE. Nativist author of the epic poem, A Assunção (1819), portraying paradise as "remarkably similar to Brazil" (Burns).

SÃO FRANCISCO RIVER. Rising in the mountains of Minas Gerais, the São Francisco is the single fluvial link between the coast and the interior along the 500 miles of its length, most of which are navigable. In its lower reaches it drops abruptly over the Itaparica and Paulo Afonso Falls, the latter a major source of hydroelectric power for the northeast. The river reaches the sea at Sergipe. Cattle raising for centuries has been the principal source of economic activity in the São Francisco Valley.

SÃO PAULO (State).   Brazil's most important political unit
since the early Republic.   The state alone dwarfs most
Latin American countries: its population of 18,000,000
in 1977 was exceeded only by Mexico, Argentina, and
Colombia.   Coffee provided the impetus for its tremendous economic thrust during the early decades of the
twentieth century; the state produced more than two-thirds
of Brazilian production at a time when Brazil garnered
as much as three-quarters of the world demand.   São
Paulo, referred to by popular political humor as the
locomotive pulling twenty empty boxcars (the number of
other states during the Republic), had led Brazil in industrial production, railroads, transportation, education,
and commerce.

SÃO PAULO ART MUSEUM.   Founded by Assis Chateaubriand
in 1947, the Museum has been called Latin America's
only picture gallery "up to international standards" (P.
Bardi), organized on didactic lines and designed to promote knowledge of the history and problems of national
and international art.

SÃO PAULO SEMINARY.   The first educational institution in
Brazil, established in the 1550's by Father Nóbrega, and
raised to the status of colégio (academy) in 1556.   Other
Jesuit colégios were founded at Rio de Janeiro and Bahia.
See also BAHIAN SEMINARY.

SÃO PAULO SHINBUN.   Japanese-language newspaper in the
city of São Paulo.

SÃO PEDRO DE ALCANTARA.   The first settlement of German immigrants in Santa Catarina, established in 1829,
on agricultural land near the coast.   Other new towns
in the region were established at Mafra, Rio Negro, and
Corrisco (1829-30), and at Piedade, Santa Isabel, and
Leopoldina (1847).   These early settlements were not exclusively German, but made up of immigrants from various parts of Europe.   The first solely German colony
was Blumenau, established in 1848.

SARAIVA, GUMERCINDO (1848-1894).   Gaúcho military figure
and caudilho who, although born to Portuguese parents,
grew up in Uruguay, and therefore spoke Portuguese
poorly, for which his enemies ridiculed him.

SARAIVA, JOSÉ ANTÔNIO (1823-1895). Statesman and Imperial-era diplomat, responsible for the 1881 Saraiva Law, an electoral reform bill, and the 1885 Saraiva-Cotegipe Law, freeing slaves who reached the age of 65.

SARAIVA LAW (1881). Provided for direct elections and lower property qualifications for voting, although the electorate still remained limited to about one percent of the population (150,000 out of 15,000,000), and the law was difficult to enforce.

SARARÁ. A light-skinned mulata with reddish, kinky hair.

SARGENTÃO. Literally, "big-deal sergeant," the insult allegedly directed at former President Hermes da Fonseca, part of a grossly insulting letter attributed by presidential candidate Artur Bernardes, whose victory contributed to the rise of the tenentes, who fought to restore the "honor" of the armed forces. The Military Club, headed by Hermes, demanded a recount of the ballots, with events eventually leading to the ex-President's arrest and the 1922 military revolt in Rio de Janeiro.

SARGENTO-MÔR. Colonial-era officer rank, corresponding to a lieutenant-colonel.

SATELLITE BLOC. A concept pertinent to the Old Republic and its highly federalist form of political organization. Leading states, strong because of their ability to tax exports and to field their own police forces (FORÇAS PUBLICAS), dominated their weaker neighbors. Thus São Paulo's satellite bloc may be said to have included the states of Paraná and Santa Catarina; Rio's, the state of Rio de Janeiro and perhaps Espiritú Santo; Bahia's Sergipe and portions of western Pernambuco and southern Piauí, where railroad tracks linked the sertão to Salvador, and Pernambuco's, the states of Alagoas, Paraíba, Ceará, and Rio Grande do Norte.

SCHERER, VICENTE CARDINAL. Archbishop of Pôrto Alegre in the 1970's, and a spokesman for the plight of the Amerindian population: in a much-criticized statement in 1977 he declared: "The long and tortuous history of Indians in our country has been one of tears, pain, and revolting justice. God save us from the blind and destructive power that exists at the decision-making levels of this nation."

SCHOLZ, WALDEMAR. The wealthiest of the Amazonian rub-

ber barons, whose home in Manaos rivaled that of European palaces; after the boom subsided, it was sold and
converted into the gubernatorial mansion.

SCLIAR, CARLOS (1920-   ). Major painter of the Cabo Frio
school.

SEABRA, JOSÉ JOAQUIM (1855-1942). Bahian state political
boss, who came to power in the wake of the Hermes da
Fonseca-salvações victory of 1910; Seabra had organized
the Hermes-Wenceslau Committee in Bahia in 1909, and
as a result was selected to run for governor in 1912.
His election divided the state party and led to events
which forced Hermes to intervene militarily in order to
place Seabra in power. As governor, he altered the
state constitution to allow him to name chief executives
of every município; as a result, he took over firm control of the state, personally naming 130 of the 141 inten-
dentes. His party's inability to control backlands coronéis, however, led to federal intervention again in 1920
and de facto coronelista political independence.

SEBASTIANISM. The propelling force behind the Canudos
insurrection in Bahia in 1896-1897, holding that Sebastião
I, a Portuguese king killed in battle against the Moors
in 1578, would appear in Brazil in a fiery day of judg-
ment, punishing wrongdoers and rewarding the faithful.
See also CANUDOS.

SECRETARIAT OF BUDGET AND FINANCE (SOF). Created
in 1968 by Treasury Secretary Roberto Campos to supervise educational spending in response to the fact that,
since 1961's Lei de Direitrizes (q. v.), decentralization
had deprived the federal Ministry of Education and Culture of authority over the sectoral distribution of funds
and over university life.

SEGALL, LASAR (1890-   ). Polish-born painter whose works,
dealing with non-academic themes in an interior manner
(compared with Portinari's external, Brazilian visages),
were first exhibited in São Paulo, in 1913, nine years
prior to the famous Semana de Arte Moderna, but with
significant impact.

SELVA. An anti-fascist law journal at the Salvador Law Faculty, established in 1938, publishing, during its brief
life, articles by such students as Carlos Lacerda (under

the pseudonym Marcos Pimenta), Aureliano Leite, Nestor
Duarte, and Luís Viana Filho--all youths who would play
major roles in state and national politics in later decades.

SEMINÁRIO, O. Weekly newspaper published by ISEB (The
Superior Institute of Brazilian Studies, or Instituto Superior de Estudos Brasileiros) during the late 1950's,
reaching a circulation of more than 60,000.

SEMINARIO DE OLINDA see COUTINHO, AZEREDO

SEMPRE VERDE ("Always green"). The name of a planted
grass used in the Northeast for forage, the seeds of
which are imported from the South. Other planted grass-
es are pangola and elephant grass.

SENZALA. Slave quarters on plantations and estâncias.
After abolition, the quarters were simply rented to agri-
cultural workers, or moradores (squatters). See also
CASA-GRANDE.

SERGIPE. Northeastern state between Alagoas and Bahia,
and considered within the political and economic sphere
of Bahia. Its capital is Aracajú.

SERINGAL. An area given to rubber extraction, in the Amazon. It was usually dominated by a barracão, or company trading post, to which the seringeiros became in-
debted.

SERINGUEIRO. Rubber gatherer of the Amazon.

SERRA DOS ORGAÕS. Late seventeenth-century quilombo,
or hidden refuge for escaped slaves, outside of Rio de
Janeiro. Many of its inhabitants were urban, or domestic
slaves, owned by city dwellers. The quilombo survived
until the first decades of the eighteenth century.

SERTANEJO. Inhabitant of the backlands, or sertão (q. v.).
The word holds a slight pejorative connotation in certain
usage, denoting a rustic or primitive, much in the manner of Euclides da Cunha's Os Sertões.

SERTANISTA. A backlands explorer, one with first-hand
knowledge of the region. Fernão Dias Paes, for example,
the bandeirante leader, was a sertanista. The word
should not be confused with sertanejo.

SERTÃO.   The backlands; a vast semi-arid zone reaching
   north from the interior of Minas Gerais and Bahia to
   Piauí and Maranhão on the Amazonian frontier.   A cattle
   raising region, the sertão has periodically been afflicted
   by drought, a calamity which, on the average of one per
   decade since the early colonial period, has driven hundreds of thousands of impoverished sertanejos to the
   coast or south in search of relief.   The popular image
   of the sertão as inhospitable desert belies the general
   salubriousness of the zone, where water is to be found
   in oases and where general life-supporting conditions are
   more favorable than on much of the tropically humid
   coast.

SERVIÇO DE ASSISTANCIA RURAL (SAR).   A leadership
   training program for rural peasants in the Northeast,
   inspired by the Bishop of Rio Grande do Norte in 1960,
   Dom Eugenio de Araujo Sales, and concerned with the
   basic education of the rural camponeses.   By 1963, a
   year before SAR was abolished by the military, it had
   organized 45,000 workers into its rural syndicates.   Its
   main organizational center was Pernambuco, where its
   labor union activities were led by two priests, Padre
   Crespo and Padre Melo, the former from Jaboatão and
   the latter from Cabo, both agro-industrial suburbs of
   Recife.

SESMARIAS.   Extensive secondary land holdings of from
   10,000 to 13,000 hectares granted to favorite subjects
   of the Portuguese Crown in order to spur settlement in
   and development of colonial Brazil.   As such, they were
   commercial enterprises, not feudal fiefdoms, since the
   grantee had to take steps to cultivate the land or it would
   ultimately revery back to the Crown.

O SEXO FEMININO.   Feminist newspaper appearing briefly
   in Rio de Janeiro during the 1870's, one of a small number of such publications edited by women in the later
   Empire.

SHAPANA   see   OMOLU

SHASHARA.   A straw wand carried by Omolu or Obaluwaiye
   or Shapana, the goddess of contagious diseases in Afro-
   Brazilian spiritist belief.

SIARÁ.   The original spelling (on sixteenth-century maps) of
   the Captaincy of CEARÁ.

SILVA, FRANCISCO MANUEL BARROSO DA   see   ALMIRANTE
BARROSO

SILVA, HÉLIO (1904-). Physician, journalist, public employee and amateur historian whose multi-volume series
of the Vargas Cycle (and other themes) have provided a
substantial body of printed documentation, minimally edited.

SILVA, LEÔNIDAS DA (1913-). Leading soccer idol of the
1930's, called the "black diamond" by the press, playing
for various Rio de Janeiro and São Paulo teams and leading the Brazilian World Cup team in France in 1938 to
a third place finish.

SILVA, ORLANDO. The most popular singer of the 1930's,
known for his romantic voice and his ability to awaken
the passions of his audiences, who frequently ripped the
clothing from his body at public appearances.

SILVA JARDIM, ANTÔNIO DA (1860-1891).   Republican pro-
pagandist and orator, and one of the most violent and
outspoken opponents of the royal family.   When the Republic came he was not offered a single post, and, in
disgust, sailed with his family for Europe.   When he
arrived in Paris, a petition calling for his return awaited
him, signed by more than 3,000 Brazilians.   Elated, he
planned to go back.   But continuing his travels to Naples,
he decided to climb Mt. Vesuvius.   At the summit, his
footing slipped, and he tumbled into the open crater.

SILVA LISBOA, JOSÉ DE.   Early nineteenth-century economic
advisor to João VI.   An admirer of Edmund Burke.   Silva
Lisboa supported Brazilian concessions to the English in
the Treaty of 1810 as a token of gratefulness for the
English role in opening Brazilian trade.

SILVA PONTES, ANTÔNIO PIRES DE.   Governor of Espíritu
Santo province in the first decade of the nineteenth century who, to facilitate navigation of the Rio Doce between
Minas Gerais and the coast, established military posts
at Lorena, the port of Sousa, and Regência Augusta for
the purpose of subduing the aboriginal tribes in the vi-
cinity.   See also ATAÍDE E MELO, PEDRO M. X DE.

SILVA TELES, JAIME DA.   Architecture student in the 1920's
who championed the new forms of French design popularized by the Parisian architectural review, L'Esprit

Nouveau. Silva Telles's advocacy led to the adoption of
buildings built on concrete columns--pilotis--and to the
invitation to Le Courbusier to come to Brazil, where he
influenced a generation of Brazilian architects.

SILVINO, ANTÔNIO (1875-1944). Born Manuel Batista de
Morais in the sertão município of Alagoa do Monteiro,
Paraíba, the youth was raised across the border in Pernambuco, a region rife with clan factionalism and conflict. His parents were well-off, owning slaves and cattle, and his father a law officer. He entered the life
of a cangaceiro after the murder of his father; after
1899 he took the name of his godfather (and uncle), one
of the most famous bandits of his day. Until 1914, when
he was betrayed and captured, he plundered the northeast, defending his family's honor. Jailed for twenty-
three years he finally was pardoned by Vargas in 1937.
After a turn as a bureaucrat in Rio he returned to the
sertão where he died impoverished. Brazilian historians
have considered him a "good" or "noble" cangaceiro,
a Brazilian Robin Hood, in contrast to the destructive
image of Lampião, a cangaceiro-avenger. By allying
himself with local coronel clans, and by directing his
violence against established authorities (including the
English-owned Great Western of Brazil Railway Company)
he managed to acquire the reputation of a popular hero,
one who, unlike Lampião, respected the "honor" of families; that is, he treated women of the elite with deference.

SIMÕES LOPES, LUIS. Rio Grande do Sul-born administrator, the first head of Vargas's civil service agency, the
Departamento Administrativo de Serviço Público (DASP),
established in 1938.

SINAGOGA PAULISTA, A. "The Paulista Synagogue," a
tract written in 1937 by Integralist leader Gustavo Barroso (q. v.), and widely distributed throughout Brazil.
See also INTEGRALISM.

"SINFONIA AMAZÔNICA." Brazil's first full-length animated
cartoon, by Mário Latini Filho, produced in 1953.

SINHÁ. Term used by slaves in addressing white women in
the Big House, rather than the conventional "senhora."
Young women, most typically the mistresses' daughters,
were called by the diminutive, "sinhazinha."

SISAL. Agave sisalana, a drought resistant, xerophytic plant

producing valuable fiber, introduced to Brazil from the
Yucatan in 1903, and harvested on plantations in the
sertão of Bahia, Pernambuco, and Paraíba. Approximately 300,000 persons were engaged in sisal agriculture
in the early 1970's.

SISSÓN, ROBERTO FALLER (1900-). Career naval officer
and Secretary-General of the ill-fated popular front, the
National Liberation Alliance (ANL). A colleague of
tenente Hercolino Cascardo, Sissón helped organize the
ANL, which served as a front for the Brazilian Communist Party although Sissón and Cascardo (and most of
its adherents) were not Party members. With the suppression of the organization in mid-1935 and the deflagra-
tion of the PCB-inspired insurrection in Natal, Recife,
and Rio de Janeiro in November, Sissón was arrested
and placed under surveillance, although he did not spend
much time in prison. He spent some years in exile in
Argentina and Uruguay. Active again during the period
of PCB legality after 1945, he returned to a life of
forced retirement and semi-incarceration, which was
limited even further after 1964. As a naval officer with
high connections, Sissón never faced the brutality shown
to others of similar political stance. But for most of
his life he was effectively excluded from political expression.

SITANTE. The owner of a small plot of land, or sítio.

SLANG. Giria, or street talk, plays an important role in
intergroup communications among Brazilians of all classes, and influences linguistic change. Giria varies widely
from region to region, but since the 1930's has been
spread with greater rapidity through the improving network of public communications. Some giria, vintage
1978, include the following terms and phrases: "estar
ligado (a)": to be deeply involved with, often in a sense
involving drugs; "não esta com nada": to be without sub-
stance, empty, as a vacuous person or institution; "estou
na pior": to be weary or depressed.
    "Vaselinar" is a coined word suggesting slipperiness,
or solicitous behavior; "barra pesada," a heavy burden,
or "trip." "Porrada" refers to a collision, as between
automobiles; "tirar sarro," to act sexually in an offensive
or gross manner. It is noteworthy that much current
giria springs from the drug culture or from strained
inter-personal behavior, although there is a second va-

riety of slang phrases describing the traditional euphoria
of everyday Brazilian language: "joia" and "barato,"
for example, both describing a state of feeling or being
sublime.

SLAVE TRADE.   Prosperous and largely in the hands of the
English by the eighteenth century, the shipment of slaves
from Portuguese colonies and trading posts in Africa
was suddenly opposed in England after 1807, when human-
itarian objections began to be raised by Wilberforce and
others.   Under English pressure the Brazilians agreed
to diminish the trade after 1830 and eliminate it entirely
by 1845, but during the period from 1840 to 1850 the
number of slave imports actually grew, with as many
as 300,000 Africans smuggled in before threat of British
intervention in 1850 finally stopped the trade.

SMITH, T. LYNN.   Professor of sociology from the United
States who, in the mid-1930's, was one of the several
foreign scholars invited to the new University of São
Paulo to help establish its academic programs.   Others
included Frenchmen Emile Coornaert and Roger Bastide.

SNYDER, RONALD.   Pseudonym for Ralph Nader who, with
Joseph Page, visited Northeastern Brazil in 1963 to inter-
view Francisco Julião.   Page was arrested and imprisoned
in a return visit a year later for having consorted with
"Snyder."

SOCIEDADE BRASILEIRA PARA CIÊNCIAS (SBPC).   The
Brazilian Society for the Advancement of Science, an
association of scientists, historians, sociologists and
other intellectuals, which has taken strong public stands
in favor of the restoration of full democratic freedoms.
It sponsored an international congress in Brazil in 1977.

SOCIEDADE DEFENSORA DA INDEPENDÊNCIA E LIBERDADE
DO BRASIL.   A political group organized in 1831 which
became the stronghold of the moderados, including José
Bonifácio, Nicolau Vergueira, and General Francisco
Lima e Silva.   Its chief mouthpiece was Evaristo da
Veiga, the outspoken editor of the Aurora Fluminense.

SOCIEDADE INTERNACIONAL DE COMÉRCIO (SOINC).   A
private German-Brazilian consortium established in 1936
to facilitate trade between the two countries, on the basis
of an exchange of coffee for railroad equipment.

SOCIOCRACY. The goal of Comtian positivism, a republic governed by a hierarchy of virtuous and capable men who had risen to the top by demonstrating their skills. Like Mexico under Diaz and his "científicos," Brazil under this ideal state would have no room for democracy, which positivists was as a "perversion of the science of mathematics."

SODRÉ, JERONYMO. A young professor at the Bahian Medical School whose call, in 1879, for parliamentary action to end slavery, is considered to have "broken the ice" of the abolitionist issue, bringing its challenge to the political arena, which heretofore had managed to keep itself as removed as possible from the gathering anger. Sodré's speech calling for legislative action attracted widespread attention and helped carry the debate to society as a whole.

SOLDADO, O see TRIBUNA MILITAR

SOMBRA, SEVERINO see LEGIÃO CEARENSE DO TRABALHO

SORBONNE. Slang for the Superior War College in Rio de Janeiro, the major stepping stone to positions of influence and power in the armed forces, especially after 1964.

SOROCABANA RAILROAD COMPANY. A line serving the coffee region of São Paulo, British-financed but purchased by the state of São Paulo, which leased it to the internationally-financed Sorocabana Railway Company Ltd. in 1907.

SORTEIO MILITAR. Brazil's universal conscription system, passed into law in 1908.

SORTILÉGIO. A one-act play, by Abdias do Nascimento, written in 1951 but staged only in 1957 after a six-year battle with censors, who labelled it immoral and revolutionary. Written expressly for Nascimento's Black Experimental Theatre, it presents a strident and emotional outcry against racial humiliations and injustices suffered by Brazilian blacks. The play underscores what the dramatist feels is the essential unity between the Afro-Brazilian and his African heritage.

SOUSA, SANCHO DE FARO. The last official to be designated Governor-General of Brazil (1718-1719). After his departure the new officeholders were named "viceroys."

SOUSA, TOMÉ DE (1515?-1573). The first governor-general of the Crown captaincy of Bahia, arriving at Salvador in 1549.

SOUTH. The region encompassing the states of Rio Grande do Sul, Santa Catarina, and Paraná.

SOUTHEAST. Region containing the states of São Paulo, Minas Gerais, Rio de Janeiro, and Espírito Santo. Formerly the region was called the Center-South; it is by far the wealthiest and most dynamic region of Brazil, and dominates the country in every sphere.

SOUZA, IRINEU EVANGELISTA DE (1813-1889). Known as Baron and Viscount Mauá, an extraordinary figure of the economic expansion of the Brazilian Second Empire from 1850 until the outbreak of the Paraguayan War. Mauá rose from simple lower-middle class origins in Rio Grande do Sul to become an importer in Rio de Janeiro, then a major industrialist, banker, and fiancier until his empire collapsed in 1875 after the central government refused to bail him out with a requested loan from the Banco do Brasil.

SOUZA E OLIVEIRA COUTINHO, AURELIANO DE (1800-1855). Foreign Minister of the Empire in the early 1840's, and a strong defender of the principle of nonintervention.

SPIRITU SANCTO, CAPTAINCY OF. The original name of the captaincy bordered on the north by Porto Seguro and on the south by Rio de Janeiro. Never a financial success, it eventually reverted to the Crown. Its modern name is Espírito Santo.

"SPOTS." An English word appropriated into the Brazilian vocabulary, usually used with reference to the fifteen- or thirty-second filmed or videotaped spots broadcast and telecast around the clock to remind Brazilians of the government's progress and of their civil and moral responsibilities. See also SUGISMUNDO; ASSESSORIA DE RELAÇÕES PÚBLICAS.

"STAGNATIONIST" SCHOOL. Identified with Celso Furtado and others connected with the Economic Commission for Latin American (ECLA) holding that the import substitution process was essentially completed in Brazil by 1962, and that industrialization had not brought the hoped for

benefits in terms of a higher standard of living for workers.   Labor absorption had been low because of the highly
capital-intensive nature of the new industries.

STERNBERG, HILGARD O'REILLY.   Berkeley-educated Brazilian geographer, who, in the 1950's, helped expose the
limitations of the solutions to the drought problem of the
Northeast through hydraulic works and reforestation,
which is impractical in a densely-populated region.

SUBSÍDIO LITERÁRIO.   A fund established in 1772 by the
Marquis of Pombal, to encourage primary and secondary
education in Brazil.   Only in 1800 did the first school
of quality--the new seminary at Olinda--open its doors;
the Pombaline educational reform had little direct effect
anywhere.

SUDENE.   The Superintendency for Development of the Northeast, a federal agency established in 1959 under the
leadership of economist Celso Furtado.   SUDENE differed
from earlier attempts to aid the drought region (see
IFOCS) in that it attempted to redistribute population,
bring industry to the region, and carry out land reform.
Furtado was dismissed in 1964 with the military coup
and SUDENE became just another bureaucratic agency.

SUGISMUNDO.   Cartoon character invented by the Assessoria
de Relações Públicas da Presidência da República (q. v.),
the official public relations arm of the executive.   Sugismundo, pictured with a dirty face and surrounded by
flies, although otherwise amiable, literally means "Dirt-
ies Everyone"; he is the hallmark of the campaign against
littering, and typical of the sophisticated use of the mass
media after 1964 to achieve mass awareness on desired
issues.

SUJEIÇÃO.   Labor performed by rural peasants as a form
of contract with the landowner.

SUMMER INSTITUTE OF LANGUAGES.   Major United States-
backed research institute for the study and teaching of
indigenous tongues, founded in 1936, for the purpose of
creating written languages so that missionaries can then
translate the Bible.   The SIL has brought Protestant
Christianity to more than 90 illiterate tribes, and is cur-
rently at work with 650 others.   In early 1978, however,
the Brazilian government cancelled permits for additional

SIL field teams to work in the Amazon: since official policy seeks to integrate indigenous tribes into Portuguese-speaking culture, the work of SIL linguists to bolster native languages has been seen as an obstacle to that integration.

SUPPLY TRAINS, MILITARY. During the Old Republic, and during the Empire, columns of troops frequently allowed women and children to accompany their men: General Amaral Savaget's column of 2,450 soldiers had in its supply train 300 women and 80 children.

SUPRA DECREE. Issued by President João Goulart on March 13, 1964, weeks before his ouster, calling for the expropriation without indemnity of all under-utilized properties of more than 1,200 acres located within six miles of major routes of communications, and lands over 70 acres within six miles of dams, irrigation, or drainage projects.

SUZANO, AZAMBUJA (1791-1873). Literary figure and precursor of the modern Brazilian romantic novel. Suzano's major work was O Capitão Silvestre e Frei Veloso ou a Plantação do Café no Rio de Janeiro.

-T-

TABA. Amerindian village.

TABAREU. A rural yokel, identified by his rustic clothing or manners when he comes into town.

TABAXARES. One of the original sixteenth-century captaincies, located at the site of the present state of Piauí, east of Ceará, and never economically viable.

TABERNA. A roadside tavern, usually in the countryside.

TABOLEIROS. Sandy tablelands of the Northeast long stripped of their forest cover, with their soils eroded from heavy rainfall and leaching by the sun.

TAÇA JULES RIMET. Created in 1928 by the International Soccer Federation, a trophy to go to the first national team to win three World Cup championships. Brazil retired the cup in 1970, fielding a team in the final match

against Italy of Félix, Carlos Alberto, Brito, Piazza,
Everaldo, Clodoaldo, the veteran Gerson, Jairzinho,
Tostão, Pelé, and Rivelino.

TAIPA.   Palm leaves, used to cover the mud or adobe
houses of the rural poor.

TAMANDARÉ, ALMIRANTE (1807-1897).   Gaúcho-born career
naval officer whose career was made by successfully suppressing various revolts and armed movement during the
early Empire--the 1824 Confederation of the Equator,
in Pernambuco; the Balaida; the Praiera revolt in 1848
and the Brazilian intervention in Uruguay in 1864 and
in the following War of the Triple Alliance against Paraguay.

TAMOIOS.   A confederation of tribes allied with the French
whose allegiance was secured through the mediation of
Padre José de Anchieta and others.   The final treaty is
known by the name of the settlement in which it was
drawn up: Iperoígue.   During a part of the negotiations,
Anchieta voluntarily remained as a semi-hostage in one
of the Tamoio villages to show his side's good faith.

TAPAJÓS, RENATO.   Filmmaker and novelist, whose "Em
Câmara Lenta" (In Slow Motion) was banned as subversive
under Article 54 of the National Security Law in 1977.
The novel treats the period (1968-1973) of urban guerrilla
activity in Brazil; Tapajós himself was peripherally connected to the Ala Vermelha (q. v.) wing of the Maoist
Partido Comunista do Brasil.

TARIFA MÓVEL.   A sliding railroad rate schedule, allowed
by the legislature of the state of São Paulo from the mid-
1890's until 1920 as an indirect government subsidy in-
suring railroads against inflation, since the system permitted rates to be raised or lowered in relation to the
exchange rate.

TARTAS, ISAAC DE CASTRO   see   LIS, JOSÉ

TAUBATÉ CONVENTION.   An accord, signed by the states
of Rio de Janeiro, Minas Gerais, and São Paulo in February 1906 to support coffee prices.   Ultimately, the
plan broke down, but the principle of "valorization" survived and was adopted by the Afonso Pena and later
Federal administrations.

TAUNAY, AFONSO D'ESCRAGNOLLE (1876-1958). Disciple of Capistrano de Abreu and author of several works on the bandeirantes; son of Alfredo, Viscount Taunay.

TAUNAY, ALFREDO D'ESCRAGNOLLE (1843-1899). Carioca-born to a noble French family, Taunay edited the Diário do Exército (Army Journal) during the Paraguayan war, and went on to write several essays and romances as well as historical commentary. His "Retreat from Laguna" (1871) is a useful (if melodramatic) account of the war. His collected works run to thirty volumes.

TAURINO DE REZENDE, GENERAL. Head of the National Commission of Investigations, in 1964 he resigned and protested publicly when his son, a faculty member at the Federal University of Pernambuco, was arrested and beaten for alleged subversion. See LOTT, HENRIQUE TEIXEIRA.

TAVARES, ANTÔNIO RAPÔSO (1598-1659?). Bandeirante leader who, during a four year period beginning in 1648, traveled the entire length of Brazil from São Vicente to Belém at the Amazon's mouth.

TAVEIRA JÚNIOR, BERNARDO (1836-1892). A nineteenth-century author and poet known as a linguist (he learned Danish, Latin, Greek and Sanskrit), and associated with the Germanophile school of Tobias Barreto.

TÁVORA, JOAQUIM. Brother of Juarez Távora, and himself a co-conspirator in the 1924 tenente insurrection in São Paulo.

TÁVORA, JUAREZ (1898-1976). Tenente leader, Prestes Column veteran, military commander of the Liberal Alliance forces in the Northeast during (and after) the 1930 coup, and presidential candidate for conservative UDN against Juscelino Kubitschek in 1955. Távora, campaigning on a platform of morality and patriotism, finished second, with some votes drained off by ex-Integralist Plínio Salgado, running from the far right, and Adhemar de Barros, the flamboyant governor of São Paulo.

TEATRO ARENA see BOAL, AUGUSTO

TEATRO EXPERIMENTAL DO NEGRO. Theater group founded by Abdias do Nascimento, to train black actors for roles outside the traditional stereotypes assigned to them in Brazilian theater.   The group was disbanded after the 1964 coup.

TEATRO NEGRO-BRASILEIRO.   The Afro-Brazilian Theater, organized in 1944 by Abdias do Nascimento in Rio de Janeiro, a frequently harassed professional company seeking to combat racial and cultural discrimination in Brazil. An anthology of plays presented by the theater group was published in 1961: Drama para Negros e Prólogo para Brancos.

TEIXEIRA, ANÍSIO (1900-1967).   The leading educator of the 1930's until his removal from his post as director of education in the Federal District for being a "bolshevik subversive." Teixeira, the only Brazilian to have studied with John Dewey, made dramatic progress in the direction of broadening the base of public education until he was fired.   In the 1950's he made a modest comeback, heading the Center for Educational Planning in Rio de Janeiro, but after 1964 he again was driven from his work.   The cause of his death in the late 1960's, possibly from suicide, possibly from a grotesque accident, is still obscured.

TELENOVELAS.   Daily soap operas, after running a year or more, in prime time in the evening as well as during the day.   Some of the most popular have been "O Direito de Nascer" ("The Right to Be Born,") and Amado's "Gabriela" (q.v.).

TENENTE.   Literally, lieutenant.   Also the name given to the insurrectionary movement of cadets and young officers which broke out in 1922 and survived through the end of the decade, when, with tenente military support, defeated presidential candidate Getúlio Vargas overthrew the incumbent administration and came to power, bringing the tenentes into the mainstream of military decision-making.

TERESA CRISTINA MARIA DE BOURBON, EMPRESS (1822-1889).   The daughter of Francisco I of the Kingdom of the two sicilies and D. Maria Isabel of Spain, she married Emperor Dom Pedro II in 1843, in Naples, with Prince D. Leopoldo acting as the Monarch's surrogate. She left for Brazil immediately afterward.   She was a popular Empress and was known as "Mãe dos Brasileiros" ("Mother of the Brazilian people").   She died in 1889 nearly as soon as the deposed royal couple arrived in their European exile. Not an attractive woman, she was rejected by Pedro in the first years of their marriage, but in time they worked out a respectful relationship.

TÊRMOS. Administrative units corresponding roughly to a county; part of a comarca, or judicial district. Têrmos were further subdivided into freguesias, or parishes; bairros, or neighborhoods; and finally wards.

TERRA CAÍDA. Breakaway floating islands of earth, common to the Amazon basin; the islands even may support tall trees--sumaumás and faveiros--upright as they journey hundreds of miles down river, or livestock, or homes and people. Eventually they break up and settle as soil-bed in a different part of the Basin.

TERRA FIRME. In the Amazon, land high enough so that it is seldom flooded.

TERRA MIXTA. Sandy soils, common to parts of the coffee growing regions in northern Paraná. These soils, in contrast to the well-known terra roxa of São Paulo and the region west of Maringá in Paraná, are less fertile; trees planted in it live for 15 or 20 years, not 50.

TERRA ROXA. "Red earth," the soil prevalent in the coffee producing areas of São Paulo and western Paraná.

TERREIRO. A terrace of stone or mud for drying coffee beans.

TERRITORIAL LIMITS OF BRAZIL. These were set, after extensive exploration of the Amazon and Paraná basins in the early seventeenth century, according to the line of settlements between Spanish and Portuguese areas. Since the Spaniards never proceeded as far east as the Portuguese did west, the present-day map of Brazil far exceeds the original juridical boundaries established by the 1494 Treaty of Tordesillas.

TERRITÓRIO DOS PASTOS BONS. "Land of good pastures," the name given to the so-called "inner sertão" in the hinterland of Bahia and Goiás--from the upper reaches of the Itapecuru and the Rio das Balsas to the Tocantins.

THIRD OF OCTOBER CLUB. Formed by tenente leaders to commemorate the outbreak and ultimate victory of the

1930 Revolution, and to serve as an organized lobby to
pressure Vargas, as provisional head of state, to fulfill
tenente goals.   Internal dissent between right- and left-
wing tenentes however, split the group and shattered its
façade of unity.   On the left, Miguel Costa and Hercolino
Cascardo advocated socialism as a tool to smash oligarchic control; on the right, Goés Monteiro and others
looked to dictatorial means to rescue Brazil from liberal
"weakness. "

TIJUCO.   Site of the first major discovery of diamonds, in
1727, in the captaincy of Minas Gerais.   Mining com-
menced in 1730, leading, in time, to the renaming of
the town Diamantina.

TIMBER.   Beginning with brazilwood, Brazil has long been
known as a prime source of timber.   It has millions of
square kilometers of forests, much of which hardwood,
and during the 1970's became one of the world's leading
suppliers of timber, mostly to Japanese mills.   Lack of
anti-pollution laws has led some foreign paper and wood
companies to open plants in Brazil for processing, rather
than to ship the wood outside.

TIPHYS PERNAMBUCANA.   Newspaper edited by Frei Caneca
in late 1823 and early 1824, attacking the Emperor for
having dissolved the Assembly, and demanding, in lofty
(and inflammatory) language, self-government in the
name of freedom.   The conflict finally exploded in the
insurrection known as the "Confederation of the Equator"
in 1824.

TOMAR ESTADO.   "To take state," the obligation of single
white women in colonial society--that is, either to marry
or enter a convent.   To guarantee that she would be able
to do so, girls were kept in seclusion to remove any
possibility of doubt about their virtue, and early marriage
was encouraged.   Should a girl choose to enter a convent,
one was selected on the basis of her social standing,
whether it would be in Portugal or Brazil (Brazilian convents accepted only pure blooded whites), and the financial
standing of her parents or sponsors.

TOMÉ-AÇU.   Site of a Japanese agricultural colony in Ama-
zônia, 45 minutes south of Belém by air.   Established
in 1929 by the KANEBO colonization company, which
sent 43 families, now numbers about 300 families, spe-

cializing primarily in the cultivation of pepper and jute.
During World War II, the lands were expropriated and
Tomé-Açu turned into a detention camp for Japanese,
German and Italian aliens.   As a result, many of the
area's farmers today are caboclos, many of the original
Japanese settlers having dispersed after the war.

TORRES, ALBERTO (1865-1917).   The father of modern Brazilian economic nationalism, and the author of O Problema
Nacional Brasileiro (1914), in which he proposed limits
on foreign investment and greater centralization of government to achieve national economic development and integration.   In the early 1930's groups linked to the tenentes
organized a Sociedade de Amigos de Alberto Torres,
which attempted to function as a lobby for nationalistic
planks in the draft constitution being worked out during
the 1933-34 constituent assembly.

TORRES HOMEM, FRANCISCO DE SALES (1811-1876).   Leading Liberal and Imperial statesman, at various times
deputy, Treasury Minister, senator, Banco do Brasil
director, chargé d'affaires in Paris, and the author of
Libello do povo, an influential attack on the centralization of power in the Conservatives' hands in the 1830's
and 1840's.

TORTA CAPIXABA.   A shellfish pie, prepared during Easter
week in the region in and around Vitória, in the state of
Espírito Santo.   Ingredients include strings of crabs--
sold by street vendors in the port--lobster meat, shrimp,
palm hearts, dendê, eggs, and coconut milk.   It is eaten
either hot or cold, and shared with neighbors and relatives.

TRABALHISMO.   "Laborism," Vargas's political program
after his return to power in 1950, a blend of social wel-
fare paternalism, centralism, economic nationalism, and
an expanded role for the president.

"TRABALHO E CONFIA."   Motto of the state of Espírito
Santo: "work and confide."

TRABUCO.   A heavy shotgun, prized by backlands bandits as
a mark of their prowess.   The trabuco, dating from the
nineteenth century, was used along with Winchester .44's
and Brownies, or Colt .45's.

"TRAGÉDIA NO MAR."   The first known Brazilian poem about

the slave trade, by Castro Alves, written in 1868, eighteen years after the trade had been abolished. Haberly
cites this as an example of Brazilian self-censorship:
in Europe literature about the slave trade's "floating
coffins" was widespread even in the seventeenth century.

TRIANGULO MINEIRO. The triangle-shaped westernmost
zone of Minas Gerais, connected economically to São
Paulo and the site of agro-pastoral development after
the 1880's. Its leading city is Uberaba.

TRIBUNA MILITAR. A semiweekly armed forces journal
which first appeared in March 1881 under the name O
Soldado (The Soldier), and which complained of obsoles-
cence and governmental negligence. It attacked the Viscount of Pelotas as having been a do-nothing War Minister
(1880-81), and encouraged higher pay for enlisted men,
most of whom were black, junior officers, and pensions
for veterans. It warned against the Argentine military
threat and demanded a protective tarriff to aid domestic
industrial development. The newspaper ceased publication without explanation in 1882.

TRINDADE, SOLANO. Recife-based poet of the 1940's and
1950's whose works, influenced by Marxist outlook, parallel those of Afro-Cuban poet Nicolás Guillén.

TRONCO DE PAU COMPRIDO. A long wooden stock into
which were locked the legs of four or five slaves; invet-
erate offenders were confined within an iron hook or
collar, a gancho. Shorter stocks were called troncos.

TROPEIRO. Dealer or driver of pack animals.

TROPICALISM. Popular music movement of the late 1960's,
led by Caetano Veloso, a reaction to the romantic bossa
nova and the socially unconscious lyrics of such popular
singers as Chico Buarque de Holanda. Veloso attacked
the official version of Brazilian reality and dared censors
to ban their songs. Tropicalism was so successful that
Chico Buarque himself took up the social cause, and was
exiled for two years in Italy. Veloso himself left the
country under pressure. By the mid-1970's, Tropicalism
had faded.

TROPICI. "Tropics," a 1969 film by an Italian, Gianni Am-
ico, which fits squarely the mood and tone of the Cinema

Nôvo. The film follows a neo-realistic approach, and
recreates the migration of an impoverished northeastern
family to São Paulo.

TUBARÃO. Brazil's only significant coal-mining region, in
the state of Santa Catarina. Coal from its mines is
principally used by industries in and around Pôrto Alegre.

TUMBEIROS. "Floating coffins," the pejorative name given
by abolitionists to slave ships during the 1830's and after,
when the slave trade was supposed to be ending.

TUPINAMBÁ. Generic term for all of the Tupí tribes that
populated the coast of Brazil in the first century of colonization.

TUXAUÁ. Also known as Tubixada, the temporal head of
the Tupi tribe.

-U-

UBÁ. A primitive canoe hollowed out of a tree trunk, used
by aboriginal Amazonian tribes.

ÚLTIMA HORA. A tabloid, pro-Goulart daily newspaper in
Rio de Janeiro in the early 1960's. Under the military
regime the paper died a slow death when advertising
revenue was driven away and its editors and owner harassed.

UMBANDA. A hybrid religious form, uniting West African
spiritualism with Brazilian Catholicism. Some writers
have called umbanda the universalization of macumba
(which is prevalent in southern Brazil), although others,
including Edison Carneiro, believe that candomblé, umbanda, and macumba are all names representing the
same religious phenomenon over time.

UMBIGADA. A navel-to-navel bump which is an essential
feature of the batuque, the African forerunner of the
modern Brazilian samba. The Bantu name for this ges-
ture, in fact, was semba, from which the word "samba"
was later derived. European observers were scandalized
by the practice, calling it "lascivious and indecent"
(Georg Wilhelm Freyreiss, a German visitor in 1815-17).

UNDESIRABLES. The term for the Jews and New Christians

who were sent to, or who migrated voluntarily to, Brazil after 1535.   Gypsies were also considered undesirable
and were transported to the New World.   Persons considered undesirable by Crown officials in Brazil were
shipped to Angola.

UNIÃO DEMOCRÁTICA NACIONAL (UDN).   The third national
political party organized after the fall of the Estado Novo,
the UDN drew support from upwardly mobile middle class
groups, especially in larger towns and urban centers.
Just before the 1964 coup it nominated for its presidential
candidate Governor Carlos Lacerda of Guanabara, who,
by that year, had moved even further to the right than
most UDN supporters.   The party's founders included
Oswaldo Aranha, Júlio Prestes, Artur Bernardes, Assis
Chateaubriand, and Francisco Campos, the author of the
1937 constitution.

UNIÃO DOS HOMEMS DE CÔR.   "Union of Men of Color,"
founded in Rio de Janeiro in 1949, and seeking to influence government officials to become more aware of limitations faced by Afro-Brazilians in the areas of education
and employment.   The group helped spur interest in an
Afro-Brazilian congress (ultimately held in 1950) but
accomplished little else, and received virtually no attention in the press.

UNIÃO FEMINISTA BRASILEIRA.   Short-lived (1935) women's
auxiliary of the Aliança Nacional Libertadora.

U. S. INVESTMENT IN BRAZIL.   In 1977, total investment
was estimated by United States sources at over 2.4 billion dollars.

UNIVERSIDADE DE MINAS GERAIS.   Established in 1927 by
bringing together existing university-level faculties, the
institution was Brazil's second de facto university although
no effort was made to operate it as a single, consolidated
unit.   See UNIVERSIDADE DE SÃO PAULO.

UNIVERSIDADE DE RIO DE JANEIRO.   Brazil's first university, created in 1920 by consolidating several independent
faculties and programs, but without overall coordination
or unification of teaching teaching faculty.   This would
come only fourteen years later, with the creation of the
University of São Paulo (USP).

UNIVERSIDADE DE SÃO PAULO (USP).   Brazil's first co-

ordinated university, established in 1934.   See FACUL-
DADE DE FILOSOFIA, CIENCIAS E LETRAS.   In 1975
it boasted 30,000 students and a staff of 3,500.

URUBÚ.   1) A black vulture.   2) Name given to small black
children, not necessarily with hostility, but serving to
harden their self-views of their racial identities.

URUBUPUNGÁ.   One of the largest hydroelectric stations
in the country, on the Paraná river, and planned to be
one of the most productive in the world.   The project
is a joint federal-state enterprise, with overall supervision by the Societá Edison, Milan.

URUÇUMIRIM.   Present-day Catete, in downtown Rio de Janeiro.   In 1567 it was one of the two principal battle
sites between the French and Portuguese whose troops
were led by the victorious Mem de Sá.

USINA.   Modern sugar refinery, the advent of which, in the
1880's and 1890's, transformed sugar production into an
agro-industrial enterprise and which drove the more rudimentary engenho mills to uncompetetive disadvantage.
Even the usinas, however, failed to restore prosperity
to the sugar regions of the Northeast and Center-South:
in spite of low labor costs, transportation difficulties
and competition from European and North American beet
sugar producers forced the federal government to subsidize usinas as well as cane planters and suppliers from
the 1930's on.

ÚTEIS.   Colonial-era militia units, made up of urban com-
mercian employees, cashiers, and other conscripts from
related occupations.   See MILÍCIAS.

-V-

VALE, JORGE MEDEIROS.   The "Bom Burgûes," one of the
most colorful figures to provide financial support for the
urban guerrilla movement of the late 1960's, and sentenced
to six years imprisonment in 1969 for the theft of funds
from the Banco do Brasil, which he used to subsidize
MR-8, a revolutionary group.   In 1977 he entered the
papal nunciature in Brasília, seeking asylum after several
threats were made on his life following his release.

VALES.   Redemption certificates.   In hard times, industria-

lists, particularly sugar usineiros, often pay wages in
the form of such script, redeemable at the company store
but worthless outside.

VALLADARES, JOSÉ (1917-1959).   Historian and art critic
on the faculty of the University of Bahia until his death
in an air crash.

VALORIZATION (Valorização).   A Brazilian-coined term referring to the subsidization of the coffee producing sector by the government of the state of São Paulo, used
especially after the announcement of plans for the Taubaté Convention of 1907.

VANDRÉ, GERALDO.   Popular singer from the Northeast
whose socially conscious songs in backlands style won
him great acclaim in the mid-1960's.   His song "Cam-
inhando" a lightly veiled call for revolution, won the 3rd
Annual Popular Music Festival in Rio de Janeiro in 1968
before it was banned; his "Disparada," a warning of coming social unrest among the downtrodden, was similarly
proscribed by the censors.   Taking refuge in Europe,
Vandré became a drug addict after 1970.

VAPOR DE DIABO.   Pejorative name given to sugar refineries
by usina (q. v.) workers.

VAQUEIRO.   Cowboy of the backlands, usually a caboclo.

VARELA, FAGUNDES (1841-1875).   Poet of secular and religious themes whose private life encompassed various
sordid affairs and led him to death from alcoholism and
exposure.   He lived in Rio de Janeiro.

VARGAS, BENJAMIN (1898-1973).   Getúlio Vargas's brother,
considered disreputable by many, whose appointment to
the post of police chief in Rio de Janeiro in 1945 contributed to the decision to oust him from power.   Benjamin's public nickname was "Beijo," or "The Kiss."

VARGAS, DARCY SARMANHO (1895-1968).   The daughter of
a São Borja rancher and businessman, married to Getúlio
Vargas at the age of fifteen after he was named state
district attorney.   Receiving a large tract of land from
her father, the couple was able to survive the meager
years of political apprenticeship, as Young points out.
In her later life she avoided the spotlight, although D.

Darcy dedicated much of her time to various charitable
groups, notably one in support of orphaned newsboys.

VARGAS, GETÚLIO DORNELES (1883-1954).   Born in São
   Borja, Rio Grande do Sul, Vargas left a military career
   to pursue one in law and state politics, and rose to become Finance Minister in the Washington Luís administration and governor of Rio Grande do Sul in 1928.   Seen
   as bland, colorless, and a loyal political follower, Vargas was named as the presidential candidate at the head
   of the opposition Liberal Alliance coalition in 1930.   Defeated at the polls, he headed a victorious civilian-military coup which overthrew the incumbency and took power
   on November 3, 1930, the event marking the end of the
   First, or Old, Republic.
      As provisional chief of state, Vargas deftly began to
   balance the conflicting elements of his victorious coalition, including the now triumphant tenentes and the civilian "liberal constitutionalists" identified with the structures of the old regime.   After the São Paulo revolt of
   1932 he agreed to call a constituent assembly in 1933,
   but he chose to ignore it and the subsequent new national
   congress installed in 1934.   Using the pretext of a threat
   from the left after the 1935 ANL insurrections, he began
   to clamp down on civil liberties and led Brazil down a
   centralized, authoritarian path culminating in the imposi-
   tion--with military backing--of the Estado Novo dictatorship on November 10, 1937, in which he, in essence,
   overthrew his own government.   Vargas flirted with the
   fascist right but broke with it in 1938 and, by 1942, had
   led Brazil into the War on the Allied side.
      When he began to exhibit populist tendencies as the
   end of the War neared, he was deposed by the same
   military chiefs who had installed him in power in 1937.
   Leaving Rio in September 1945, he returned to his home
   state, where he was elected to the Senate (he also represented São Paulo and three other states in the Congress
   during the period from 1945 to 1950).   In that year, supported by two of the three national parties he had helped
   create, the PTB and PSD, he was elected president, the
   first time he was voted chief of state after holding that
   position from 1930 to 1945.   Assuming a more nationalistic posture, and exploiting his (doubled-edged) program
   of social legislation enacted during the 1930's, he rode
   to power at the head of an urban working and middle-
   class coalition fired by nationalism.   Unable to face the
   pressures and crises which flared up during the early

1950's, and with the military lurking in the background,
Vargas committed suicide at his residence in August
1954, leaving a note blaming "hidden forces" and "foreign interests" for his death. Until the 1960's, Vargas's
name enjoyed great popularity among urban voters who
remembered his paternalism and his creation of thousands
of bureaucratic jobs, but after 1964 his public image was
allowed to fade: he was not remembered by the new
generation of apolitical youths who came to political awareness after the 1964 coup, and he was considered too
colorful for the austere military leaders who came to
hold power.

VARGAS, MANUEL DO NASCIMENTO (1845-1924?). Getúlio
Vargas's father, a rancher and local political boss in
the frontier town of São Borja, Rio Grande do Sul. For
service during the Paraguayan War, Manuel Vargas was
named an honorary general by Floriano Peixoto; he was
a faithful follower of state chieftain Júlio de Castilhos.

VARGAS, PROTÁSIO (1877-1970). Another Vargas brother,
who avoided a public career and acted principally as a
behind-the-scenes advisor to brother Getúlio.

VARGAS, YEDA MARIA (1944-). Winner of the "Miss
Universe" contest in Miami in 1963. Her selection as
Miss Brazil prior to that competition provoked some
degree of controversy, since the public favorite was a
mulata, raising comments in the press that even if the
mulata were more attractive, Ms. Vargas should represent Brazil abroad. "After all," wrote the social col-
umnist of the Jornal do Brasil, "we don't want the rest
of the world to think that Brazilian society is composed
of a bunch of pickaninnies."

VARIG. Brazil's major commercial airline, now the largest
in South America, with service to 18 foreign countries
and a total of 102 cities. Formerly a private airline
established with joint Brazilian and German capital during the 1930's in the state of Rio Grande do Sul, VARIG
--in 1977 the 14th largest airline in the world--became
a wholly Brazilian-owned corporation after the Second
World War and a semi-public entity.

VATAPÁ. Succulent dish made with manioc powder, dendê
oil, peppers, peanuts, and meat or fish. Afro-Brazilian
in origin; common in Bahian cuisine.

VAZ, ROCHA. Author of a 1935 educational reform code,
   which served to stimulate primary and secondary education and to modify curricula. The act made provisions
   for the creation of new universities, and created the
   Departamento Nacional de Ensino under the Justice Ministry, the antecedent of the future Ministry of Education.

VEIGA, EVARISTO DA (1799-1837). Founder and publisher
   of the Aurora Fluminense in 1827, a newspaper whose
   criticism of Pedro I helped lead to his abdication in
   1831. In the following year da Veiga was shot at and
   wounded, but he escaped death.

VELHO, DOMINGOS JORGE (1614-1698?). Paulista commander
   of the bandeirante forces hired as mercenaries to attack
   and destroy the "republic" of escaped slaves at Palmares.
   Royal officials allegedly reneged on their promises for
   payment, and it took Velho several years to collect his
   due. The bandeirante campaign took three years (1692-
   1694) before attaining victory, and this only after being
   reinforced by additional militia troops.

VELLOSO, JOÃO PAULO DOS REIS (1931-). Yale-trained
   economist and Minister of Planning under Garrastazú
   Medici and Ernesto Geisel. The only cabinet minister,
   in fact, to be held over from the Médici administration.
   Velloso has urged the President to maintain Brazil's
   somewhat dangerous policy of heavy borrowing--by 1979
   Brazil's debt servicing will total almost $8 billion annual-
   ly--on the grounds that Brazil's economic managers are
   able to sustain Brazil's real economic growth rate at an
   average of 10 percent per year.

VELOSO, CAETANO see TROPICALISM

VELOSO, FREI JOSÉ MARIANO DA CONCEIÇÃO (1741-1811).
   Brazilian-born, Portuguese-trained botanist whose Flora
   fluminensis appeared in eleven volumes between 1825 and
   1827, in Lisbon.

VENDAS. Stores, during the colonial period and after.

VERGUEIRO, NICOLAU (1778-1859). Paulista fazendeiro responsible for one of the first colonization schemes in
   the coffee region, contracting several score of Swiss and
   German colonists and making them sharecroppers on his
   property, pledged to repay their passage through labor.

The system faltered; in 1857 the dissatisfied sharecroppers revolted, and fled the plantation. Other planters avoided Vergueiro's scheme in fear that such a spirit of freedom might infiltrate the minds of their slaves, as well. Buarque de Holanda blames the failure of the project in part from an inability of the European immigrants to adapt to tropical conditions.

VERÍSSIMO, ÉRICO (1906-1976). Major regional novelist, from Rio Grande do Sul. His Time and the Wind and other works reflect the cultural environment of gaúcho life during the Vargas period and after.

VERÍSSIMO, JOSÉ (1857-1916). Educator and literary critic from Pará and author of História de Literatura Brasileira, a major work of its day.

VESPUCCI, AMÉRIGO (1451-1512). Although much-praised (in the words of Oliveira Marques), Vespucci never discovered much of anything in spite of his fame as an explorer. Legend (and some old text books) suggest that he may have sighted the Brazilian coast before Cabral, but recent scholarship holds that he never even reached the coast east of present-day French Guiana, and even this is suspect.

VESTIBULAR. National university entrance examination, given annually under an atmosphere of intense pressure and competition, so much so that widespread cheating and corruption has been reported in recent years. The vestibular examinations are given in several subjects, a combination of which is required for admission to university faculties, assuming that places (vagas) are available. Some students who pass the vestibular examination still do not win admission. To pass the exams, most students take private cram courses, many of which are taught by university personnel.

VIAMÃO see CAMPOS DO VIAMÃO

VIEIRA, ANTÔNIO (1608-1697). A Jesuit father who won fame as an eloquent spokesman against enslavement of the Amerindian population. He spent many years traveling in the Amazon and along the Northern coast; in 1661 Maranhão planters drove the Jesuits out of their captaincy for their anti-slavery preachments, and Vieira, who went to Portugal to protest, and to defend his leniency toward

New Christians, was imprisoned for four years.   In 1667
he was released and went to Rome to plead the cause of
the New Christians; he was given a safe-conduct pass by
the Pope to return, and he died among his beloved native tribes in 1697, at ninety years of age.

VIGILENGAS.   One-masted sailboats plying the Middle Amazon
carrying foodstuffs and other products to markets.

VILA BELA.   One of the two populated districts of the captaincy of Mato Grosso, the other Cuiabá, which became
the leading population center after the discovery of gold
in 1718.   Vila Bela, despite its small size (7,000 inhabitants in 1800), was made the capital of the captaincy in
1746 owing to its strategic position on the banks of the
Guaporé River, near the Spanish-populated dominions to
the southwest.

VILA BOA.   Colonial-era capital of Goiás, in the southern
portion of the captaincy where gold was discovered in
1725.

VILA CIPÓ.   Rural hamlet in Rio de Janeiro state where
Carolina Maria de Jesus (q. v.) is buried in a pauper's
grave.

VILA DO LUGAR DA BARRA.   "Village near the river's
mouth," the eighteenth-century name for the settlement
later renamed Manaos.

VILA FRANCA.   Village on the Tapajós, in the Amazonian
Basin, chosen by the Jesuits in colonial times as their
administrative center from where they supervised 10,000
Indians practicing agriculture and handicrafts.   When
Pombal expelled the Jesuits the town immediately was
plunged into a decline; ultimately it gave way to Santarém,
on the protected, southern side of the Bay of the Tapajós.

VILA KENNEDY.   A housing project outside of Rio de Janeiro
built by the United States Agency for Internation Development (AID) in the 1960's, and often cited by Brazilians
and non-Brazilians as an example of the glaring weaknesses of the concept of such aid.   The community, constructed at a cost of $3.5 million, is located about 30
miles from the heart of the city, forcing its 19,000 residents, which were removed from favelas in the city's
center, sometimes forcibly, to spend up to six hours a

day commuting to jobs, at a cost of from 30 to 40 percent of their salaries for bus fare.   Since the Brazilian
work day for laborers and domestics begins at 6 A.M.
or earlier, workers have to leave their homes around
3 A.M.   Furthermore, the community was built with no
infrastructre of shops, schools, or jobs; it lies isolated
and bare beyond the reach of city services.   No Brazilian
agency felt obliged to take over such organization once
AID completed its project, leaving a legacy of bitterness
and cynicism about the entire foreign aid process.

VILA RICA.   Town in the gold mining region of Minas Gerais,
later renamed Ouro Preto (q.v.), for the dark pigmentation of its ore.   The town is famous for its magnificent
baroque-style churches, and has become a center of
tourism and artisanship.

VILARES, DÉCIO.   Painter and designer of the Republican
flag of Brazil, the present-day banner portraying the
stars of the Southern Cross and the positivist motto,
Order and Progress, on a yellow and green field.   The
idea for the flag was suggested by Army Capitain Benjamin Constant, who usually is given credit for its design
although Vilares actually carried it out.

VILAS BOAS BROTHERS.   Cláudio, Orlando, and Leonardo,
who have devoted their careers to the protection of the
interests of Brazil's aboriginal population.   Although
their methods of achieving "pacification" have been criticized both by anthropologists and progress-minded officials, for differing reasons, they have distinguished themselves for their humane dedication to their work.   See
INDIAN PROTECTIVE ASSOCIATION; ABORIGINAL POP-
ULATION.

VILLA-LOBOS, HEITOR (1887-1959).   Major Brazilian classical composer whose more than 1700 works draw on
indigenous themes.   His most acclaimed work is his
"Bachianas Brasileiras" (q.v.).   Villa-Lobos gained attention as a participant in the modernists' Modern Art Week
of São Paulo (1922).

VINTEQUATRO.   A large poisonous ant, native to the middle
and upper Amazon, whose bite produces what its name
("twenty-four") suggests: twenty four hours of severe
pain, swelling, and fever.

VIRACOPOS.   International airport serving São Paulo, near
the city of Campinas, 85 kilometers from the state capital.

VISCONTI, ELISEU (1867-1944). Painter of the optic school, fascinated with color and light, and known for his landscapes of Teresópolis, in the mountains beyond Guanabara Bay.

VISIGOTHS. One of the several Germanic tribes that swept across the Iberian peninsula after the fall of Rome in 410. The Visigoths, Christians of the Arian sect, converted to orthodox Christianity under their King, Reccared. They were fierce people who preferred rural to urban social organization; during their three century domination of Hispania feudalism was introduced. They were driven out in the eighth century by the Moslems.

VISSUNGOS. Work songs chanted by slaves in the gold regions of Minas Gerais; some, in Bantu dialect, had survived in rural Minas through the 1940's. Few of the singers, however, any longer understood the meaning of the words.

VITAL, DOM see GONÇALVES DE OLIVEIRA, DOM VITAL

VIVEIROS DE CASTRO, AUGUSTO OLYMPIO. Rio law professor and Catholic lay leader who, in the 1920's, spoke out against work performed outside of the home by women as "unnatural, anti-social, and uneconomic."

VOLAGE. The British frigate which carried D. Pedro I and his immediate family back to Portugal, after his abdication in April 1831.

VOLANTES. "Flying columns" of police troops, used to comb the backlands for bandits in the 1920's and 1930's.

VOLKSDEUTSCHE. German-born Brazilians, numbering between 800,000 and 1,000,000 (estimated) in the mid-1930's, and hoped-for supporters of a domestic fascist regime by such Nazi sympathizers as Felinto Müller and Plínio Salgado. Most of the Volksdeutsche, although they were concentrated in the states south of São Paulo and almost universally maintained their German social customs, including their language, proved loyal to the Vargas administration and did not oppose the suppression of the Nazi and Integralist movements after 1938.

VOLTA REDONDA. Brazil's major steel producing center, located in the Paraíba Valley between Rio de Janeiro and Sao Paulo, and federally owned. Volta Redonda's original

plant was part of the lend-lease arrangement delivered,
at the conclusion of the Second World War, in gratitude
for Brazil's entry in the War on the Allied side.   The
steel plants have recently been modernized; they are administered by a government trust, the Companhia Side-
rúgica Nacional.

VON MARTIUS, KARL FRIEDRICH PHILIP (1794-1868).   A
Bavarian botanist who, with colleague Johan Baptiste von
Spix, came to Brazil with Princess Leopoldina, daughter
of the Austrian Emperor and fianceé of Pedro I, and
produced an eighty-volume study on indigenous flora,
Flora Brasiliensis, for generations the standard work
on the subject.

VON SPIX, JOHAN BAPTISTE (1781-1826) see VON MAR-
TIUS, KARL FRIEDRICH PHILIP

VOTO DE CABRESTO.   A "halter vote," where citizens
voted under instruction by political bosses or coronéis,
an abuse of expanded suffrage under the Republic.

VOYAGES DANS L'INTÉRIEUR DU BRÉSIL (1852)   see
SAINT-HILAIRE, AUGUSTE DE

VRIJBURG PALACE   see PALÁCIO FRIBURGO

-W-

WALLACE DA GAMA COCHRANE, IGNÁCIO.   Conservative
Imperial deputy from São Paulo, and outspoken
critic of the Republic.   Cochrane expressed dis-
belief that Brazil's 14,000,000 citizens could allow the
Empire to fall without protest, and blamed events on
lack of public spirit and patriotism.

WAR OF THE TRIPLE ALLIANCE see PARAGUAYAN WAR

WEBB, JAMES W.   United States Minister of Brazil in 1863
who predicted, not without bias, a rising tide of republicanism, and that Pedro II would be the last Emperor.
The Republican party was actually organized in 1870 by
dissident liberals in São Paulo, echoing the fall of the
French Empire and the rise of the Third Republic.

WHALING.   A royal monopoly in colonial times, operated

on a contract basis to concessionaires. Caio Prado notes that one expedition in the 1760's caught 523 whales. The oldest whaling ports were in Bahia, at the harbor bar and at Itaparica; later installations were established at Praia Grande (now Niterói), Santos, and at Santa Catarina. By 1800, the whale population along the coast had been greatly reduced--although at the same time restrictions were lifted, throwing open the industry to all comers. By the last quarter of the century, whaling all but disappeared because of the virtual extinction of the mammals from Brazilian waters.

WHITAKER, JOSÉ MARIA. A Paulista banker and Vargas's first Minister of the Treasury. In spite of his family name, he spoke no English, to the chagrin of British diplomats who took the fact for granted.

WOLNEY, ABÍLIO. One of the two main coronel chieftains hired by authorities to pursue the Prestes Column with jagunço guerrillas. Wolney, from Goiás, skirmished frequently with the Column but failed to overtake it or win any major victories. See also MATOS, HORÁCIO DE.

-X-

XANGÔ. An Afro-Brazilian vodun cult centered in Pernambuco. See also CANDOMBLÉ.

XAQUE-XAQUE. A dumbbell-shaped metal rattle, used in Afro-Brazilian cult ceremonies.

XAVIER, CHICO see KARDECISM

XAVIER, JOAQUIM JOSÉ DA SILVA (1746-1792). "Tiradentes," or "tooth-puller," a cavalry officer and leader of the Inconfidência Mineira who, after the conspiracy was betrayed, was hanged, his body drawn and quartered, his home razed, and its site strewn with salt. As such, the would-be conspirator was turned into a martyr and, after the passage of time, a national hero as a precursor of Independence and republicanism.

XICRIABÁ TRIBE. Dominant on the western bank of the Tocantins, in Maranhão, hostile, and given to raids on population centers on the eastern bank as well. These attacks restricted westward penetration by settlers, and terrorized the Portuguese until the early nineteenth century.

XOKLÉNG TRIBE.   Massacred by professional riflemen hired by land colonization companies in Paraná and Santa Catarina, in the early years of this century.   The event helped contribute to the sense of national anger which in turn led to the creation of the Indian Protective Service.   See also RONDON.

XUXÚ (or CHUCHÚ).   A pale green vegetable, called chayote in English.   One of the few vegetables served in traditional Brazilian cuisine, where diets usually consisted of meat or dried cod, rice, and manioc--even in the homes of the affluent.   Xuxú in taste and texture resembles the green squash, and is usually served with little seasoning.

-Y-

YANAMANÖ.   An Amerindian tribe--also known as Guaharibo or Waika--who live in the tropical area bordered by the Rio Negro and the Orinoco, and who for hundreds of years have managed to fend off attacks from the warlike Caribs and Arawak.   To the 1970's, they also successfully managed to isolate themselves from coastal civilization.

YELLOW FEVER PROPHYLAXIS SERVICE.   Formed in 1903 under the direction of Oswaldo Cruz, in Rio, to carry out the anti-mosquito campaign and to divide the city into sanitary districts, with the goal of isolating yellow fever patients.   Although discussion of the bill creating the service was angry--many legislators were unconvinced of the efficacy of the Walter Reed-Carlos Findlay methods--it ultimately served as model for a national yellow fever campaign.

YORDIM.   Israeli Jews who emigrated to Brazil after 1950, some settling in the Amazon region and others moving to the larger cities.   About 1,000 of these immigrants are known to have entered Brazil between 1950 and 1960.

YPANEMA IRON FACTORY.   Built in São Paulo early in the nineteenth century under Imperial auspices, but never successful; under the Republic it was closed.

-Z-

ZAMBI see ZUMBI

ZEBU. Brazil's principal strain of beef cattle, developed
    after cross-breeding with bulls imported from India. The
    Zebu can reach a weight of one ton in less than three
    years.

ZIRALDO, ALVES PINTO (1932-). Social and political
    cartoonist and poster artist.

ZONA. Slang for red-light district.

ZONA BRAGANTINA. An Amazonian sub-region, named for
    the town of Bragança, east of Belém, and the last out-
    post of coastal civilization until the construction of the
    trans-Amazon highway in the late 1960's.

ZONA DA MATA. The narrow coastal strip running from
    Rio Grande do Norte to Bahia along the northeast. Hu-
    mid and fertile, this is the traditional zone given to
    sugar agriculture, the home of the engenho (sugar mill)
    and the hierarchical pattern of master-slave relations
    described by Gilberto Freyre.

ZONA FRANCA DE MANAOS. The duty-free zone of the
    Amazonian city of Manaos, created in the mid-1960's
    to attract Brazilian visitors lured by low prices for im-
    ported goods.

ZONA NORTE. Industrial and lower class residential area
    of Rio de Janeiro, composed of districts such as Penha,
    Meier, Engenho Nôvo, Madureira, and Bangú.

ZUMBI (?-1695). Chieftain of the free black "republic"
    (quilombo) at Palmares. Stories of his heroic suicide
    before insurmountable odds at the end of the republic's
    life, however, are inventions; in reality he was captured
    and executed a year after its defeat, in 1695.

"ZUM-ZUM." Slang term for a slave insurrection, or mass
    protest.

ZUR ISRAEL. One of two synagogues established in Recife
    in the early 1630's under Maurice of Nassau. The sec-
    ond was Mogen Abraham.

ZWEIG, STEFAN. Austrian-Jewish writer who escaped to Brazil and wrote a book which became well-known in English: Brazil: Land of the Future. Despondent at the news of the war, he committed suicide in Petrópolis in 1943.

BIBLIOGRAPHY

To facilitate use, I have divided the bibliography into sixteen categories, as listed below in the Table of Contents. Many entries could well have been placed in two or more sections, and the reader would do well to peruse related categories for material. The bibliography is cross-referenced at the conclusion of each part in the case of entries whose subjects clearly overlap other sections.

Books and articles considered particularly useful have been starred (*). Readers will note that the bibliography is restricted to published works appearing in English. Dissertations are excluded, since they are easily retrieved through use of catalogs issued by the University Microfilms Corporation in Ann Arbor. A parallel bibliography of Portuguese-language sources, not to mention other languages, could easily be compiled to equal this volume's bibliography in length. Few research projects on Brazil of any thoroughness could possibly be accomplished without the use of Portuguese-language works.

TABLE OF CONTENTS

KEY TO FREQUENTLY CITED JOURNALS

AA	American Anthropologist
AAG/A	Association of American Geographers/Annals
ASR	American Sociological Review
AUFS	American Universities Field Staff
CSSH	Comparative Studies in Society and History
EDCC	Economic Development and Cultural Change
HAHR	Hispanic American Historical Review
HT	The History Teacher
IAEA	Inter-American Economic Affairs
IJAS	International Journal of African Studies
ISSJ	International Social Science Journal
JAH	Journal of African History
JDH	Journal of Developing Areas
JEH	Journal of Economic History
JIAA	Journal of Inter-American Affairs
JIASWA	Journal of Inter-American Studies and World Affairs
JIH	Journal of Interdisciplinary History
JNH	Journal of Negro History
LARR	Latin American Research Review
LBR	Luso-Brazilian Review
NACLA	North American Congress on Latin America
PCCLAS	Pacific Coast Conference on Latin American Studies
RIB	Revista Interamericana de Bibliografia
R/RI	Revista/Review Interamericana
SJA	Southwestern Journal of Anthropology
TA	The Americas
WPQ	Western Political Quarterly

I. BIBLIOGRAPHY; HISTORIOGRAPHY; RESEARCH AIDS

1 Bacceches, B. Bibliography of Brazilian Bibliographies, Detroit, 1978.

2 Burns, E. Bradford. "A Working Bibliography for the Study of Brazilian History," TA, 22 (July 1965), 54-88.

3 _____, ed. Perspectives on Brazilian History, New York, 1967.

4 Byars, Robert S. and Joseph L. Love. Quantitative Social Science Research on Latin America, Urbana, Illinois, 1973.

5 Catholic University of America. Bibliographical and Historical Description of the Rarest Books in the Oliveira Lima Collection at the Catholic University in America (comp. by Ruth E. Holmes), Washington, 1926.

6 Dorn, Georgette M. Latin America, Spain and Portugal: An Annotated Bibliography of Paperback Books, 2nd ed., Hispanic Foundation, Washington, 1976.

7 Esquenazi-Mayo, Roberto and Michael C. Meyer, eds. Latin American Scholarship since World War II: Trends in History, Political Science, Literature, Geography, and Economics, Lincoln, Nebraska, 1971.

8 Fuerst, René. Bibliography of the Indigenous Problem and Policy of the Brazilian Amazon Region (1957-1972), Geneva and Copenhagen, 1972.

9 Gillett, Theresa. Catalog of Luso-Brazilian Material in the University of New Mexico Libraries, Albuquerque, 1970.

10 Graham, Richard and Virginia Valiela. Brazil in the Lon-

don Times, 1850-1905: A Guide, Carbondale, Ill., 1969.

11 *Griffin, Charles C., ed. Latin America: A Guide to the Historical Literature, Austin, 1971.

12 *Handbook of Latin American Studies, V. 1-14, Cambridge, Massachusetts; V. 15- , Gainesville, Florida, 1936- .

13 Hill, Roscoe R., ed. The National Archives of Latin America, Cambridge, Massachusetts, 1945.

14 Hilton, Ronald. Who's Who in Latin America. Part VI: Brazil, 3rd ed., Stanford, 1948.

15 Hutchinson, Harry W. Field Guide to Brazil, National Academy of Sciences, Washington, 1960.

16 Ianni, Octávio. "Research and Race Relations in Brazil," in M. Mörner, ed., Race and Class in Latin America, New York, 1970, pp. 256-278.

17 *Jackson, William V. Library Guide for Brazilian Studies, Pittsburgh, 1964.

18 Jones, C. K. A Bibliography of Latin American Bibliographies, Baltimore, 1922; 2nd ed., Washington, 1942.

19 Levine, Robert M. Brazil: Field Research Guide in the Social Sciences, Institute of Latin American Studies, Columbia University, New York, 1966.

20 _____. "Letter from Recife," LBR, 7:2 (Dec. 1970), 114-121.

21 Lombardi, Mary. Brazilian Serial Documents: A Selected and Annotated Guide, Bloomington, 1977.

22 Manchester, Alan K., ed. "Descriptive Bibliography of the Brazilian Section of the Duke University Library," HAHR, 13:2/3 (May and Nov. 1933), 238-266; 495-523.

23 Manning, William R., ed. Diplomatic Correspondence of the United States Concerning the Independence of the Latin-American Nations, 3 vols., New York, 1925.

24 Morse, Richard M. "Some Themes of Brazilian History," South Atlantic Quarterly, 61:2 (1962).

25 Pan American Union. Columbus Memorial Library.
    Index to Latin American Periodical Literature, 1929-
    1960, 8 vols. , Boston, 1962.

26 Phillips, Philip L. A List of Books, Magazine Articles,
    and Maps Relating to Brazil, 1800-1900, Washington,
    1901.

27 Pierson, Donald. Survey of the Literature on Brazil of
    Sociological Significance Published up to 1940, Cam-
    bridge, Massachusetts, 1945.

28 Rodrigues, José Honório. "Brazilian Historiography,"
    in M. Diegues Júnior and B. Wood, eds. , Social
    Science in Latin America, New York, 1967, pp. 217-
    240.

29 Sable, Martin H. , ed. A Guide to Latin American Studies
    U. C. L. A. Latin American Studies Center, Reference
    Series #4, 2 vols. , Los Angeles, 1967.

30 *Skidmore, Thomas E. "The Historiography of Brazil,
    1889-1964," Part I, HAHR, 55:4 (Nov. 1975), 716-
    748; Part II, HAHR, 56:1 (Feb. 1976), 81-109.

31 Souza, Amaury de. "Annotated Bibliography on the Bra-
    zilian Political Movement of 1964," Report #2, Latin
    American Research Program, University of California,
    Riverside, 1966.

32 Stein, Barbara H. Latin America: Social Sciences and
    Humanities Serials Currently Received in the Princeton
    University Library, Princeton, 1964.

33 *Stein, Stanley J. "The Historiography of Brazil, 1808-
    1889," HAHR, 40:2 (May 1960), 234-278.

34 *_____. "Latin American Historiography," in Social
    Science Research on Latin America (ed. by C. Wagley),
    New York, 1964, pp. 88-124.

35 *_____. "The Tasks Ahead for Latin American His-
    torians," HAHR, 41:4 (Nov. 1961), 424-433.

36 Steward, Julian, ed. Handbook of South American In-
    dians, 2 vols. , Washington, 1946-48.

37 Texas, University of. Library. Catalog of the Latin

American Collection of the University of Texas Library, 36 volumes, Boston, 1971.

38   Topete, José M. A Working Bibliography of Brazilian Literature, Gainesville, 1957.

39   Trask, David F. , Michael C. Meyer, and Roger R. Trask, eds. A Bibliography of United States-Latin American Relations Since 1810, Lincoln, Nebraska, 1968.

39a   Wilgus, A. Curtis.   The Historiography of Latin America: A Guide to Historical Writing, 1500-1800, Metuchen, N. J. , 1975.

39b   _____. Latin America in the Nineteenth Century: A Selected Bibliography of Books of Travel and Description Published in English, Metuchen, N. J. , 1973.

39c   _____. Latin America, Spain and Portugal: A Selected and Annotated Bibliographical Guide to Books Published in the United States, 1954-1974, Metuchen, N. J. , 1977.

40   Wirth, John D.   "Brazil, the Republic," in Latin America: A Guide to the Historical Literature (ed. by C. Griffin), Austin, 1971, pp. 607-618.

41   Wood, Bryce and Manuel Diegues Júnior, eds.   Social Science in Latin America, New York, 1967.

42   Zubatsky, David.   "A Bibliography of Cumulative Indexes to Luso-Brazilian Journals of the 19th and 20th centuries," LBR, 8:2 (Dec. 1971), 71-81.

SEE ALSO: 155, 578, 668, 868.

II.   GENERAL TREATMENTS

43   *Alden, Dauril and Warren Dean, eds.   Essays Concerning the Socioeconomic History of Brazil and Portuguese India, Gainesville, 1977.

44   *Azevedo, Fernando de.   Brazilian Culture, New York, 1950.

45   *Baklanoff, Eric N. , ed.   New Perspectives of Brazil, Nashville, 1966.

46 _____. The Shaping of Modern Brazil, Baton Rouge, 1969.

47 Bello, José Maria. A History of Modern Brazil, 1889-1964, (tr. by J. L. Taylor, with a new concluding chapter by Rollie E. Poppino), Stanford, 1966.

48 Bender, Lynn Darrell. "Brazil: Giant in Pursuit of Greatness," R/RI, 7:1 (Spring 1977).

49 Bernstein, Harry. Modern and Contemporary Latin America, Part III, New York, 1965.

50 _____. Modern Brazil: An Emerging Nation, New York, 1964.

51 Bishop, Elizabeth. Brazil, New York, 1962.

52 Blakemore, Harold A., ed. Portugal and Brazil: An Introduction, Oxford, 1953.

53 Burns, E. Bradford. A Documentary History of Brazil, New York, 1966.

54 * _____. A History of Brazil, New York, 1970.

55 _____. Nationalism in Brazil: A Historical Survey, New York, 1968.

56 _____. Perspectives on Brazilian History, New York, 1967.

57 Calogeras, João Pandia. A History of Brazil (tr. and ed. by P. A. Martin), Chapel Hill, N.C., 1939.

58 Carless, H. and Peter Flynn. Modern Brazil, New York, 1970.

59 Céspedes, Gillermo. "Brazil: The View from Spanish American History," HT, 2:3 (March 1969), 44-49.

60 Chilcote, Ronald H., ed. Protest and Resistance in Angola and Brazil, Berkeley, 1972.

61 Cole, J. P. Latin America: An Economic and Social Geography, New York, 1956, pp. 323-370.

62 Denis, Pierre. Brazil (tr. by B. Miall), London, 1941.

63 Flynn, Peter. Brazil: A Political Analysis, London, 1978.

64 Freyre, Gilberto. Brazil: An Interpretation, New York, 1947.

65 _____. New World in the Tropics: The Culture of Modern Brazil, New York, 1959.

66 _____. The Portuguese and the Tropics (tr. by H. D'O Matthew and F. de Mello Moser), Lisbon, 1961.

67 *Furtado, Celso. The Economic Growth of Brazil: A Survey from Colonial to Modern Times (tr. by R. de Aguiar and E. C. Drysdale), Berkeley, 1963.

68 Gardel, Luis Delgado. Brazil, Chicago, 1969.

69 Godfrey, Walter. Brazil, Overseas Economic Survey, London, 1954.

70 Graham, Richard, ed. A Century of Brazilian History Since 1865: Issues and Problems, New York, 1969.

71 Hill, Lawrence F., ed. Brazil, Berkeley, 1947.

72 James, Preston E. "Portuguese South America," in Latin America, 4th ed., New York, 1969.

73 Jobim, José. Brazil in the Making, New York, 1943.

74 Keith, Henry H. and S. F. Edwards, eds. Conflict and Continuity in Brazilian Society, Charlestown, S. C., 1969.

75 Kingsbury, Robert C. and Ronald M. Schneider. An Atlas of Latin American Affairs, New York, 1965, pp. 106-123.

76 Lacombe, Américo Jacobina, Brazil: A Brief History, Rio de Janeiro, 1954.

77 Lévi-Strauss, Claude. Tristes Tropiques (tr. by J. Russell), New York, 1964.

77a Martin, P. A., "Brazil," in Argentina, Brazil and Chile (ed. by A. Curtis Wilgus), Washington, 1935; reprinted 1963.

78   Martins, Wilson.   "Brazilian Politics," LBR, 1:2 (Dec. 1964).

79   Marshall, Andrew.   Brazil.   London, 1966.

80   Oliveira Lima, Manoel D.   The Evolution of Brazil Compared with That of Spanish and Anglo-Saxon America, Stanford, 1914.

81   *Poppino, Rollie E.   Brazil: The Land and People, 2nd ed., New York, 1973.

82   Prado Júnior, Caio.   Economic History of Brazil, Berkeley, 1945.

83   *_____.   Formation of Contemporary Brazil, Berkeley, 1942.

84   Rodrigues, José Honório.   Brazil and Africa (tr. by R. Nazzara and S. Hileman), Berkeley, 1967.

85   _____.   The Brazilians: Their Character and Aspirations (tr. by E. Dimmick), Austin, 1967.

86   Roiter, Fúlvio, ed.   Brazil, New York, 1971.

87   Saunders, John, ed.   Modern Brazil: New Patterns and Development, Gainesville, 1971.

88   Sayers, Raymond B., ed.   Portugal and Brazil in Transition, Minneapolis, 1968.

89   Schurz, William L.   Brazil, the Infinite Country, New York, 1961.

90   *Smith, T. Lynn.   Brazil, People and Institutions, 4th ed., Baton Rouge, 1972.

91   _____.   Brazilian Society, Albuquerque, 1975.

92   _____ and A. Marchant, eds.   Brazil, Portrait of Half a Continent, New York, 1951.

93   Tavares de Sá, Hernane.   The Brazilians: People of Tomorrow, New York, 1947.

94   Vellinho, Moises.   Brazil South: Its Conquest and Settlement, New York, 1968.

95 *Wagley, Charles. An Introduction to Brazil, 2nd ed.,
   New York, 1971.

96 Webb, Kempton. The Changing Face of Northeast Brazil. New York, 1974.

97 Weil, Thomas E. Area Handbook for Brazil, Washington, 1971.

98 Worcester, Donald E. Brazil: From Colony to World
   Power, New York, 1973.

99 Young, Jordan. "Brazil: World Power 2000?" Intellect. 105:2385 (June 1977).

100 Zweig, Stefan. Brazil: Land of the Future (tr. by A.
    St. James), New York, 1941.

III. TRAVEL AND CONTEMPORARY ACCOUNTS

101 Adalbert, Prince of Prussia. Travels in the South of
    Europe and in Brazil, With a Voyage up the Amazon
    (tr. by R. H. Schomburgk and J. E. Taylor), 2 vols.,
    London, 1849.

102 Agassiz, Louis. Scientific Results of a Journey to Bra-
    zil, Boston, 1870.

103 *   and Elizabeth C. Agassiz. A Journey to Bra-
    zil, Boston, 1871.

104 Andrews, Christopher Columbus. Brazil: Its Condition
    and Prospects, New York, 1887.

105 *Armitage, John. The History of Brazil from the Ar-
    rival of the Bragança Family in 1808 to 1831, 2
    vols., London, 1836.

106 Ashe, Thomas. A Commercial View and Geographical
    Sketch of the [sic] Brazil in South America, London,
    1812.

107 Assú, Jacaré. Brazilian Colonization from a European
    Point of View, London, 1873.

108 Baker, John M. A View of the Commerce Between the
    United States and Rio de Janeiro, Washington, 1838.

109 Barrows, John. A Voyage to Cochinchina in the Years
     1792 and 1793, London, 1806.

110 Bates, Henry W. The Naturalist on the River Amazon,
     London, 1863.

111 Bennett, Frank, Forty Years in Brazil, London, 1914.

112 Bezerra dos Santos, Lindalvo. "People and Scenes of
     Brazil," Revista Brasileira de Geografia (1945),
     137-138.

113 Bigg-Wither, Thomas Plantagenet. Pioneering in South
     Brazil: Three Years of Forest and Prairie Life
     in the Province of Paraná, 2 vols. , London, 1878.

114 Boyce, William D. , Illustrated South America, Chicago
     and New York, 1912.

115 *Burton, Richard F. Exploration of the Highlands of
     the Brazil, 2 vols. , London, 1869.

116 *Calcott, Maria Graham. Journal of a Voyage to Bra-
     zil and Residence There During Part of the Years
     1821, 1822, 1823, London, 1824; reprinted, New
     York, 1969.

117 Chamberlain, Henry. Views and Costumes of the City
     and Neighborhood of Rio de Janeiro, London, 1822.

118 Codman, John. Ten Months in Brazil, Boston, 1867.

119 Cooke, Morris L. Brazil on the March, A Study in
     International Cooperation, New York, 1944.

120 Dampier, William. A New Voyage Round the World,
     London, 1927.

121 Dent, H. C. , A Year in Brazil, London, 1886.

122 Dundas, Robert, Sketches of Brazil, Including New
     Views on Tropical and European Fever, London,
     1852.

123 Dundonald, Thomas (Lord Cochrane). Narrative of Ser-
     vice in the Liberation of Chile, Peru, and Brazil,
     2 vols. , London, 1859.

124 Dunn, Ballard S. Brazil, the Home for Southerners, New York, 1866.

125 Edmundson, George, ed. , Journal of the Travels and Labours of Father Samuel Fritz in the River of the Amazons between 1686 and 1723, London, 1922.

126 Elliott, L. E. Brazil: Today and Tomorrow, New York, 1917.

127 Ewbank, Thomas. Life in Brazil, New York, 1856; reprinted, Detroit, 1971.

128 Fawcett, Percy H. Exploration Fawcett. London, 1969.

129 Foster, William, ed. The Voyage of Sir James Lancaster to Brazil and to the East Indies, 1591-1603, London, 1940.

130 Gardner, George. Travels in the Interior of Brazil, London, 1846.

131 Gaston, James McFadden. Hunting a Home in Brazil. The Agricultural Resources and Other Characteristics of the Country; also, the Manners and Customs of the Inhabitants, Philadelphia, 1867.

132 Gibson, Hugh. Rio, Garden City, 1937.

133 Granville, Charles G. "English-speaking Travellers in Brazil, 1851-1887," HAHR, 40:4 (Nov. 1960), 533-547.

134 Guenther, Konrad. A Naturalist in Brazil: The Flora and Fauna and the People of Brazil (tr. by B. Miall), London, 1931.

135 Hadfield, William. Brazil, the River Plate, and the Falkland Islands, London, 1854.

136 _____. Brazil and the River Plate in 1868, London, 1869.

137 _____. Brazil and the River Plate, 1870-76, London, 1877.

138 Heaton, Herbert. "A Merchant Adventurer in Brazil, 1808-1818," JEH, 6 (May 1946), 1-23.

139   _____, ed., The Discovery of the Amazon, New
          York, 1934.

140   Henderson, James. A History of Brazil, London, 1821.

141   Herndon, William Lewis and Lardner Gibbon, Explora-
          tion of the Valley of the Amazon, 3 vols., Washing-
          ton, 1854.

142   Holdridge, Desmond. Feudal Island. New York, 1939.

143   Hurford, Alice V. "First Impressions of São Paulo,"
          South America, 3 (Feb. 1915), 202-204.

144   *Kidder, Daniel P. and James C. Fletcher. Brazil
          and the Brazilians, Portrayed in Historical and De-
          scriptive Sketches, 8th ed., Boston, 1868.

145   Kipling, Rudyard. Brazilian Sketches, New York, 1940.

146   Koebel, William H. The Great Southland: The River
          Plate and Southern Brazil of Today, New York, 1920.

147   *Koster, Henry. Travels in Brazil, London, 1817, 2
          vols.; reprinted, Carbondale, Illinois, 1966.

148   Luccock, John. Notes on Rio de Janeiro and the South-
          ern Parts of Brazil Taken During a Residence of
          Ten Years, 1808 to 1818, London, 1820.

149   Mansfield, Charles Blackford. Paraguay, Brazil and
          the Plate; Letters Written in 1852-1853, Cambridge,
          England, 1856.

150   Mathison, Gilbert F. Narrative of a Visit to Brazil,
          Chile, Peru, and the Sandwich Islands During 1821
          and 1822, London, 1825.

151   Mawe, John. Travels in the Interior of Brazil, Par-
          ticularly in the Gold and Diamond Districts of That
          Country, London, 1812.

152   Mulhall, Michael G. Rio Grande do Sul and Its German
          Colonies, London, 1873.

153   Nelson, Margaret. "The Negro in Brazil as Seen
          Through the Chronicles of Travelers," JNH, 30:2
          (April 1945), 203-218.

154 Phelps, Gilbert. The Last Horizon: A Brazilian Journey, 2nd ed. , London, 1973.

155 *Poppino, Rollie. Bibliographic essay in Brazil: The Land and People, New York, 1973, pp. 342-349.

156 Roosevelt, Theodore. Through the Brazilian Wilderness, New York, 1914. Reprinted, New York, 1969.

157 Scully, William. Brazil: Its Provinces and Chief Cities; the Manners and Customs of the People; Agricultural, Commercial, and Other Statistics, Taken from the Latest Official Documents; with a Variety of Useful and Entertaining Knowledge, Both for the Merchant and the Emigrant, London, 1866.

158 Smith, Herbert H. Brazil, the Amazons and the Coast, New York, 1879.

159 *Southey, Robert. History of Brazil, London, 1918; reprinted, New York, 1969.

160 *Spix, J. B. von and C. F. P. von Martins. Travels in Brazil in the Years 1817-1820, 2 vols. , London, 1824.

161 [Staden, Hans]. Hans Staden, the True Story of His Captivity, (tr. and ed. by M. Letts), London, 1928.

162 Stein, Barbara H. "Brazil Viewed from Selma, Alabama, 1867," Princeton University Library Journal, 27:2 (Winter 1966), 66-85.

163 Stewart, C. S. A Visit to the South Seas During the Years 1829 and 1830, 2 vols. , London, 1831.

164 Tjarks, Alicia. "Brazil: Travel and Description, 1800-1899," Revista de História de América, 83 (1968).

165 Wallace, Alfred. A Narrative of Travels on the Amazon and the Rio Negro, 2 vols. , London, 1853.

166 Walsh, Robert. Notices of Brazil in 1828 and 1829, 2 vols. , Boston, 1831.

167 Waterton, Charles. Wanderings in South America, London, 1903.

168 Walter, Richard, ed. Anson's Voyage Round the World, London, 1928.

169 Warren, J. E. Pará, New York, 1851.

170 Wells, James William. Exploring and Travelling Three Thousand Miles Through Brazil from Rio de Janeiro to Maranhão. With an Appendix Containing Statistics and Observations on Climate, Railways, Central Sugar Factories, Mining, Commerce, and Finance; the Past, Present, and Future, and Physical Geography of Brazil, London, 1886. 2 vols.

171 Wied-Neuwied, Maximilian von. Travels in Brazil in 1815, 1816, and 1817, London, 1820.

172 Wilkes, Charles. Narrative of the United States Exploring Expedition During the Years 1838-1842, 5 vols., New York, 1856.

173 Winter, Nevin Otto. Brazil and Her People of To-Day: An Account of the Customs, Characteristics, Amusements, History and Advancement of the Brazilians, and the Development and Resources of Their Country, Boston, 1910.

174 Woodruffe, Joseph F. The Upper Reaches of the Amazon, London, 1914.

175 Wright, Marie Robinson. The New Brazil: Its Resources and Attractions, Historical, Descriptive and Industrial, 2nd ed., Philadelphia, 1907.

SEE ALSO: 26, 803.

IV. HISTORY, 1500-1808

176 Alden, Dauril. "The Population of Brazil in the Late Eighteenth Century: A Preliminary Survey," HAHR, 43:2 (May 1963), 173-205.

177 * _____. Royal Government in Colonial Brazil, Berkeley, 1968.

178 * _____, ed. The Colonial Roots of Modern Brazil, Berkeley, 1973.

179 *Boxer, Charles. The Dutch in Brazil, 1624-1654, Oxford, 1957.

180 * _____. The Golden Age of Brazil, Berkeley, 1965.

181 * _____. A Great Luso-Brazilian Figure: Padre Antônio Vieira, S. J. , London, 1957.

182 * _____. The Portuguese Seaborne Empire, London, 1969.

183 * _____. Salvador de Sá and the Struggle for Brazil and Angola, 1602-1686, London, 1952.

184 Chandler, C. L. "List of United States Vessels in Brazil, 1792-1805," HAHR, 26 (1946), 599-617.

185 Costa, Luis Edmundo da. Rio in the Time of the Viceroys (tr. by D. Momsen). Rio, 1936.

186 Diffie, Bailey W. Latin American Civilization: Colonial Period, Harrisburg, 1946; reprinted, New York, 1967.

187 * _____. Prelude to Empire: Portugal Overseas Before Henry the Navigator, Lincoln, Nebraska, 1961.

188 Dominian, Helen G. Apostle of Brazil: The Biography of José de Anchieta, New York, 1958.

189 Dutra, Francis A. "Duarte Coelho Pereira," TA, 29:4 (April 1973), 415-451.

190 Greenlee, William B. , ed. The Voyage of Pedro Alvares Cabral to Brazil and India, London, 1938.

191 Johnson, H. B. "The Donatary System in Perspective," HAHR, 52:2 (May 1972), 203-214.

192 Kennedy, John N. "Bahian Elites, 1750-1822," HAHR, 53:4 (Nov. 1972), 415-439.

193 Ley, Charles David, ed. Portuguese Voyages, 1498-1663, New York, 1947.

194 *Marchant, Alexander. From Barter to Slavery: The

Economic Relations of Portuguese and Indians in the Settlement of Brazil, 1500-1580, Baltimore, 1942.

195   *Maxwell, Kenneth.   Conflicts and Conspiracies: Brazil and Portugal, 1750-1808, Cambridge, 1973.

196   _____.   "The Generation of the 1790's and the Idea of Luso-Brazilian Empire," in Colonial Roots (ed. by D. Alden), Berkeley, 1973.

197   _____.   "Pombal and the Nationalization of the Luso-Brazilian Economy," HAHR, 48:4 (Nov. 1968), 608-631.

198   *Morse, Richard M.   The Bandeirantes: The Historical Role of the Brazilian Pathfinders.   New York, 1965.

199   Nash, Roy.   The Conquest of Brazil, New York, 1926; reprinted, New York, 1968.

200   Ramos, Donald.   "Marriage and the Family in Colonial Vila Rica," HAHR, 55:2 (May 1975), 200-225.

201   _____.   "Social Revolution Frustrated: The Conspiracy of the Tailors in Bahia, 1798," LBR, 13:1 (Summer 1976), 74-90.

202   Russell-Wood, A. J. R.   "Black and Mulatto Brotherhoods in Colonial Brazil: A Study in Collective Behavior," HAHR, 54:4 (Nov. 1974), 567-602.

203   _____.   "Colonial Brazil," in Neither Slave nor Free (ed. by D. W. Cohen and J. P. Greene), Baltimore, 1972, pp. 84-133.

204   *   _____.   Fidalgos and Philanthropists: The Santa Casa de Miseracôrdia of Bahia, 1550-1755, Berkeley, 1968.

205   *   _____, ed.   From Colony to Nation: Essays on the Independence of Brazil, Baltimore, 1975.

206   Schwartz, Stuart B.   "Cities of Empire: Mexico and Bahia in the Sixteenth Century," JIAS, 11 (1960), 616-637.

207   _____.   "Free Labor in a Slave Economy: The Lav-

radores de Cana of Colonial Bahia," in Colonial Roots (ed. by D. Alden), Berkeley, 1973, pp. 147-198.

208 * _____ . Sovereignty and Society in Colonial Brazil, Berkeley, 1973.

209 Smith, David Grant. "Old Christian Merchants and the Foundation of the Brazil Company, 1649," HAHR, 54:2 (May 1974), 233-259.

210 Soeiro, Susan A. "The Social and Economic Role of the Convent: Women and Nuns in Colonial Bahia, 1677-1800," HAHR, 54:2 (May 1974), 209-232.

211 Vianna Moog, Clodomir. Bandeirantes and Pioneers (tr. by L. Barrett), New York, 1964.

212 White, Robert Allan. "Fiscal Policy and Royal Sovereignty in Minas Gerais," TA, 34:2 (Oct. 1977), 201-229.

213 Winius, George, "India or Brazil: Priority for Imperial Survival," American Portuguese Cultural Society Journal, 2 (1976), 34-42.

214 Witznizer, Arnold. Jews in Colonial Brazil, New York, 1960.

215 _____ . "The Number of Jews in Dutch Brazil, 1630-1654," Jewish Social Studies, 16:2 (1954), 107-114.

216 _____ . Records of the Earliest Jewish Community in the New World, New York, 1954.

SEE ALSO: 43, 53-57, 82-83, 88, 94, 98, 258-259, 447, 498, 520, 659, 821.

V.   HISTORY, 1808-1889

217 Barman, Roderick. "The Brazilian Peasantry Reexamined: The Implications of the Quebra-Quilo Revolt, 1874-1875," HAHR, 57:3 (Aug. 1977). 401-424.

218 _____ and Jean Barman. "Critique of Thomas

Flory's 'Judicial Politics in Nineteenth-Century Brazil,'" HAHR, 57:4 (Nov. 1977), 695-701.

219 Bartley, Russell H. "The Inception of Russo-Brazilian
     Relations (1808-1828), HAHR, 56:2 (May 1976), 217-
     240.

220 Bernstein, Harry. Dom Pedro II, New York, 1973.

221 Boehrer, George C. A. "The Church and the Over-
     throw of the Brazilian Monarchy," HAHR, 48:3 (Aug.
     1968), 380-401.

222 _____. "The Flight of the Brazilian Deputies from
     the Cortes Gerais of Libson, 1822," HAHR, 40:4
     (Nov. 1960), 497-512.

223 _____. "José Carlos Rodrigues and O Novo Mundo,
     1870-1880," JIAS, 9:1 (Jan. 1967), 127-144.

224 Burns, E. Bradford. "The Role of Azeredo Coutinho
     in the Enlightenment of Brazil," HAHR, 44:2 (May
     1964), 145-160.

225 Cardozo, Manoel. "The Holy See and the Question of
     the Bishop-Elect of Rio, 1833-1839," TA, 10 (July
     1953), 3-74.

226 _____. "Oliveira Lima and the Catholic University
     of America," JIAS, 11:2 (April 1969), 209-222.

227 Costa, Sérgio Corrêa. Every Inch a King (tr. by S.
     Putnam), New York, 1950.

228 *Dean, Warren. "Latifundia and Land Policy in Nine-
     teenth Century Brazil," HAHR, 51:4 (Nov. 1971),
     606-625.

229 Dudley, William S. "Institutional Sources for Officer
     Discontent in the Brazilian Army, 1870-1889," HAHR,
     50:1 (Feb. 1975), 44-65.

230 Flory, Thomas. "Judicial Politics in Nineteenth Cen-
     tury Brazil," HAHR, 50:4 (Nov. 1975), 664-692.

231 _____. "Race and Social Control in Independent
     Brazil," JLAS, 9:2 (Nov. 1977), 199-224.

232 Freyre, Gilberto. "Social Life in Brazil in the Middle
     of the Nineteenth Century," HAHR, 5:4 (Nov. 1922),
     597-630.

233 *Graham, Richard. Britain and the Onset of Moderni-
     zation in Brazil, 1850-1914, Cambridge, England,
     1968.

234 _____. "Government Expenditures and Political
     Change in Brazil, 1880-1899," JIASWA, 19:3 (Aug.
     1977), 339-368.

235 _____. Independence in Latin America: A Compara-
     tive Approach, New York, 1972.

236 _____. "Landowners and the Overthrow of the Em-
     pire," LBR, 6:2 (Dec. 1970), 44-56.

237 _____. "Sepoys and Imperialists: Techniques of
     British Power in Nineteenth-Century Brazil," IAMEA,
     23:2 (Autumn 1969), 23-37.

238 _____, ed. A Century of Brazilian History Since
     1865: Issues and Problems, New York, 1969.

239 Hahner, June E. "The Brazilian Armed Forces and
     the Overthrow of the Monarchy: Another Perspec-
     tive," TA, 26:2 (Oct. 1969), 171-182.

240 Harding, Bertita. Amazon Throne: The Story of the
     Braganzas of Brazil, Indianapolis, 1941.

241 Haring, Clarence H. Empire in Brazil, Cambridge,
     Massachusetts, 1958.

242 Hill, Lawrence F. Diplomatic Relations Between the
     United States and Brazil, Durham, 1931.

243 Humphreys, Robert A. "Monarchy and Empire," in
     Portugal and Brazil: An Introduction (ed. by H. A.
     Blakemore), Oxford, 1953, pp. 301-320.

244 Levi, Darrell E. "The Prado Family, European Cul-
     ture and the Rediscovery of Brazil, 1860-1930,"
     Revista de História, 52 (Oct.-Dec. 1975), 803-824.

245 *Manchester, Alan K. British Pre-eminence in Brazil,

Its Rise and Decline: A Study in European Expansion, Chapel Hill, N. C., 1933; reprinted, Chapel Hill, N. C., 1964.

246 _____. "The Growth of Bureaucracy in Brazil, 1808-1821," JLAS, 4:1 (May 1972), 77-83.

247 _____. "The Recognition of Brazilian Independence," HAHR, 31:1 (Feb. 1951), 80-96.

248 Marchant, Anyda. "Dom João's Botanical Garden," HAHR, 41:2 (May 1961), 259-274.

249 _____. Viscount Mauá and the Empire of Brazil, A Biography of Irineu Evangelista de Sousa, 1813-1889, Berkeley, 1965.

250 Martin, Percy A. "Causes of the Collapse of the Brazilian Empire," HAHR, 4:1 (Feb. 1921), 4-48.

251 Morton, F. W. O. "The Military and Society in Bahia, 1800-1821," JLAS, 7:2 (Nov. 1975), 249-269.

252 Munn, B. W. "Graça Aranha, Nabuco, and the Brazilian Rapprochment with the United States," LBR, 6:2, Dec. 1969, 66-72.

253 Nabuco, Carolina, The Life of Joaquim Nabuco, Stanford, 1950.

254 Palmer, Thomas W. "A Momentous Decade in Brazilian Administrative History, 1831-1840," HAHR, 30:2 (May 1950), 209-217.

255 *Pang, Eul-Soo and Ron L. Seckinger. "The Mandarins of Imperial Brazil," CSCH, 4:1 (March 1972).

256 Ridings, Eugene W. "Interest Groups and Development: The Case of Brazil in the Nineteenth Century," JLAS, 9:2 (Nov. 1977), 225-250.

257 _____. "Elite Conflict and Cooperation in the Brazilian Empire: The Case of Bahia's Businessmen and Planters," LBR, 12:1 (Summer 1975), 80-99.

258 Rogers, Edward J. "The Iron and Steel Industry in Colonial and Imperial Brazil," TA, 19:3 (Oct. 1962), 172-184.

259 Silva Dias, Maria Odila. "The Establishment of the Royal Court in Brazil," in From Colony to Nation (ed. by A. J. R. Russell-Wood), Baltimore, 1975, pp. 89-108.

260 *Stein, Stanley J. Vassouras, a Brazilian Coffee County, 1850-1900, Cambridge, Massachusetts, 1957.

261 Strauss, Norman, "The Rise of American Growth in Brazil: The Decade of the 1870's," TA, 32:1 (Jan. 1976), 437-444.

262 Tambs, Lewis A. "Rubber, Rebels, and Rio Branco: The Contest for the Acre," HAHR, 46:3 (Aug. 1966), 254-273.

263 Turner, J. Michael. "Arab Documents in Bahian Archives," ITAS (1975).

264 Viotti da Costa, Emília. "The Political Emancipation of Brazil," in A. J. R. Russell-Wood, ed. , From Colony to Nation, Baltimore, 1975, pp. 43-88.

265 Williams, Mary W. Dom Pedro the Magnanimous, Second Emperor of Brazil, Chapel Hill, N. C. , 1937; reprinted, New York, 1966.

SEE ALSO: 33, 43, 53-57, 70, 82-83, 88, 98, 445-447, 563, 750, 752, 755, 763, 807-808, 810, 822, 840.

VI.   HISTORY, 1889-1964

266 Alexander, Robert J. Communism in Latin America, New Brunswick, 1957.

267 _____. Prophets of the Revolution, New York, 1962.

268 Bemis, George W. From Crisis to Revolution: Monthly Case Studies, School of Public Administration, University of Southern California, Los Angeles, 1964.

269 Bonilla, Frank. Jânio Vem Aí: Brazil Elects a President, AUFS, 1966.

270 Bourne, Richard. Getúlio Vargas of Brazil: 1883-1954, London, 1974.

271   Burns, E. Bradford, "Manaus, 1910: Portrait of a
      Boom Town," JIAS, (July 1965), 400-421.

272   _____. The Unwritten Alliance: Rio Branco and
      Brazilian-American Relations, New York, 1966.

273   Busey, William. "Brazil's Reputation for Political Sta-
      bility," WPQ, 18 (Dec. 1965), 866-880.

274   Chilcote, Ronald H., ed. The Brazilian Communist
      Party: Conflict and Integration, 1922-1972, New
      York, 1974.

275   _____. Protest and Resistance in Angola and Bra-
      zil: Comparative Studies, Berkeley, 1972.

276   Conniff, Michael L. "Voluntary Associations in Rio,
      1870-1945," JIASWA, 17:1 (Feb. 1975), 64-81.

277   _____. "The Tenentes in Power: A New Perspective
      on the Brazilian Revolution on 1930," JLAS, forth-
      coming.

278   Cortés, Carlos. Gaúcho Politics in Brazil: The Role
      of Rio Grande do Sul in National Politics, Albuquer-
      que, 1974.

279   Crawford, H. P. "Comments on the Constitution of
      Brazil," General Legal Bulletin, United States De-
      partment of Commerce, C.L. 517, G.L. 126, Wash-
      ington, April 15, 1935.

280   Davis, Horace B. "Brazil's Political and Economic
      Problems," Foreign Policy Reports, 11:1 (March 13,
      1935), 1-12.

281   *Dean, Warren. "The Planter as Entrepreneur: The
      Case of São Paulo," HAHR, 46:2 (May 1966), 138-
      152.

282   Dell, E. "Brazil's Partly United States," Political
      Quarterly, 33:3 (July 1962), 282-293.

283   *Della Cava, Ralph. Miracle at Joaseiro, New York,
      1970.

284   Donald, Carr Lowe. "Brazilian Local Self-Government:
      Myth or Reality?" WPQ, 13:4 (Dec. 1960), 1043-1055.

Bibliography   252

285 Dubnic, Vladimir Reisky de. Political Trends in Brazil, Washington, 1968.

286 Dulles, John W. F. Unrest in Brazil: Political-Military Crises, 1955-1964, Austin, 1970.

287 _____. Vargas of Brazil: A Political Biography, Austin, 1967.

288 Flynn, Peter. "The Revolutionary Legion and the Brazilian Revolution of 1930," in Latin American Affairs (ed. by R. Carr), No. 22, Oxford, 1970.

289 Freels, Peter W., Jr. "The Many Shades of Revolutions in Brazilian Political Literature," University of California, Riverside, Latin American Research Program, Report No. 1, Oct. 1966.

290 Gauld, Charles A. "Brazil Takes a Census," Journal of Geography (April 1941), 138-144.

291 Hahner, June E. Civilian-Military Relations in Brazil, 1889-1898, Columbia, South Carolina, 1969.

292 _____. "Jacobins versus Gallegos: Urban Radicals versus Portuguese Immigrants in Rio de Janeiro in the 1890's," JIASWA, 18:2 (1976), 125-154.

293 Hambloch, Ernest. His Majesty the President of Brazil: A Study of Constitutional Brazil, London, 1935.

294 Harding, Timothy. "Revolution Tomorrow: the Failure of the Left in Brazil," Studies of the Left, 4:4 (Fall 1964), 30-54.

295 Hewitt, Cynthia N. "Brazil: the Peasant Movement in Pernambuco, 1961-1964," in Latin American Peasant Movements (ed. by H. A. Landsberger), Ithaca, 1961.

296 Hilton, Stanley E. "Ação Integralista Brasileira," LBR, 9:2 (Dec. 1972), 3-29.

297 _____. Brazil and the Great Powers, 1930-1939, Austin, 1975.

298 _____. "Military Influence on Brazilian Economic

Policy, 1930-1945: a Different View," HAHR, 53:1
(Feb. 1973), 71-94.

299 Holloway, Thomas H. The Brazilian Coffee Valorization of 1906, Madison, 1975.

300 Johnson, J. H. "Brazil in an Election Year: 1960,"
Current History, 38 (March 1968), 134-139.

301 Johnson, John J. "The Military in Brazil," in The
Military and Society in Latin America, Stanford,
1964, pp. 175-243.

302 _____. Political Change in Latin America: The
Emergence of the Middle Sectors, Stanford, 1961.

303 Levine, Robert M. "Brazil's Jews During the Vargas
Era and After," LBR, 5:1 (June 1968), 45-58.

304 _____. Pernambuco in the Brazilian Federation,
1889-1937, Stanford, 1978.

305 _____. "Some Views on Race and Immigration During
the Old Republic," TA, 27:4 (April 1971), 373-380.

306 _____. The Vargas Regime: The Critical Years,
1934-1938, New York, 1970.

307 Lipson, Leslie. "Government in Contemporary Brazil,"
Journal of Economics and Political Science, 22
(1956), 183-198.

308 Love, Joseph L. "An Approach to Regionalism," in
New Approaches to Latin American History (ed. by
R. Graham and P. H. Smith), Austin, 1974, pp.
137-155.

309 * _____. "Political Participation in Brazil, 1881-
1969," LBR, 7:2 (Dec. 1970), 3-24.

310 * _____. Rio Grande do Sul and Brazilian Regionalism, 1882-1930, Stanford, 1971.

311 * _____. São Paulo in the Brazilian Federation, 1889-
1937, Stanford, 1979.

312 *Lowenstein, Karl, Brazil Under Vargas, New York,
1942.

313 Ludwig, Armin K. "The Kubitschek Years, 1956-1961," in Cultural Change in Brazil, Ball State University, Muncie, Indiana, 1969, pp. 101-113.

314 Maack, Reinhard. "The Germans of South Brazil: A German View," Quarterly Journal of Inter-American Relations, 1:3 (July 1968), 5-23.

315 Macaulay, Neill. The Prestes Column, New York, 1974.

316 McCann, Frank D., Jr. "Aviation Diplomacy: The United States and Brazil, 1939-1941," IAMEA, 21:4 (Spring 1968), 35-50.

317 * _____. The Brazilian-American Alliance, 1937-1945, Princeton, 1973.

318 _____. "The Nation in Arms: Obligatory Military Service During the Old Republic," in Essays Concerning the Socio-economic History of Brazil and Portuguese India (ed. by D. Alden and W. Dean), Gainesville, 1977.

319 _____. "Vargas and the Destruction of the Brazilian Integralista and Nazi Parties," TA, 26:1 (July 1969), 15-34.

320 McClain, W. Douglas, Jr. "Alberto Torres, ad hoc Nationalist," LBR, 4:2 (Dec. 1967), 17-34.

321 McCloskey, Michael B. "The United States and the Brazilian Naval Revolt, 1893-1894," TA, 2:1 (Jan. 1946), 296-321.

322 Maram, Sheldon L. "Anarcho-Syndicalism in Brazil," PPCLAS, 4 (1975), 101-116.

323 _____. "Labor and the Left in Brazil, 1890-1921: A Movement Aborted," HAHR, 57:2 (May 1977), 254-272.

324 Martin, Percy A. "Federalism in Brazil," HAHR, 18:2 (May 1938), 143-163.

325 Matoon, Robert H., Jr. "Railroads, Coffee, and the Growth of Big Business in São Paulo, Brazil," HAHR, 57:2 (May 1977), 273-295.

326 Maybury-Lewis, David. "Growth and Change in Brazil
     Since 1930: An Anthropological View," in Portugal
     and Brazil in Transition (ed. by R. S. Sayers),
     Minneapolis, 1968, pp. 159-172.

327 Melby, John. "Rubber River: An Account of the Rise
     and Collapse of the Amazon Basin," HAHR, 22:3
     (Aug. 1942), 452-469.

328 Murphy, Charles. "Letter from Recife, Intrigue on
     the Bulge," Fortune, 23:6 (June 1941), 36-38.

329 Nachman, Robert G. "Positivism, Modernization, and
     the Middle Class in Brazil," HAHR, 57:1 (Feb.
     1977), 1-23.

330 _____. "Positivism and Revolution in Brazil's First
     Republic," TA, 34:1 (July 1977), 20-39.

331 Nunn, Frederick M. "Military Professionalism and
     Professional Militarism in Brazil, 1870-1970,"
     JLAS, 4:1 (May 1972), 29-54.

332 O'Neill, Sister M. Ancilla. Tristão de Athayde and
     the Catholic Social Movement in Brazil, Washington,
     1939.

333 Page, Joseph A. The Revolution That Never Was:
     Northeast Brazil, 1955-1964, New York, 1972.

334 Pang, Eul-Soo. "The Changing Role of Priests in the
     Politics of the Northeast, 1889-1964," TA, 30:3
     (Jan. 1974), 341-372.

335 _____. "Coronelismo in Northeast Brazil," in The
     Caciques (ed. by R. Kern), Albuquerque, 1972.

336 _____. "The Revolt of the Bahian Coroneis and the
     Federal Intervention of 1920," LBR, 8:2 (Winter
     1971), 3-25.

337 Patric, Anthony. Toward the Winning Goal, Rio, 1940.

338 Prestes, Luis Carlos. The Struggle for Liberation in
     Brazil, New York, 1936.

339 Putnam, Samuel, "The Vargas Dictatorship in Brazil,"
     Science and Society, 5:2 (Spring 1941), 97-116.

340 Quadros, Jânio. "Brazil's New Foreign Policy," Foreign Affairs, 40:1 (Oct. 1961), 19-27.

341 Redmont, Bernard S. "Brazilian Communist Outlines Party Policy in Latin America," World Report (Oct. 8, 1946), 18-19.

342 Saunders, John V. D. "A Revolution of Agreement among Friends: The End of the Vargas Era," HAHR, 44:2 (May 1964), 197-213.

343 Sharp, Walter R. "Brazil 1940: Whither the New State?" Inter-American Quarterly, 2:4 (October 1940), 5-17.

344 Skidmore, Thomas E. "Eduardo Prado: A Conservative Nationalist Critic of the Early Brazilian Republic, 1889-1901," LBR, 12:2 (Winter 1975), 149-164.

345 * _____ . Politics in Brazil, 1930-1964: An Experiment in Democracy, New York, 1967.

346 Singlemann, Peter. "Political Structure and Social Banditry in Northeast Brazil," JLAS, 7:1 (May 1975), 59-83.

347 Smith, Joseph. "Britain and the Brazilian Naval Revolt of 1893-94," JLAS, 2:2 (Nov. 1970), 175-198.

348 Tiller, Ann Q. "The Igniting Spark: Brazil 1930," HAHR, 45:3 (Aug. 1965), 384-392.

349 Turner, Charles W. Ruy Barbosa: Brazilian Crusader for the Essential Freedoms, New York, 1945.

350 Vargas, Getúlio. Suicide note, in New York Times, Aug. 25, 1954, p. 2.

351 Waddell, Agnes S. "The Revolution in Brazil," Foreign Policy Association Information Service, 6:26 (1931), 489-506.

352 Wagley, Charles. "The Brazilian Revolution: Social Change Since 1930," in Social Change in Latin America Today (ed. by R. Adams, et al.), New York, 1960, pp. 177-230.

353 Wileman, J. P. , comp. The Brazilian Year Book, 1908-1909, 2 vols. , Rio de Janeiro and London, n. d.

354 *Wirth, John D. Minas Gerais in the Brazilian Federation, 1889-1937, Stanford, 1977.

355 *_____. The Politics of Brazilian Development, 1930-1954, Stanford, 1970.

356 _____. "Tenentismo in the Brazilian Revolution of 1930," HAHR, 44:2 (May 1964), 161-179.

357 Young, Jordan M. The Brazilian Revolution of 1930 and the Aftermath, New Brunswick, 1967.

SEE ALSO: 40, 47, 53-57, 70, 98, 260, 474, 502, 529-530, 536, 548-549, 704, 727-728, 749, 796, 808, 854, 868, 896, 905.

VII. HISTORY, SINCE 1964

358 Álves, Márcio Moreira. "Brazil: What Terror Is Like," The Nation, March 15, 1971.

359 *_____. A Grain of Mustard Seed, New York, 1973.

360 Amnesty International, Report on Torture, London, 1975.

361 Arraes, Miguel. Brazil: The People and the Power, London, 1969.

362 Barnet, Richard. "Letter from Rio," Harper's, 245: 1468 (Sept. 1972), 16-21.

363 Berryman, Philip. "The 'Miracle,'" America, 132:20 (May 24, 1975), 397-399.

364 Bolton, R. H. "Brazilian Torture," Christian Century, 87 (April 1, 1970), 387-388.

365 "Brazil: The Dead Side of the Miracle," Brazilian Information Bulletin, Berkeley (Winter 1974).

366 Burns, E. Bradford. "Brazil: The Imitative Society," The Nation, July 10, 1972, 17-20.

367 _____. "Tradition and Variation in Brazilian Foreign Policy," JIAS, 9:2 (April 1967), 295-312.

368 Cardoso, Fernando Henrique. "The Consumption of

Dependency Theory in the United States," LARR, 12:3 (1977), 7-24.

369 Cooper, Richard N. "Novel Exchange Rate System Supports the Economic Surge," The Americana Annual, 1974, New York, 1974, pp. 55-57.

370 De Broucker, José. Dom Helder Câmara: The Violence of a Peacemaker, New York, 1969.

371 Della Cava, Ralph. "Brazil: The Struggle for Human Rights," Commonweal, 102:20 (Dec. 19, 1975), 623-626.

372 _____. "Letters to the Editors," Commonweal, 92:16 (Aug. 7, 1970).

373 _____. "Torture in Brazil," Commonweal, 92:6 (April 24, 1970), 135-141.

374 Fiechter, Georges-André. Brazil Since 1964: Modernisation Under a Military Regime (tr. by A. Braley), New York, 1975.

375 Flynn, Peter. "Brazil: Authoritarianism and Class Control" JLAS, 6:2 (Nov. 1974), 315-353.

376 Gordon, Lincoln. "Letter to the Editors," Commonweal, 92:16 (Aug. 7, 1970).

377 Horowitz, Irving L. Revolution in Brazil: Politics and Society in a Developing Nation, New York, 1964.

378 Ianni, Octavio. Crisis in Brazil, New York, 1970.

379 Keith, Henry and Robert A. Hays, eds. Perspectives on Armed Politics in Brazil, Center for Latin American Studies, Tempe, Arizona, 1976.

380 Lens, Sidney. "Brazil's Police State," The Progressive, Dec. 1966.

381 Levine, Robert M. "Booming Brazil," The Americana Annual, 1974, New York, 1974, pp. 46-53; 57.

382 _____. "Brazil at the Crossroads," Current History, 64:378 (Feb. 1973), 53-56; 86.

383 _____. "Brazil: the Aftermath of 'Decompression,'"
        Current History, 70:413 (Feb. 1976), 53-56; 81.

384 Marighela, Carlos. For the Liberation of Brazil. Lon-
        don, 1971.

385 Martins, Carlos E. "Brazil and the United States from
        the 1960's to the 1970's," in Latin America and the
        United States: The Changing Political Realities (ed.
        by J. Cotler and R. Fagen), Stanford, 1974, pp.
        269-301.

386 Melo, Antônio. The Coming Revolution in Brazil, New
        York, 1970.

387 Moraes, Clodomir. "Peasant Leagues in Brazil," in
        Agrarian Problems and Peasant Movements in Latin
        America (ed. by R. Stavenhagen), Garden City, N.
        Y., 1970.

388 Poppino, Rollie. "Brazil: New Model for National
        Development?" Current History, February 1972.

389 Quartim, João. Dictatorship and Armed Struggle in
        Brazil, New York, 1971.

390 Rodman, Selden. "After the Prosperity, the Problems,"
        National Review, 24 (May 12, 1972).

391 *Roett, Reardon A. , ed. Brazil in the Sixties, Vander-
        bilt, 1972.

392 _____, ed. Brazil: Politics in a Patrimonial So-
        ciety, Boston, 1972.

393 Rosenbaum, H. Jon. "Brazil's Foreign Policy and
        Cuba," IAEA, 23:3 (Winter 1969), 25-46.

394 _____. "Brazil's Foreign Policy: Developmentalism
        and Beyond," Orbis, 16 (Sept. 1972), 58-84.

395 _____. "A Critique of the Brazilian Foreign Service,"
        Journal of Developing Areas, 2 (April 1968), 377-
        392.

396 * _____ and William G. Tyler, eds. Contemporary
        Brazil: Issues in Economic and Political Develop-
        ment, New York, 1972.

397   Rowe, James. "Revolution and Counterrevolution in
      Brazil," in Latin American Politics (ed. by R. D.
      Tomasek), New York, 1970, pp. 532-538.

398   _____. "The 'Revolution' and the 'System,'" in
      Latin American Politics (ed. by R. D. Tomasek),
      New York, 1970, pp. 491-515.

399   *Schmitter, Philippe C. Interest Conflict and Political
      Change in Brazil, Stanford, 1971.

400   *Schneider, Ronald M. Brazil: Foreign Policy of a
      Future World Power, New York, 1977.

401   * _____. The Political System of Brazil's Emergence
      as a "Modernizing" Authoritarian Regime, 1964-1970,
      New York, 1971.

402   Selcher, Wayne. Afro-Asian Dimensions of Brazilian
      Foreign Policy, Gainesville, 1974.

403   Steiner, H. J. and D. M. Trubeck, "Brazil: All Power to
      the Arsenals," Foreign Affairs, 49 (April 1971), 464-79.

404   Stepan, Alfred C. and Luigi R. Einaudi. "Latin Amer-
      ican Institutional Development: Changing Military
      Perspectives in Peru and Brazil," Rand Corporation
      Study R-586-DOS, April 1971.

405   *Stepan, Alfred C. The Military in Politics: Changing
      Patterns in Military-Civilian Relations in Brazil,
      Princeton, 1971.

406   * _____, ed. Authoritarian Brazil: Origins, Policies,
      and Future, New Haven, 1973.

407   Távora, Araken. How Brazil Stopped Communism, Rio
      de Janeiro, 1964.

408   United States Congress. Senate. Committee on For-
      eign Relations. Brazil and United States Policies,
      Washington, 1962.

409   _____. Policies and Programs in Brazil, Hearings,
      May 4, 5, and 11, 1971, Washington, 1971.

410   Wagley, Charles. Brazil: Crisis and Change, New
      York, 1964.

411 Weffort, Francisco. "State and Mass in Brazil," in
     Studies in Comparative International Development,
     2:12 (1966), St. Louis, 1966.

SEE ALSO: 31, 275, 557, 674, 711-716, 795.

VIII. SLAVERY AND RACE RELATIONS

412 Alexander, Herbert B. "Brazilian and United States
     Slavery Compared," JNH, 7 (Oct. 1922), 349-364.

413 Bastide, Roger. African Civilizations in the New World,
     London, 1971.

414 _____. "The Development of Race Relations in Bra-
     zil," in Industrialisation and Race Relations: A
     Symposium (ed. by Guy Hunter), London, 1965.

415 _____. "Dusky Venus, Black Apollo," Race, 3 (Nov.
     1961).

416 _____. "Race Relations in Brazil," ISSJ, 9:4 (1957),
     495-512.

417 _____ and P. van den Berghe. "Stereotypes, Norms,
     and Inter-Racial Behavior in São Paulo, Brazil,"
     ASR, 22 (Dec. 1957).

418 Bethell, Leslie M. The Abolition of the Brazilian
     Slave Trade, 1807-1869, Cambridge, England, 1970.

419 _____. "Britain, Portugal and the Suppression of
     the Brazilian Slave Trade: The Origins of Lord
     Palmerston's Act of 1839," English Historical Re-
     view, 80 (1965), 761-784.

420 _____. "The Mixed Commissions for the Suppression
     of the Transatlantic Slave Trade in the Nineteenth
     Century," JAH, 7 (1966), 79-93.

421 *Boxer, Charles R. Race Relations in the Portuguese
     Colonial Empire, 1415-1825, London, 1963.

422 Braztel, John F. and Daniel M. Masterson. "O Ex-
     emplo: Afro-Brazilian Protest in Pôrto Alegre,"
     TA, 33:4 (April 1977), 58-92.

423   Cardozo, Manoel. "Slavery in Brazil as Described by
      Americans," TA, 17:1 (Jan. 1961), 241-260.

424   Chapman, Charles E. "Palmares: the Negro Numantia,"
      JNH, 3:1 (Jan. 1918), 29-32.

425   Clarana, José. "Letter from Brazil," The Crisis
      (April 1918), 276-278.

426   Conrad, Robert. "The Contraband Slave Trade to Bra-
      zil, 1831-1845," HAHR, 49:4 (Nov. 1969), 617-638.

427   *_____. The Destruction of Brazilian Slavery, 1850-
      1888, Berkeley, 1972.

428   *_____. "Neither Slave nor Free: The Emancipados
      of Brazil, 1818-1868," HAHR, 53:1 (Feb. 1973), 50-
      70.

429   _____. "Nineteenth-Century Brazilian Slavery," in
      Slavery and Race Relations in Latin America, (ed.
      by R. B. Toplin), Westport, Connecticut, 1974, pp.
      146-173.

430   *Corwin, Arthur F. "Afro-Brazilians: Myths and
      Realities," in Slavery and Race Relations in Latin
      America (ed. by R. B. Toplin), Westport, Connecti-
      cut, 1974, pp. 385-438.

431   Costa Eduardo, Octávio de. The Negro in North Bra-
      zil: A Study in Acculturation, American Ethnologi-
      cal Society Monograph No. 16, New York, 1940.

432   *Curtin, Philip D. The Atlantic Slave Trade: A Cen-
      sus, Madison, Wisconsin, 1969.

433   _____. "Epidemiology and the Slave Trade," PSQ,
      83:2 (June 1968), 190-216.

434   *Davis, David Brion. The Problem of Slavery in West-
      ern Culture, Ithaca, 1966.

435   *Degler, Carl. Neither Black nor White: Slavery and
      Race Relations in Brazil and in the United States,
      New York, 1971.

436   Diggs, Irene. "Zumbi and the Republic of Palmares,"
      Phylon, 14:1 (1953), 62-69.

437   Donald, Cleveland, Jr. "Slave Resistance and Abolitionism in Brazil: The Campista Case, 1879-1888,"
LBR, 13:2 (Winter 1976), 182-193.

438   Dzidzienyo, Anani. The Position of Blacks in Brazilian
Society, London, 1971.

439   Eisenberg, Peter L. "Abolishing Slavery: The Process
on Pernambuco's Sugar Plantations," HAHR, 52:4
(Nov. 1972), 580-597.

440   Fernandes, Florestan. "Beyond Poverty: The Negro
and the Mulatto in Brazil," in Slavery and Race Relations in Latin America (ed. by R. B. Toplin),
Westport, Connecticut, 1974, pp. 277-298.

441 *   . The Negro in Brazilian Society (tr. by J.
Skiles), New York, 1969.

442   Frazier, E. Franklin. "A Comparison of Negro-White
Relations in Brazil and in the United States," in
On Race Relations: Selected Writings (ed. by G.
Franklin Edwards), Chicago, 1968, pp. 88-102.

443   . "The Negro Family in Bahia," ASR, 7 (Aug.
1942), 465-478.

444   . "Some Aspects of Race Relations in Brazil,"
Phylon, 3 (1942), 284-286.

445   Freyre, Gilberto. "The Brazilian Melting Pot," The
Atlantic Monthly (Feb. 1946).

446 *   . The Mansions and the Shanties (tr. by H.
de Onis), New York, 1963.

447 *   . The Masters and the Slaves: A Study in
the Development of Brazilian Civilization (tr. by S.
Putnam), New York, 1946.

448 *   . Order and Progress (tr. by R. W. Horton),
New York, 1970.

449   Galloway, J. H. "The Last Years of Slavery on the
Sugar Plantations of Northeast Brazil," HAHR, 51:4
(Nov. 1971), 586-605.

450   Garcia-Zamor, Jean Claude. "Social Mobility of Ne-

groes in Brazil," JIASWA, 12 (April 1970).

451 Gordon, Eugene. An Essay on Race Amalgamation,
       Pan American Union, Rio de Janeiro, 1951.

452 *Graham, Richard. "Brazilian Slavery Reexamined,"
       JSH, 3:2 (Summer 1970), 431-453.

453 *_____. Causes for the Abolition of Negro Slavery
       in Brazil: An Interpretive Essay," HAHR, 46:2
       (May 1966), 123-137.

454 Haberley, David T. "Abolitionism in Brazil: Anti-
       Slavery and Anti-Slave," LBR, 9:2 (Dec. 1972), 30-
       46.

455 *Hamilton, Russell. "Afro-Brazilian Cults in the Novels
       of Jorge Amado," Hispania, 2 (May 1937).

456 Harris, Marvin. "Race Relations in Minas Velhas,"
       in Race and Class in Rural Brazil (ed. by C. Wag-
       ley), 2nd ed., New York, 1963.

457 _____. "Racial Identity in Brazil," LBR, 1:1 (Sum-
       mer 1964), 21-28.

458 _____. "Referential Ambiguity in the Calculus of
       Brazilian Racial Identity," SJA, 26:1 (1970), 1-14.

459 _____ and Conrad Kottak. "The Structural Signifi-
       cance of Brazilian Racial Categories," Sociologia,
       25:2 (1963), 203-209.

460 Hill, Lawrence F. "The Abolition of the African Slave
       Trade to Brazil," HAHR, 11:2 (May 1931), 169-197.

461 Holub, Norman. "The Brazilian Sabinada: Revolt of
       the Negro Masses," JNH, 54:3 (July 1969), 275-283.

462 *Jesus, Carolina Maria de. Child of the Dark (tr. by
       D. St. Clair), New York, 1962.

463 Karasch, Mary. "Black Worlds in the Tropics: Gil-
       berto Freyre and the Woman of Color in Brazil,"
       PCCLAS, 3 (1974), 19-30.

464 Kent, R. K. "Palmares: An African State in Brazil,"
       JAH, 6:2 (1965), 161-175.

465 *Klein, Herbert S. "The Colored Freedman in Bra-
     zilian Slave Society, " JSH, 3:2 (Fall 1969).

466 _____. "The Internal Slave Trade in Nineteenth Cen-
     tury Brazil, " HAHR, 51:4 (Nov. 1971).

467 _____. "The Portuguese Slave Trade from Angola in
     the Eighteenth Century," JEH, 32:4 (Dec. 1972), 892-918.

468 _____. "The Trade in African Slaves to Rio de Ja-
     neiro, 1795-1811, " JAH, 10:4 (1969), 533-549.

469 Kottack, Conrad P. "Race Relations in a Bahian Fish-
     ing Village, " LBR, 4:2 (Dec. 1967), 35-52.

470 Johnston, H. The Negro in the New World. London, 1910.

471 Lacerda, João Baptista de. "The Metis, or Half-Breeds,
     of Brazil, " in Papers on Inter-Racial Problems Com-
     municated to the First Universal Races Congress
     Held at the University of London, July 26-29, 1911,
     London and Boston, 1911.

472 Leacock, Seth and Ruth Leacock. Spirits of the Deep:
     A Study of an Afro-Brazilian Cult, New York, 1972.

473 *Leff, Nathaniel. "Long-Term Viability of Slavery in a
     Backward Colonial Economy, " JIH, 1:1 (Summer 1974).

474 Levine, Robert M. "The First Afro-Brazilian Congress, "
     Race, 15:2 (1973), 185-193.

475 Lloyd, Christopher. The Navy and the Slave Trade,
     London, 1949.

476 MacLachlan, Colin M. "African Slave Trade and Eco-
     nomic Development in Amazonia, 1700-1800, " in Slav-
     ery and Race Relations in Latin America (ed. by R. B.
     Toplin), Westport, Connecticut, 1974, pp. 112-45.

477 Manchester, Alan K. "Racial Democracy in Brazil, "
     South Atlantic Quarterly, 94:1 (Winter 1965).

478 Martin, Percy A. "Slavery and Abolition in Brazil, "
     HAHR, 13:2 (May 1933), 151-196.

479 Mathieson, William L. Great Britain and the Slave
     Trade, 1839-1865, London, 1929.

480 Metall, R. A. and M. Paranhos da Silva, "Equality of
     Opportunity in a Multi-Racial Society: Brazil,"
     International Labour Review, 93 (Jan. -June 1966).

481 Monk, Abraham. Black and White Race Relations in
     Brazil, SUNY/Buffalo Special Studies, #4, Buffalo,
     1971.

482 Mörner, Magnus. Race Mixture in the History of the
     New World, Boston, 1967.

483 Morse, Richard M. "The Negro in São Paulo, Brazil,"
     JNH, 38:2 (July 1953).

484 Nascimento, Abdias do. "Afro-Brazilian Culture,"
     Black Image, 3-4 (Autumn-Winter 1972).

485 _____. "The Negro Theater in Brazil," African
     Forum, 4 (Spring 1967).

486 Nogueira, Oracy. "Skin Color and Social Class," Pan
     American Union Monographs #7, Washington, D. C.,
     1959.

487 Olinto, Antônio. "The Negro Writer and Negro Influence
     in Brazilian Literature," African Forum, 4 (Spring
     1967).

488 Pescatello, Ann, ed. The African in Latin America,
     New York, 1976.

489 *Pierson, Donald. Negroes in Brazil: A Study of Race
     Contact at Bahia, Carbondale, Illinois, 1967.

490 *Ramos, Artur. The Negro in Brazil (tr. by R. Pattee),
     Washington, 1939.

491 *Reis, Jaime. "Abolition and the Economics of Slave-
     holding in North East Brazil," Boletin de Estudos
     Latino-Americanas y del Caribe, 17 (Dec. 1974),
     3-20.

492 Rout, Leslie B. , Jr. "The Black Bishops Mystery,"
     LBR (Sept. 1972), 86-92.

493 _____. "Brazil: Study in Black, Brown, and Beige,"
     Negro Digest, 19 (Feb. 1970), 21-73.

494 _____. "Race Relations in Southern Brazil: The Pôrto Alegre Experience," PCCLAS, 4 (1975), 89-100.

495 _____. "Sleight of Hand: Brazilian and American Authors Manipulate the Brazilian Racial Situation," TA, 4:4 (1973), 471-489.

496 Russell-Wood, A. J. R. "Race and Class in Brazil, 1937-1967," Race, 10:2 (Oct. 1968), 185-191.

497 _____. "Technology and Society: The Impact of Gold Mining on the Institution of Slavery in Portuguese America," JEH, 37:1 (March 1977).

498 *Schwartz, Stuart B. "The Manumission of Slaves in Colonial Brazil: Bahia, 1684-1745," HAHR, 54:4 (Nov. 1974), 603-635.

499 Schuyler, George. Afro-Brazilians report, in Pittsburgh Courier, 24:34 (Aug. 21, 1948) and 36 (Sept. 4, 1948).

500 _____. Black and Conservative. New Rochelle, 1966.

501 *Skidmore, Thomas E. Black into White: Race and Nationality in Brazilian Thought, New York, 1974.

502 *_____. "Gilberto Freyre and the Early Brazilian Republic: Some Notes on Methodology," CSSH, 6:4 (July 1964), 490-505.

503 _____. "Toward a Comparative Analysis of Race Relations Since Abolition in Brazil and the United States," JLAS, 4:1 (May 1972), 1-28.

504 _____, ed. "The Death of Brazilian Slavery, 1866-1888," in Latin American History: Select Problems (ed. by F. Pike), New York, 1969, pp. 134-173.

505 Staley, Austin J. Racial Democracy in Marriage: A Sociological Analysis of Negro-White Intermarriage in Brazilian Culture, Ann Arbor, 1960.

506 Sternberg, Hilgard O'Reilly. A Geographer's View of Race and Class in Latin America, Berkeley, 1970.

507   *Tannenbaum, Frank.   Slave and Citizen: The Negro
      in the Americas.   New York, 1946.

508   "To Be Poor," Ebony (December 1966).

509   *Toplin, Robert Brent.   The Abolition of Slavery in
      Brazil, New York, 1973.

510   _____. "Upheaval, Violence and the Abolition of
      Slavery in Brazil: The Case of São Paulo," HAHR,
      49:4 (Nov. 1969), 639-655.

511   *_____, ed. Slavery and Race Relations in Latin
      America, Westport, Connecticut, 1974.

512   Turner, Doris J.   "Symbols in Two Afro-Brazilian Lit-
      erary Works: Jubaibá and Sortilégio, " in Teaching
      Latin American Studies (ed. by M. Williford and J.
      D. Casteel), Gainesville, 1977, pp. 41-58.

513   Turner, J. Michael.   "Reversing the Trend: Afro-Bra-
      zilian Influences in West Africa," in The Thematic
      Conceptual Approach to African History (ed. by L.
      Goggins), Dubuque, Iowa, 1978.

514   Universal Races Congress, London.   Papers on Inter-
      Racial Problems Communicated to the First Universal
      Races Congress, Held at the University of London,
      July 26-29, 1911, London and Boston, 1911.

515   Warren, Donald.   "The Negro and Religion in Brazil,"
      Race (Jan. 1965).

516   Williams, Mary W.   "The Treatment of Negro Slaves
      in the Brazilian Empire.   A Comparison with the
      United States," JNH, 15 (July 1930), 315-336.

517   Zamor, Jean-Claude.   "Social Mobility of Negroes,"
      JIASWA, 12:2 (April 1970), 242-254.

518   Zimmerman, Ben.   "Race Relations in the Arid Sertão,"
      in Race and Class in Rural Brazil (ed. by C. Wag-
      ley), Paris, 1952.

SEE ALSO: 16-44, 53-56, 64-66, 81, 88, 95, 124, 153, 162,
      194, 202-203, 207, 231-232, 253, 260, 263, 305,
      543, 619, 808, 810-811, 830, 834, 843, 852, 894,
      899.

IX. RELIGION AND MESSIANIC MOVEMENTS

519   Antoine, Charles. Church and Power in Brazil (tr. by P. Nelson), New York, 1973.

520   *Auferderheide, Patricia. "True Confessions: The Inquisition and Social Attitudes in Brazil at the Turn of the Century," LBR, 10:2 (Dec. 1973), 208-240.

521   Azevedo, Thales de. "Catholicism in Brazil," Thought, 27 (1953), 253-274.

522   Bachmann, Theodore E. Lutherans in Brazil, Minneapolis, 1970.

523   Bear, James E. Mission to Brazil, Nashville, 1961.

524   *Bruneau, Thomas C. The Political Transformation of the Brazilian Catholic Church, Cambridge, England, 1974.

525   _____. "Power and Influence: Analysis of the Church in Latin America and the Case of Brazil," LARR, 8:2 (Summer 1973), 25-51.

526   *De Kadt, Emanuel. Catholic Radicals in Brazil, New York, 1970.

527   _____. "Religion, the Church, and Social Change in Brazil," in The Politics of Conformity in Latin America (ed. by C. Veliz), London, 1967, pp. 192-220.

528   *Della Cava, Ralph. "Brazilian Messianism and National Institutions," HAHR, 48:3 (Aug. 1968), 402-420.

529   * _____. "Catholicism and Society in Twentieth Century Brazil," LARR, 11:2 (1976), 7-50.

530   Gammon, Samuel R. The Evangelical Invasion of Brazil, Richmond, 1910.

531   Gross, Daniel. "Ritual and Conformity: A Religious Pilgrammage to Northeast Brazil," Ethnology, 10:2 (1971), 129-148.

532   Gross, Sue Anderson. "Religious Sectarianism in the Sertão, 1815-1966," JIAS, 10:3 (July 1968), 369-383.

533 Krischke, Paulo J. "Nationalism and the Catholic
     Church: The Preparation for Democracy in Brazil,"
     in The Church and Politics in Latin America, Latin
     American Research Unit Studies, Toronto, 1977, pp.
     62-92.

534 Lima Vaz, Henrique C. "The Church and Conscienti-
     zação," America, 118:17 (April 27, 1968), 578-581.

535 Mutchler, D. E. "Roman Catholicism in Brazil," Stud-
     ies in Comparative International Development, St.
     Louis, 1:8 (1965).

536 *Queiroz, Maria Isaura Pereira de. "Messiahs in Bra-
     zil," Past and Present, 31 (July 1965), 62-86.

537 Read, William R. and Frank A. Inerson. Brazil 1980:
     The Protestant Handbook, MARC, Monrovia, Califor-
     nia, 1975.

538 Ribeiro, René. "Brazilian Messianic Movements," in
     Millenial Dreams in Action (ed. by S. Thrupp),
     s'Gravenhage, 1962.

539 Sanders, Thomas G. "Brazil's Catholic Left," America,
     117:1 (Nov. 18, 1967), 598-601.

540 Thornton, Maria C. The Church and Freemasonry in
     Brazil, 1872-1875. A Study in Regalism, Washington,
     1948.

541 Toop, Walter R. "Organized Religious Groups in a
     Village of Northeastern Brazil," LBR, 9:2 (Dec.
     1972), 58-77.

542 Vieira, David G. "Some Protestant Missionary Letters
     Relating to the Religious Question in Brazil, 1872-
     1875," TA, 24:4 (April 1958), 337-353.

543 Warren, Donald, Jr. "The Negro and Religion in Bra-
     zil," Race, 6:3 (1965).

544 *_____. "Portuguese Roots of Brazilian Spiritism,"
     LBR, 5:2 (Dec. 1968), 3-34.

545 Wiarda, Howard J. The Brazilian Catholic Labor Move-
     ment, Amherst, 1969.

546 Willems, Emílio. Followers of the New Faith: Culture
     Change and the Rise of Protestantism in Brazil and
     Chile, Nashville, 1967.

547 _____. "Protestantism as a Factor of Culture Change
     in Brazil," Economic Development and Cultural
     Change, 3 (July 1955), 321-333.

548 *Williams, Margaret Todaro. "Integralism and the Bra-
     zilian Catholic Church," HAHR, 54:3 (Aug. 1974),
     431-452.

549 *_____. "The Politicalization of the Brazilian Cath-
     olic Church: The Catholic Electoral League,"
     JIASWA, 16:3 (Aug. 1974), 301-325.

SEE ALSO: 44, 183, 188, 214-216, 221, 225, 226, 283,
     303, 332, 334, 370, 472, 515, 852.

X. INDIGENOUS POPULATIONS

550 Aborigines Protection Society of London, Tribes of the
     Amazon Basin in Brazil, London, 1973.

551 Bodard, Lucien. Green Hell, New York, 1971.

552 Brooks, Edwin. "Twilight of Brazilian Tribes," Geo-
     graphical Magazine, 45:4 (Jan. 1973), 304-310.

553 _____. "The Brazilian Road to Ethnicide," Contem-
     porary Review, 224 (May 1974), 2-8.

554 _____. "Frontiers of Ethnic Conflict in the Brazilian
     Amazon," International Journal of Environmental
     Studies, 7 (1974), 63-74.

555 Cowell, Adrian. The Tribe That Hides from Man, New
     York, 1974.

556 Chiappino, Jean. The Brazilian Indigenous Problem
     and Policy: The Aripuanã Park, Geneva/Copenhagen,
     1974.

557 *Davis, Shelton. Victims of the Miracle: Development
     and the Indians of Brazil, New York, 1977.

558 Goodland, R. J. A. and H. S. Irwin, Amazon Jungle,
     Amsterdam, 1975.

559 *Hanbury-Tension, Robin. A Question of Survival for
     the Indians of Brazil, New York, 1973.

560 *Hopper, Janice H., ed. Indians of Brazil in the Twen-
     tieth Century, Washington, 1967.

561 Junqueira, Carmen. The Brazilian Indigenous Problem
     and Policy: The Example of the Xingú National
     Park, Geneva/Copenhagen, 1973.

562 Kando, Ata. Slave or Dead? Amsterdam, 1971.

563 Kieman, Mathias C. "The Status of the Indians in Bra-
     zil After 1820," TA, 21:3 (Jan. 1965), 263-273.

564 Lathrap, D. W. Upper Amazon, New York, 1970.

565 Lévi-Strauss, Claude. World on the Wane, London,
     1961.

566 Lizot, Jaques. The Yanomani in the Face of Ethnocide,
     Copenhagen, 1976.

567 *Maybury-Lewis, David. The Savage and the Innocent,
     Boston, 1968.

568 Meggers, Betty J. Amazonia: Man and Culture in a
     Counterfeit Paradise, Chicago, 1971.

569 Oberg, Kalervo. The Terena and the Caduveo of Southern
     Mato Grosso, Brazil, Washington, 1949.

570 Primitive People's Fund. Report of a Visit to the In-
     dians of Brazil, London, 1971.

571 Ribeiro, Darcy. "Brazil's Indian Frontier," Americas,
     6:3 (1954).

572 Vilas Boas, Orlando and Cláudio. "Saving Brazil's
     Stone Age Tribes from Extinction," National Geo-
     graphic, 134:3 (Sept. 1968), 424-444.

573 _____. Xingú: The Indians, Their Myths, New
     York, 1973.

574 Von Puttkamer, W. Jesco. "Brazil Protects Her Cintas
     Largas Indians," National Geographic, 140:3 (Sept.
     1971).

575 _____. "Brazil's Kreen-Akárores: Requiem for a Tribe?" National Geographic, 147:2 (Feb. 1975), 254-268.

576 *Wagley, Charles and Eduardo Galvão. The Tenetehara Indians of Brazil, New York, 1949.

577 Wycliffe Bible Translators. Brazil's Tribes, Summer Institute of Linguistics, Campinas, 1967.

SEE ALSO: 8, 36, 44, 77, 95, 110, 139, 158, 165, 174, 194, 198-199, 211, 327, 476, 617, 631, 633, 639, 641-643, 697, 703, 783, 793, 820, 855.

XI. SOCIETY, POPULATION, AND THE QUALITY OF LIFE

578 Arriaga, Eduardo. New Life Tables for Latin American Populations in the Nineteenth and Twentieth Centuries, Berkeley, 1968.

579 Ávila, F. J. de. "Brazil," The Economics of Internal Migration (ed. by B. Thomas), London, 1958.

580 Azevedo, Thales de. "Family, Marriage, and Divorce in Brazil," in Contemporary Cultures and Societies in Latin America (ed. by D. Heath and R. Adams), New York, 1965, 288-310.

581 _____. "Italian Colonization in Southern Brazil," Anthropological Quarterly, 34 (1961), 60-68.

582 *_____. Social Change in Brazil, Monograph #22, University of Florida, Gainesville, 1962.

583 Bastos de Ávila, Fernando. Economic Impact of Immigration: The Brazilian Immigration Problem, The Hague, 1954.

584 Bonilla, Frank. "Rio's Favelas," AUFS, FB-1-61 (Aug. 1961).

585 _____. "Rural Reform in Brazil: Diminishing Prospects for a Democratic Solution," Dissent, 9 (Autumn 1962).

586 Burns, E. Bradford. "Brazil: The Imitative Society," in South America: Problems and Prospects (ed. by I. Isenberg), New York, 1975.

587 *Castro, Josué de. Death in the Northeast, New York, 1966.

588 _____. The Geography of Hunger, Boston, 1952.

589 Chardon, Roland E. "Changes in the Geographic Distribution of Population in Brazil, 1950-1960," in New Perspectives of Brazil (ed. by E. N. Baklanoff), Nashville, 1966, 155-178.

590 Chaffee, Wilbur Jr. "The Cartorial State: A Study of the Growth of the Brazilian Middle Class," R/RI, 1 (1972), 116-123.

591 Cooper, Donald. "Oswaldo Cruz and the Impact of Yellow Fever on Brazilian History," Bulletin of Tuland University Medical Faculty, 26 (Feb. 1967), 49-52.

592 Cowell, Bainbridge, Jr. "Cityward Migration in the Nineteenth and Twentieth Century: The Case of Recife, Brazil," JIASWA, 17:1 (Feb. 1975), 43-63.

593 Davis, Horace B. and M. R. Davis. "Scale of Living of the Working Class in São Paulo, Brazil," Monthly Labor Review (Jan. 1937), 245-253.

594 Deffontaines, Pierre. "Origin and Growth of the Brazilian Network of Towns," Geographical Review, 28 (July 1938), 379-399.

595 Ferenczi, Imre and Walter Wilcox. International Migrations, National Bureau of Economic Research, New York, 1929.

596 *Forman, Shepard. The Brazilian Peasantry, New York, 1975.

597 _____. "Disunity and Discontent: A Study of Peasant Political Movements in Brazil," JLAS, 3:1 (May 1971), 3-24.

598 _____. The Raft Fisherman: Tradition and Change in the Brazilian Peasant Economy, Bloomington, 1970.

599 Free, Lloyd A. Some International Implications of the Political Psychology of Brazilians, Princeton, 1961.

600 Freyre, Gilberto. "Brazilian National Character in the Twentieth Century," Annals of the A. A. P. S. S., 370 (March 1967), 57-62.

601 _____. "The Patriarchal Basis of Brazilian Society," in Politics of Change in Latin America (ed. by J. Maier and R. Weatherhead), New York, 1964.

602 Fujii, Yokio and T. Lynn Smith. The Acculturation of the Japanese Immigrants in Brazil, Gainesville, 1959.

603 Galjart, Benno. "Class and Following in Rural Brazil," América Latina (July-Sept. 1964).

604 Greenfield, Sidney M. "Differentiation, Stratification, and Mobility in Traditional Brazilian Society," LBR, 6:2 (Winter 1969).

605 _____. "Patronage, Politics, and the Articulation of Local Community and National Society in Pre-1968 Brazil," JIASWA, 19:2 (May 1977), 139-172.

606 *Harris, Marvin. Town and Country in Brazil, New York, 1956.

607 Hutchinson, Harry W. "The Patron-Dependant Relationship in Brazil," Sociologia Ruralis, 6:1 (1966).

608 *_____. Village and Plantation Life in Northeastern Brazil, Seattle, 1957.

609 Iutaka, S. "Social Mobility and Differential Occupational Opportunity in Urban Brazil," Human Organizations, 24 (Summer 1965).

610 Kahl, Joseph A. The Measurement of Modernism: A Study of Values in Brazil and Mexico, Austin, 1968.

611 Johnson, Allen W. Sharecroppers of the Sertão, Stanford, 1971.

612a _____ and Bernard Siegel. "Wages and Income in Ceará, Brazil," SJA, 25:1 (Spring 1969).

612 Kottack, Conrad P. "Kinship and Class in Brazil," Ethnology, 6:4 (1967), 427-443.

613 *Leeds, Anthony. "Brazilian Careers and Social Structure," AA, 66:6 (Dec. 1964), 1321-1347.

614 Leslie, Thomas M. Population Growth Along the Bra-
sília-Belém Highway, Los Angeles, 1973.

615 McDonough, Josefina F. "A Transitional Model of the
Ecology of Delinquency: The Case of Rio de Janeiro,"
LBR, 13:2 (Winter 1976), 129-137.

616 Malloy, James M. "Social Security Policy and the
Working Class in the Twentieth Century," JIASWA,
19:1 (Feb. 1977), 35-60.

617 Moran, Emílio F. "The Adaptive System of the Amazonian Caboclo," in C. Wagley, ed., Man in the
Amazon, Gainesville, 1974.

618 Mortara, G. "The Brazilian Birth Rate," in Culture
and Human Fertility (ed. by F. Lorimer, et al.),
Paris, 1954.

619 Nascimento, Edson Arantes do (Pelé) and Robert L.
Fish. My Life and the Beautiful Game, Garden
City, 1977.

620 Nichols, Glenn A. Class and Mass in Pre-1964 Brazil: The Case of Rio de Janeiro, JIASWA, 18 (Aug.
1976), 323-356.

621 Oberg, Kalervo. "The Marginal Peasant in Rural Brazil," AA, 67 (1965), 1417-1427.

622 Perlman, Janice E. The Myth of Marginality: Urban
Poverty and Politics in Rio de Janeiro, Berkeley,
1976.

623 *Pierson, Donald, et al. Cruz das Almas, a Brazilian
Village, Washington, 1951.

624 Price, Robert. Rural Unionization in Brazil, Land
Tenure Center, University of Wisconsin, #14 (Aug.
1964).

625 *Riegelhaupt, Joyce F. and Shepard Forman. "Bodo
Was Never Brazilian: Economic Integration and
Rural Development Among a Contemporary Peasan-
try." JEH, 30 (March 1970), 100-116.

626 Rosen, Bernard and Manoel Berlinck. "Modernization

and Family Structure in the Region of São Paulo, Brazil," América Latina, 11:3 (July-Sept. 1968), 75-96.

627 Salmen, Lawrence. "A Perspective on the Resettlement of Squatters in Brazil," América Latina, 12:1 (Jan.-March 1969), 73-95.

628 Salzano, Francisco M. Problems in Human Biology: A Study of Brazilian Populations, Detroit, 1970.

629 Sánchez-Albornoz, Nicolás. The Population of Latin America, (tr. by W. Richardson), Berkeley, 1974.

630 Sanders, Thomas J. "Brazilian Interior Migration: Three Frontier Cities on the Belém-Brasília Highway," AUFS, 15:2 (1971).

631 _____. "Colonization on the Transamazonian Highway," AUFS, 17:4 (1973).

632 _____. "Japanese in Brazil," AUFS, 14:3 (1970).

633 _____. "The Northeast and Amazonian Integration," AUFS, 17:3 (1973).

634 _____. "Population Review 1970: Brazil," AUFS, 14:6 (1970).

635 Santos, John F. "A Psychologist Reflects on Brazil and the Brazilians," in E. Baklanoff, ed., New Perspectives of Brazil, Nashville, 1966.

636 Shirley, Robert W. The End of Tradition: Culture, Change and Development in the Município of Cunha, São Paulo, Brazil, New York, 1970.

637 Siegel, Bernard J. "Migration Dynamics in the Interior of Ceará, Brazil," SJA, 27:3 (1971).

638 Sims, Harold D. "Japanese Postwar Migration to Brazil: An Analysis of Data Presently Available," International Migration Review, 6 (Fall 1972), 246-266.

639 *Wagley, Charles. Amazon Town: A Study of Man in the Tropics, New York, 1964.

640 _____. "Brazil," in Most of the World (ed. by R. Linton), New York, 1949.

641 _____. "The Folk Culture of the Brazilian Amazon," Proceedings of the XXIX Congress of Americanists, Chicago, 1952.

642 _____. The Latin American Tradition, New York, 1968.

643 *_____, ed. Man in the Amazon, Gainesville, 1974.

644 *_____, ed. Race and Class in Rural Brazil, Paris, 1952.

645 _____ and M. Harris. Minorities in the New World, New York, 1949.

646 Willems, Emílio. "Assimilation of German Immigrants in Brazil," Sociology and Social Research, 25:2 (1940), 125-132.

647 _____. "The Rise of a Rural Middle Class in a Frontier Society," in Brazil in the Sixties (ed. by R. Roett), Nashville, 1972, pp. 325-344.

648 _____. "Some Aspects of Culture Conflict and Acculturation in Southern Rural Brazil," Rural Sociology, 7 (1942), 375-385.

649 *_____. "The Structure of the Brazilian Family," Social Forces, 31 (1953), 339-345.

SEE ALSO: 27, 44-45, 81, 88-92, 95, 144, 160, 173, 214-217, 244, 260, 290, 326, 346, 352, 366, 406, 411, 541, 654, 656, 657, 660, 756, 770, 819, 846, 852.

XII. ROLE OF WOMEN

650 Blachman, Morris J. "Eve in an Adamocracy: Women and Politics in Brazil," Occasional Papers, No. 5, New York University, Ibero-American Language and Area Center, New York, 1973.

651 Friedan, Betty. "Go Home Yankee Lady!," McCalls, 94:1 (Oct. 1971), 69-72.

652 *Hahner, June E. "Women and Work in Brazil, 1850-1920," in Essays Concerning the Socioeconomic His-

tory of Brazil and Portuguese India (ed. by D. Alden and W. Dean), Gainesville, 1977, pp. 87-117.

653 Karasch, Mary. "Rio's Black Brasileiras," in The African in Latin America (ed. by A. Pescatello), New York, 1975, pp. 168-172.

654 *Landes, Ruth. The City of Women, New York, 1947.

655 _____, ed. "A Woman Anthropologist in Brazil," in Women in the Field (ed. by P. Golde), Chicago, 1970.

656 MacLachlan, Colin. "The Feminine Mystique in Brazil: A Middle-Class Image," PCCLAS, 2 (1973), 61-73.

657 Pescatello, Ann, ed. Female and Male in Latin America, Pittsburgh, 1972.

658 _____. "The Female in Ibero-America: An Essay on Research," LARR, 7:2 (Spring 1972), 125-141.

659 Russell-Wood, A. J. R. "Women and Society in Colonial Brazil," JLAS, 9:1 (May 1977), 1-34.

660 Safiotti, Heleieth Iara Bongiovani. "Status of Women in Brazil," in Women Cross-Culturally: Change and Challenge (ed. by R. R. Leavitt), The Hague, 1975.

SEE ALSO: 95, 200, 210, 463, 829-830, 849.

XIII. EDUCATION

661 Dunne, George H. "Happening in São Paulo," America, 117:13 (Sept. 23, 1967), 306-313.

662 Faust, A. F. Brazil: Education in An Expanding Economy, Washington, 1963.

663 *Freire, Paulo. The Pedagogy of the Oppressed (tr. by M. B. Ramos), New York, 1969.

664 *Haar, Jerry. The Politics of Higher Education in Brazil, New York, 1977.

665 Harrell, William A. The Brazilian Educational System: A Summary, Washington, 1970.

Bibliography   280

666 *Havighurst, Robert and A. J. Gouveia. Brazilian
    Secondary Education and Socio-Economic Develop-
    ment, New York, 1969.

667 *Havighurst, Robert and J. Roberto Moreira. Society
    and Education in Brazil, Pittsburgh, 1965.

668 Leão, A Carneiro. "The Evolution of Education in Bra-
    zil," in Brazil: Portrait of Half a Continent (ed. by
    T. L. Smith and A. Marchant), New York, 1951, pp.
    313-333.

669 McNeill, Malvina Rosat. Guidelines to Problems of
    Education in Brazil, Teachers College, Columbia
    University, New York, 1970.

670 Myhr, Robert O. "The University Student Tradition in
    Brazil," JLAS, 12:1 (Jan. 1970), 126-140.

671 O'Neil, Charles. "Educational Innovation and Politics
    in São Paulo, 1933-1934," LBR, (Summer 1971),
    56-68.

672 Ribeiro, Darcy. "Universities and Social Development,"
    in Elites in Latin America (ed. by S. Lipset and A.
    Solari), New York, 1967, pp. 343-381.

673 Rios, José Arthur. The University Student and Bra-
    zilian Society, Monograph No. 6, Latin American
    Studies Center, Michigan State University, East
    Lansing, 1971.

674 Wedge, Bryant. "The Case Study of Student Political
    Violence: Brazil, 1964 and the Dominican Republic,
    1964," World Politics, 21:2 (Jan. 1969), 183-206.

SEE ALSO: 534.

XIV. ECONOMIC, REGIONAL, AND
      NATIONAL DEVELOPMENT

675 Aartsen, J. P. V. "Northeastern Brazil," in Neder-
    landsch Aardrijkskindig Genootschap, Amsterdam,
    76:3 (1959), 228-242.

676 Abouchar, Alan. "Inflation and Transportation Policy
    in Brazil," EDCC, 18:1 (Oct. 1969), 92-109.

281   Bibliography

677 American Chamber of Commerce for Brazil, São Paulo.
     The Take-Off Is Now, São Paulo, 1971.

678 Arruda, Marcos, et al. Multinationals and Brazil, Tor-
     onto, 1975.

679 Baer, Werner. The Development of the Brazilian Steel
     Industry, Nashville, 1969.

680 _____. "Furtado Revisited," LBR, 11:1 (Summer
     1974), 114-121.

681 *_____. Industrialization and Economic Development
     in Brazil, Homewood, Illinois, 1965.

682 _____. "Regional Inequality and Economic Growth in
     Brazil," ECCC, 12:3 (April 1964), 268-285.

683 _____ and Mário Henrique Simonsen. "American
     Capital and Brazilian Nationalism," Yale Review,
     53 (1964), 192-198.

684 _____ and Annibal Vilela. "Industrial Growth and
     Industrialization: Revisions in the Stages of Brazil's
     Economic Development," JDA, 8:2 (1973), 217-234.

685 _____, et al. "The Changing Role of the State in
     the Brazilian Economy," World Development, I
     (Nov. 1973), 23-34.

686 Bergsman, Joel. Brazil: Industrialization and Trade
     Policies, London, 1970.

687 _____ and A. Candal. "Industrialization: Past Suc-
     cess and Future Problems," in The Economy of
     Brazil (ed. by H. S. Ellis), Berkeley, 1968.

688 Bharta, Sarvan K. Democracy, Development and Plan-
     ning with Special Reference to Brazil and India, Savan-
     nah, Georgia, 1970.

689 Black, Edie and Fred Goff. "The Hanna Industrial Com-
     plex: Operations in Brazil," NACLA's Latin Amer-
     ican and Empire Report, New York, 1969, pp. 1-6.

690 Bonilla, Frank. "A National Ideology for Development,"
     in K. H. Silvert, ed., Expectant Peoples: National-
     ism and Development, New York, 1963, pp. 232-264.

691 Branner, John G. The Railways of Brazil, Chicago, 1887.

692 Brazilian Embassy. A Survey of the Brazilian Economy, Washington, 1966.

693 Campbell, Gordon. Brazil Struggles for Development, London, 1973.

694 Cardoso, Fernando Henrique. "The Industrial Elite in Latin America," in H. Bernstein, ed., Underdevelopment and Development: The Third World Today, London, 1973, pp. 191-204.

695 *_____. "The Structure and Evolution of Industry in São Paulo, 1930-1960," Studies in Comparative International Development, St. Louis, I:5 (1965), 43-47.

696 Chacon, Vamireh. "State Capitalism and Bureaucracy in Brazil," (tr. from Estado e Povo no Brasil, 1937-1964), Rio de Janeiro, 1977.

697 Collier, Richard. The River that God Forgot, London, 1968.

698 Cunningham, Susan M. "Planning Brazilian Regional Development During the 1970's," Geography, 61 (July 1976), 163-166.

699 Daland, Robert T. Brazilian Planning: Development Politics and Administration, Chapel Hill, 1967.

700 _____. "Development Administration and the Brazilian Political System," WPQ, 12:2 (June 1968), 25-39.

701 Dos Santos, Teotonio. "Brazil," in Latin America: The Struggle with Dependency and Beyond (ed. by R. Chilcote and J. Edelstein), New York, 1974, pp. 409-490.

702 _____. "Foreign Investment and the Large Enterprise in Latin America: The Brazilian Case," in Latin America: Reform or Revolution? (ed. by J. Petras and M. Zeitlin), New York, 1968, pp. 431-453.

703 Davis, Shelton and Robert O. Matthews. The Geological Imperative: Anthropology and Development in the Amazon Basin, Cambridge, Massachusetts, 1976.

283   Bibliography

704 *Dean, Warren. The Industrialization of São Paulo,
      1880-1945, Austin, 1969.

705 *_____. "Remittances of Italian Immigrants: from
      Brazil, Argentina, Uruguay, and U. S. A., 1884-
      1914," New York University Ibero-American Language
      and Area Center, Occasional Paper #14, New York,
      1974.

706 Denevan, William. "Development and the Imminent
      Demise of the Amazon Rainforest," The Professional
      Geographer, 25 (1973), 130-135.

707 Dordick, H. S. Engineering in Regional Development:
      The Brazilian Northeast, RAND Corporation, Santa
      Monica, 1967.

708 Economic Commission for Latin America. Basic Equip-
      ment in Brazil, New York, 1963.

709 Ellis, Howard E., ed. The Economy of Brazil, Berke-
      ley, 1968.

710 Epstein, David G. Brasília, Plan and Reality: A
      Study of Planned and Spontaneous Urban Development,
      Berkeley, 1973.

711 *Erickson, Kenneth Paul. The Brazilian Corporative
      State and Working-Class Politics, Berkeley, 1977.

712 _____. "Corporatism and Labor in Development,"
      in Contemporary Brazil (ed. by H. J. Rosenbaum
      and W. G. Tyler), New York, 1972, pp. 139-166.

713 _____. "Political Strikes in Brazil, 1960-1964,"
      New York University Ibero-American Language and
      Area Center, Occasional Paper No. 17, New York,
      1975.

714 *_____. "Populism and Political Control of the Work-
      ing Class in Brazil," PCCLAS, 4 (1975), pp. 117-
      144; reprinted in Ideology and Social Change in Latin
      America (ed. by J. Nash and J. Corradi), Vol. II,
      New York, 1975, pp. 91-127.

715 _____ and Patrick V. Peppe. "Dependent Capitalist
      Development, U.S. Foreign Policy, and Repression

of the Working Class in Brazil and Chile," Latin
American Perspectives, 3 (Spring 1976), 19-44.

716 Evans, Peter B. "The Military, the Multinationals,
     and the 'Miracle': The Political Economy of the
     'Brazilian Model' of Development," Studies in Com-
     parative International Development, 9 (1974), 26-45.

717 Fischlowitz, E. S. "Manpower Problems in Brazil,"
     International Labour Review (April 1959).

718 *Fishlow, Albert. "Brazilian Size Distribution of In-
     come," American Economic Review, 62 (May 1972),
     391-402.

719 _____. "Origins and Consequences of Import Sub-
     stitution in Brazil," in International Economics and
     Development, New York, 1972, pp. 312-365.

720 Forman, Shepard and Joyce F. Riegelhaupt. "Market-
     place and Marketing System," CSSH, 12:12 (1970).

721 Frank, Andre G. Capitalism and Underdevelopment in
     Latin America: Historical Studies of Chile and Bra-
     zil, New York, 1967.

722 _____. "On the Mechanisms of Imperialism: The
     Case of Brazil," Monthly Review (Sept. 1964).

723 Furtado, Celso. "Adventures of a Brazilian Economist,"
     International Social Science Journal, 25:1-2 (1973),
     28-38.

724 _____. Diagnosis of the Brazilian Crisis, Berkeley,
     1965.

725 _____. "Political Obstacles to the Economic Develop-
     ment of Brazil," in Obstacles to Change in Latin
     America (ed. by C. Veliz), New York, 1965, pp.
     144-161.

726 Galeano, Eduardo. "The De-Nationalization of Brazilian
     Industry," Monthly Review, 21:7 (Dec. 1969), 11-30.

727 Gauld, Charles A. The Last Titan: Percival Farqua-
     har, American Entrepreneur in Latin America, Stan-
     ford, 1964.

728 Goode, Liesel. The General Electric Company in Bra-
     zil, New York, 1967.

729 Goodman, David E. "The Brazilian Economic 'Miracle'
     and Regional Policy: Some Evidence from the Urban
     Northeast," JLAS, 8:1 (May 1976), 1-27.

730 Gordon, Lincoln and Englebert Grommers. U. S. Man-
     ufacturing Investment in Brazil, 1946-1960, Boston,
     1962.

731 Graham, Douglas H. and Sérgio Buarque de Holanda
     Filho. Regional and Urban Growth and Development
     in Brazil, 2 vols., São Paulo, 1971.

732 Graham, Lawrence S. Civil Service Reform in Brazil,
     Austin, 1968.

733 Harrigan, John J. "Geography and Planning in Bra-
     zilian Urban and Regional Development," LBR, 12:1
     (Summer 1975), 108-125.

734 Hirschman, Albert O. "Brazil's Northeast," in Journeys
     Toward Progress, New York, 1963, pp. 11-91.

735 _____. "Industrial Development of the Brazilian
     Northeast and the Tax Credit Scheme of Article 34/
     18," Journal of Development Studies, 5 (Oct. 1968),
     1-28.

736 Hofford, William. "Brasília, a New Capital City for
     Brazil," Architectural Review, 122 (1957), 394-402.

737 Hollowood, Bernard. The Story of Morro Velho. Lon-
     don, 1955.

738 Jaguaribe, Hélio. "A Brazilian View," in How Latin
     America Views the U.S. Investor (ed. by R. Vernon),
     New York, 1966, pp. 67-93.

739 *_____. "The Dynamics of Brazilian Nationalism,"
     in Obstacles to Change in Latin America, (ed. by
     C. Veliz), New York, 1965.

740 _____. Economic and Political Development: A
     Theoretical Approach and a Brazilian Case Study,
     Cambridge, Massachusetts, 1968.

741 James, Preston E. and Speridão Faissol. "The Problem of Brazil's Capital City," Geographical Review, 46:3 (1956), 301-317.

742 Johnson, J. J. "Politics and Economics in Brazil," Current History, 42 (1962), 89-95.

743 Jones, Clarence F. "The Evolution of Brazilian Commerce," Economic Geography, 2 (1926), 550-574.

744 Krasner, Stephan. "Manipulating International Commodity Markets: Brazilian Coffee Policy, 1906-1962," Public Policy, 21 (Fall 1973), 493-523.

745 Kuznets, Simon. Economic Growth: Brazil, India, Japan, Durham, 1955.

746 Lafer, Celso. The Planning Process and the Political System in Brazil: A Study of Kubitschek's Target Plan, 1956-1961, Ithaca, 1970.

747 Lambert, Francis. "Trends in Administrative Reform in Brazil," JLAS, 1:2 (Nov. 1969), 168-188.

748 Lando, Barry. Change in Latin America: The Example of Northeastern Brazil, Toronto, 1964.

749 Leff, Nathaniel H. The Brazilian Capital Goods Industry, 1929-1964, Cambridge, Massachusetts, 1968.

750 _____. "Economic Development and Regional Inequality: Origins of the Brazilian Case," Quarterly Journal of Economics, 86 (May 1972), 243-262.

751 _____. Economic Policy-Making and Development in Brazil, 1947-1964, New York, 1968.

752 _____. "Economic Retardation in Nineteenth-Century Brazil," Economic History Review, 25 (Aug. 1972).

753 _____. "Long-Term Brazilian Economic Development," JEH, 29:3 (1969), 473-493.

754 _____. "Marginal Savings Rates in the Development Process: The Brazilian Experience," Economic Journal (1968).

755 _____. "Tropical Trade and Development in the

Nineteenth Century: The Brazilian Experience,"
Journal of Political Economy, 81 (May-June 1973).

756 Lever, Janet. "Soccer: Opium of the Brazilian People," Trans-Action (Dec. 69), 36-43.

757 Ludwig, Armin K. "The Planning and Creation of Brasília: Toward a New and Unique Regional Environment," in New Perspectives of Brazil (ed. by E.
Baklanoff), Nashville, 1966.

758 McCrary, Ernest. "The Amazon Basin--New Mineral
Province for the 70's," Engineering and Mining Journal (Feb. 1972), 80-83.

759 Marchant, Alexander. "Industrialism, Nationalism,
and the People of Brazil," JIAA, 9:1 (1955).

760 Margolis, Maxine L. The Moving Frontier, Gainesville, 1973.

761 Mikesell, Raymond. "Iron Ore in Brazil: The Experience of Hanna Mining Company," in Foreign Investment in the Petroleum and Mineral Industries, Baltimore, 1971, pp. 345-364.

762 Momsen, Richard P., Jr. Routes over the Serra do
Mar: The Evolution of Transportation in the Highlands of Rio de Janeiro, Rio de Janeiro, 1964.

763 Morse, Richard M. "Cities and Society in Nineteenth
Century Latin America: The Illustrative Case of
Brazil," in The Urbanization Process in America
(ed. by J. Hardoy and R. P. Schaedel), Buenos
Aires, 1969.

764 * _____. From Community to Metropolis: A Biography of São Paulo, Brazil, Gainesville, 1958. Revised, New York, 1974.

765 _____. "Trends and Issues in Latin American Urban
Research, 1965-1970," LARR, 6:1-2 (Spring-Fall
1971), 3-52; 19-76.

766 Motta Lima, Pedro. "Marxism, Leninism, and Its
Influence in Cultural Life in Brazil," World Marxist
Review, 5 (Oct. 1962), 19-25.

767   Nader, Ralph. "Recife," Christian Science Monitor
      (Sept. 30, 1963).

768   Newfarmer, Richard S. and Willard F. Mueller. Multi-
      national Corporations in Brazil and Mexico, Commit-
      tee on Foreign Relations, U. S. Senate, Washington,
      1975.

769   Normano, João F. Brazil: A Study of Economic Types,
      Chapel Hill, N. C., 1935; reprinted, New York, 1968.

770   Page, Joseph A. The Revolution That Never Was:
      Northeast Brazil, 1955-1964, New York, 1972.

771   Pelaez, Carlos Manuel. "The Theory and Reality of
      Imperialism in the Coffee Economy of Nineteenth-
      Century Brazil," Economic History Review, 29 (May
      1976), 276-290.

772   Pinto, Rogério F. S. The Political Ecology of the
      Brazilian National Bank for Development (BNDE),
      Washington, 1969.

773   Pyle, Gerald F. "Approaches to Understanding the
      Urban Roots of Brazil," Geographical Research on
      Latin America, Ball State University, Muncie, In-
      diana, 1971, pp. 378-396.

774   Pokshishevskiy, V. V. "The Major Economic Regions
      of Brazil," Soviet Geography, I (Jan. - Feb. 1960),
      48-68.

775   Rippy, J. Fred. British Investment in Latin America,
      1822-1949, Minneapolis, 1959.

776   Robock, Stephan H. Brazil's Developing Northeast: A
      Study of Regional Planning and Foreign Aid, Wash-
      ington, 1963.

777   _____. "Recent Economic Trends in Northeast Bra-
      zil," IAEA, 16 (Winter 1962), 65-89.

778   _____. "The Rural Push for Urbanization in Latin
      America: The Case for Northeast Brazil," Michigan
      State University, Latin American Center, Occasional
      Paper No. 1 (1968).

779   Roett, Riordan A. The Politics of Foreign Aid in the
      Brazilian Northeast, Nashville, 1972.

780 Rosen, Bernard. "The Achievement Syndrome and
     Economic Growth in Brazil," Social Forces, 42:3
     (March 1964), 341-354.

781 Rosenbaum, H. Jon and William G. Tyler, eds. Con-
     temporary Brazil: Issues in Economic and Political
     Development, New York, 1972.

782 Simonsen, Roberto C. Brazil's Industrial Revolution,
     São Paulo, 1939.

783 Smith, Anthony. Mato Grosso: The Last Virgin Land,
     New York, 1971.

784 Smith, Peter S. "Brazilian Oil: From Myth to Real-
     ity?" IAEA, 30:4 (Spring 1977).

785 _____. Oil and Politics in Brazil, Toronto, 1976.

786 _____. "Petrobrás, 1953-1967," Business History
     Review (Summer 1972).

787 Soares, Glaucio Ary Dillon. "The New Industrialization
     and the Brazilian Political System," in Latin Amer-
     ica: Reform or Revolution? (ed. by J. Petras and
     M. Zeitlin), New York, 1968, pp. 186-201.

788 Spiegel, Henry William. The Brazilian Economy:
     Chronic Inflation and Sporadic Industrialization,
     Philadelphia, 1949.

789 Stein, Stanley J. "Brazilian Cotton Textile Industry,
     1850-1950," in Economic Growth: Brazil, India,
     Japan (ed. by S. Kuznets), Durham, 1955, pp. 430-
     447.

790 _____. The Brazilian Cotton Manufacture. Textile
     Enterprise in an Underdeveloped Area, 1850-1950,
     Cambridge, Massachusetts, 1957.

791 Stepan, Alfred C., ed. "The Continuing Problem of
     Brazilian Integration," in Latin American History:
     Select Problems (ed. by F. Pike), New York, 1969,
     pp. 260-297.

792 Stepan, Nancy. Beginnings of Brazilian Science, New
     York, 1976.

793 Sternberg, Hilgard O'Reilly. The Amazon River of
     Brazil, Germany, 1975.

794 Syvrud, Donald. Foundations of Brazilian Economic
     Growth, Stanford, 1974.

795 Tambs, Lewis. "Geopolitics of the Amazon," in Man
     in the Amazon (ed. by C. Wagley), Gainesville, 1974.

796 Tendler, Judith. Electric Power in Brazil: Entre-
     preneurship in the Public Sector, Cambridge, Massa-
     chusetts, 1969.

797 Tuthill, John W. "Economic and Political Aspects of
     Development in Brazil, and United States Aid," JIAS,
     11:2 (April 1969), 186-208.

798 United States Senate, Committee on Foreign Relations.
     Multinational Corporations and United States Foreign
     Policy, Washington, 1973.

799 Vaz da Costa, Rubens. "Population and Development:
     The Brazilian Case," Population Reference Bureau,
     Washington, 25 (1969).

800 Wells, J. "Distribution of Earnings, Growth, and the
     Structure of Demand in Brazil During the 1960's,"
     World Development, 2 (Jan. 1974), 9-24.

801 Winpenny, J. T. Brazil: Manufactured Exports and
     Government Policy Since 1939, London, 1972.

802 _____. "Industrialization in Brazil," JLAS, 2:2
     (Nov. 1970), 199-208.

803 Wirth, John D. "A German View of Brazilian Trade
     and Development, 1935," HAHR, 47:2 (May 1967),
     225-235.

804 Wythe, George, et al. Brazil: An Expanding Economy,
     New York, 1949.

SEE ALSO: 67, 81-83, 90, 92, 95, 180, 194-195, 197, 204,
     209, 210, 212-213, 228, 233, 234, 237, 245, 249,
     258, 280, 281, 310-311, 325, 354-355, 368, 369,
     388-391, 476, 587-588, 625, 805-808, 857, 861, 886.

XV. AGRICULTURE AND LAND TENURE

805 Benton, Peggie. One Man Against the Backlands:
     Struggle and Achievement in Brazil, London, 1972.

806 CIDA (Inter-American Committee for Agricultural De-
     velopment), Land Tenure Conditions and Socio-Eco-
     nomic Development: Brazil, Washington, 1965.

807 Dean, Warren. "Latifundia and Land Policy in Nine-
     teenth-Century Brazil," HAHR, 51:4 (Nov. 1971),
     606-625.

808 *_____ . Rio Claro: A Brazilian Plantation System,
     1820-1920, Stanford, 1976.

809 Diegues, Manuel, Jr. "Land Tenure and Use in the
     Brazilian Plantation System," in Plantation Systems
     of the New World, Pan American Union, Social
     Science Monograph No. 7, Washington, 1959.

810 Eisenberg, Peter. The Sugar Industry in Pernambuco:
     Modernization Without Change, 1840-1910, Berkeley,
     1974.

811 Feder, Ernest. The Rape of the Peasantry, Garden
     City, N. Y., 1971.

812 Galloway, J. H. "Northeast Brazil 1700-1750: The
     Agricultural Crists Re-Examined," Journal of His-
     torical Geography, I:1 (1975), 21-38.

813 _____ . "The Sugar Industry in Pernambuco During
     the Nineteenth Century," AAG/A, 58 (1968), 285-303.

814 Greenfield, Sidney. "On Monkeys, Fish, and Brazilian
     Agriculture," Journal of Developing Areas (July 1971).

815 Gross, Daniel and Barbara A. Underwood. "Technolo-
     gical Change and Caloric Costs: Sisal Agriculture
     in Northeastern Brazil," AA, 73:3 (June 1971), 725-
     740.

816 James, Preston E. "Patterns of Land Use in Northeast
     Brazil," AAG/A, 43 (1953), 98-126.

817 Ludwig, Armin K. and Harry W. Taylor. Brazil's New
     Agrarian Reform, New York, 1969.

818   Margolis, Maxine. "The Coffee Cycle on the Paraná Frontier," LBR, 9:1 (June 1972), 3-12.

819   Mitchell, Simon. "The Influence of Kinship in the Social Organization of North East Brazilian Fishermen," JLAS, 6:2 (Nov. 1974), 301-313.

820   *Moran, Emílio F. "Agricultural Development in the Transamazon Valley," Latin American Studies Working Papers, Indiana University, Bloomington, October 1976.

821   Nichols, William H. and Ruy Miller Paiva. Ninety-nine Fazendas: The Structure and Productivity of Brazilian Agriculture: 1963, Nashville, 1969.

822   Pearse, Arno S. Cotton in North Brazil, London, 1923.

823   Reichmann, Felix. Sugar, Gold, and Coffee: Essays on the History of Brazil, Ithaca, 1959.

824   Schuh, G. Edward and Alves, Eliseu R. The Agricultural Development of Brazil, New York, 1970.

825   Taylor, Kit Sims. "Brazil's Northeast: Sugar and Surplus Value," Monthly Review (March 1969), 20-29.

826   Webb, Kempton E. "Origins and Development of a Food Economy in Central Minas Gerais," AAG/A, 49 (1959), 409-419.

SEE ALSO: 81, 217, 238, 260, 262, 281, 299, 325, 387, 439, 447, 449, 491, 596-598, 608, 621, 720, 770, 771, 774, 789, 790, 870.

XVI.   CULTURE: ART, LITERATURE, IDEAS

827   Aldridge, A. Owen, ed. The Ibero-American Enlightenment, Urbana, 1971.

828   Alencar, José Martiano de. Iracema (tr. by I. Burton), London, 1886; (tr. by D. da Cruz), New York, 1959.

829   Amado, Jorge. Dona Flôr and Her Two Husbands (tr. by H. de Onis), New York, 1969.

830 _____. Gabriela, Clove and Cinnamon (tr. by W. Grossman and J. L. Taylor), New York, 1962.

831 _____. Home Is the Sailor (tr. by H. de Onis), New York, 1964.

832 _____. Shepherds of the Night (tr. by H. de Onis), New York, 1964.

833 _____. Tent of Miracles (tr. by H. de Onis), New York, 1975.

834 _____. The Two Deaths of Quincas Wateryell (tr. by B. Shelby), New York, 1965.

835 _____. The Violent Land (tr. by S. Putnam), New York, 1945; revised ed., New York, 1965.

836 Andrade, Mário de. Hallucinated City (tr. by J. Tomlins), Nashville, 1968.

837 Azevedo, Aluísio de. A Brazilian Tenement (tr. by H. W. Brown), New York, 1926.

838 Bandeira, Manoel. A Brief History of Brazilian Literature, Pan American Union, Washington, 1958; reprinted, New York, 1964.

839 Bardi, P. M. Profile of the New Brazilian Art, Rio de Janeiro, 1970.

840 Barman, Roderick. "Politics on the Stage: The Late Brazilian Empire as Dramatized by França Júnior," LBR, 13:2 (Winter 1976), 244-260.

841 Bishop, Elizabeth and Emanuel Brasil, eds. An Anthology of Twentieth-Century Brazilian Poetry, Middletown, Connecticut, 1972.

842 Brandt, Alice. The Diary of "Helen Morley," (tr. by E. Bishop), New York, 1957.

843 Caldwell, Helen. The Brazilian Othello of Machado de Assis: A Study of Dom Casmurro, Berkeley, 1960.

844 Callado, Antônio. Don Juan's Bar, New York, 1972.

845 _____. Quarup (tr. by B. Shelby), New York, 1970.

846 Callenbach, Ernest. "Comparative Anatomy of Folk-Myth Films: Robin Hood and Antônio das Mortes," Film Quarterly, 23 (1969-70), 42-47.

847 Cândido, Antônio de Melo e Sousa. "Literature and the Rise of Brazilian Brazil National Self-Identity," LBR, 4:1 (Summer 1968), 27-43.

848 Corcão, Gustavo. Who If I Cry Out? Austin, 1967.

849 Corteau, Joanna. "The Image of Woman in the Novels of Graciliano Ramos," Interamerican Review, 4:2 (1974), 162-176.

850 Coutinho, Afranio. An Introduction to Literature in Brazil (tr. by G. Rabassa), New York, 1969.

851 Cruz Costa, João. A History of Ideas in Brazil (tr. by S. Macedo), Berkeley, 1964.

852 *Cunha, Euclides da. Rebellion in the Backlands (tr. by S. Putnam), Chicago, 1944.

853 De Beer, Gabriela. José Vasconcelos and His World, New York, 1966.

854 Dimmick, Ralph E. "The Brazilian Literary Generation of 1930," Hispánia, 34 (May 1951), 181-187.

855 Driver, David M. The Indian in Brazilian Literature, New York, 1942.

856 Ellison, Fred P. Brazil's New Novel: Four Northeastern Masters, Berkeley, 1954.

857 Evenson, Norma. Two Brazilian Capitals, New Haven, 1973.

858 Ferreira de Castro, Antônio. Jungle (tr. by C. Duff), New York, 1935.

859 Goldberg, Isaac. Brazilian Literature, New York, 1922.

860 _____, ed. Brazilian Tales, New York, 1922.

861 Goodwin, Philip L. Brazil Builds: Architecture New and Old, 1652-1942, New York, 1943.

862 Graça Aranha, José Pereira de. Canaan (tr. by M.
     J. Lorente), Boston, 1920.

863 Graham, Robert B. Cunningham. A Brazilian Mystic,
     London, 1920.

864 Guimarães Rosa, João. The Devil to Pay in the Back-
     lands (tr. by J. Taylor and H. de Onis), New York,
     1963.

865 _____. Sagarana (tr. by H. de Onis), New York,
     1966.

866 _____. The Third Bank of the River and Other Stor-
     ies (tr. by B. Shelby), New York, 1968.

867 Johnson, Phil Brian. "Up-Tight About Ruy: An Essay
     on Brazilian Cultural Nationalism and Mythology,"
     JIASWA, 15:2 (May 1973), 191-204.

868 Kelly, John R. "An Annotated Bibliography of the Early
     Writings of José Lins do Rêgo," LBR, 9:1 (Summer
     1972), 72-85.

869 Kent, Rockwell. Portinari--His Life and Art, Chicago,
     1940.

870 Lins do Rêgo, José. Plantation Boy (tr. by E. Baum),
     New York, 1966.

871 Loos, Dorothy Scott. The Naturalistic Novel of Brazil,
     New York, 1963.

872 Lowe, Elizabeth. "The 'New' Jorge Amado," LBR,
     6:2 (Dec. 1969), 73-82.

873 Lucas, Fábio. "Cultural Aspects of Brazilian Litera-
     ture," Triquarterly, Evanston, Illinois, 13-14 (1968-
     1969), 33-53.

874 Luper, Albert T. The Music of Brazil, Washington,
     1943.

875 Machado, José Bittencourt. Machado of Brazil: The
     Life and Times of Machado de Assis, New York, 1953.

876 Machado de Assis, Joaquim María. Dom Casmurro
     (tr. by H. Caldwell), New York, 1953.

877 _____. Esau and Jacob (tr. by H. Caldwell), Berkeley, 1965.

878 _____. Epitaph of a Small Winner (tr. by W. Grossman), New York, 1952. Reprinted, New York, 1967.

879 _____. Philosopher or Dog? (tr. by C. Wilson), New York, 1954.

880 _____. The Psychiatrist and Other Stories (tr. by W. Grossman and H. Caldwell), Berkeley, 1963.

881 Mindlin, Henrique F. Modern Architecture in Brazil, Rio de Janeiro, 1956.

882 Monteiro, Mário Ypiranga. "The Influence of Intellectuals in the Events of Brazil," in Artists and Writers in the Evolution of Latin America (ed. by E. D. Terry), University, Alabama, 1969.

883 Nist, John, ed. Modern Brazilian Poetry, Bloomington, 1962.

884 * _____. The Modernist Movement in Brazil, Austin, 1967.

885 Onis, Harriet de. The Golden Land: An Anthology of Latin American Folklore in Literature, New York, 1948.

886 Parker, Barry. "Town Planning Experiences in Brazil," Architects Journal, 51 (1920), 48-52.

887 Prowess, M. Cavalcanti, Tony Frank, and Harry O'-Fields. McLuhanaima: The Solid Gold Hero; or, O Heroi Com Bastante Carater (Uma Fuga), New Haven, 1976.

888 *Putnam, Samuel. Marvelous Journey: A Survey of Four Centuries of Brazilian Writing, New York, 1948.

889 Papadaki, Stamo. Oscar Niemeyer, New York, 1960.

890 Queiroz, Rachel de. The Three Marias (tr. by F. Ellison), Austin, 1963.

891 Ramos, Graciliano. Anguish (tr. by L. C. Kaplan), New York, 1946.

892 _____. Barren Lives (tr. by R. E. Dimmick),
        Austin, 1965.

893 Rodman, Selden. Genius in the Backlands: Popular
        Artists of Brazil, Old Greenwich, Connecticut, 1977.

894 Sayers, Raymond S. The Negro in Brazilian Literature,
        New York, 1956.

895 Shaw, Paul Van Orden. "European and Asian Influences
        in the Economic and Cultural Development of Bra-
        zil," Brazilian-American Survey, 12 (1960), 39-40.

896 Skidmore, Thomas E. and Thomas H. Holloway. "New
        Light on Euclides da Cunha: Letters to Oliveira
        Lima," LBR 8:1 (Summer 1971), 30-55.

897 Suassuna, Ariano. The Rogues' Trial (tr. by D. Rat-
        cliff), Berkeley, 1965.

898 Taunay, Alfredo d'Escragnolle. Innocence (tr. by H.
        Chamberlain), New York, 1945.

899 Vassberg, David E. "African Influence on the Music
        of Brazil," LBR, 13:1 (Summer 1976), 35-54.

900 Verissimo, Erico. Consider the Lilies of the Field
        (tr. by J. N. Karnoff), New York, 1947.

901 _____. Crossroads (tr. by L. C. Kaplan), New
        York, 1943.

902 _____. His Excellency, the Ambassador, New York,
        1967.

903 _____. Night, New York, 1956.

904 _____. The Rest Is Silence (tr. by L. C. Kaplan),
        New York, 1946.

905 _____. Time and the Wind (tr. by L. L. Barrett),
        New York, 1951.

SEE ALSO: 38, 196, 224, 244, 455, 462, 485, 487, 501,
        512, 600, 766.